I0035920

Hermann von Berg's

Demythologizing Marx

The Book that Shattered Communism in Eastern

Europe

Copyright © 1986, Hermann von Berg,
Translation copyright © 2010, J.J. Keith,
Herculaneum Publishing Company

All rights reserved

For information about permission to reproduce selections from this
book, write to:
Herculaneum Publishing Company
2744 Hylan Boulevard
Suite #132
Staten Island, NY 10306

Website address: http://www.karlmarxandengels.com

Publisher: Herculaneum Publishing Company

Berg, Hermann von:
Demythologizing Marx: The Book that Shattered Communism in

Eastern Europe, Hermann v. Berg, 1986

ISBN 978-0-578-06858-9

Cover design: Ronald Sansone

Printed and e-book-published in the United States of America

About the Author:

The renowned economist of former Soviet East Germany cast a look back in anger in this book, his main work: A relentless as well as sarcastic discussion of Marxism-Leninism which he calls a half-German and half-Russian ideology. Hermann von Berg recounts here what he considers the sum of his life's research and experience, politically as well as theoretically. Thus, he does not limit himself to polemics, but he refutes hypotheses and claims of the former countries of the "real-existing Socialism" in examining the classic writers Marx, Engels, Lenin, as well as Communist Party proclamations and practices.

Hermann von Berg was born in 1933. He studied History, Philosophy and Economics at the Karl-Marx-University of Leipzig. He then received his Ph.D. and his Doctor of Economics. From 1970 onward Berg has been a university lecturer; in 1972 he was made Professor at Humboldt University, Berlin. His professional experiences include: co-ordination in the Ministry of Foreign Trade of the German Democratic Republic [G.D.R.] for the preparation of the negotiations between the European Community and the COMECON States. He has published variously on economic and historical topics. He was barred from exercising his profession in East Germany because of his dissident views. He was expatriated to West Germany in 1985, shortly after having finished this work.

Table of Contents:

Hermann von Berg:

The Economist To End All Economics!

No Cold War thriller could really capture the sheer all-pervasive paranoia of that period, although some have given it a fair shot. In constant survival mode at the time Berlin citizens in all four sectors, U.S., British, French, Soviet, developed a peculiar brand of black humor: Why is Berlin the safest city on the planet? Because no one power could throw a nuclear bomb without equally blowing up the other sectors! What this kind of dire political irony couldn't hide was the fact that if a nuclear holocaust were to happen it would most likely happen there. From 1945 to 1989, i.e., from the End of World War II to the Fall of the Iron Curtain, it was as if the Cuban Missile Crisis had frozen in time. The writer of this book was literally born on what would later become the Iron Curtain, he was born in the heart of Germany, and his life and work came to epitomize the world conflict that would engulf this area during much of the 20th century. That he managed to do what he did, and that he managed to survive is a tale that defies all probability!

Hermann von Berg strikes anyone who has ever met him in the flesh as a force of nature rather than a human being. Conan Doyle's Professor Challenger of *The Lost World* fame would come to mind if Professor von Berg were not altogether unique. Another difference would be that Challenger found a fictitious lost continent in the 19th century still peopled with dinosaurs – an idea that Spielberg later explored further and popularized in his *Jurassic Park* movies – while von Berg has set out to map a new world of social justice and productive abundance for all beyond our badly-shaken post-Cold-War world against the lizard-eyed phantom apparatchiks of a now defunct system. At the time of writing, the U.N. estimates that close to one third of the present world population of roughly 7 billion people lives on poverty row on less than two dollars a day. One barrel of oil on the world market has hit the all-time record high of $145.29 in July of 2008. Millions of people in the U.S. alone have lost their homes through the housing crisis, the ensuing debt crisis and the crisis of the world financial markets. Most first-rate economic experts agree that we are in for it for a long haul. They also agree - and they do so regardless of their ideological persuasions - that we can do better than that.

But how so?

The question here is: will the crisis last only a couple of years or will it be an entire bad decade or worse? A Great Recession we have had, and if a depression is not averted it will be a second Great Depression, and, indeed, as we are adults and not children who need comforters and lullabies to stop crying over bogeymen, we may look the facts fairly and squarely in the face – we may be in for a national and global crisis that shall make the Great Depression look like a cakewalk. These statements are made not by professional doomsayers. These facts are admitted even by economic experts who are getting paid millions to make us believe that everything is honky-dory at all times, even now, when for large masses of the world population it patently isn't. And the crisis has squeezed not just the lower or the middle strata of society; it has hit hard many members of the upper stratum, as well. According to anthropologist Jared Diamond the consumption factors between "first world" and "third world" populations have a varying discrepancy of 32 to 1. The discrepancy of the production factors runs along analogous lines. If, economically speaking, the "emerging nations" like India, China, Brazil, et al, come on board with a consumption factor of, say, only 16, and if we look at the worldwide availability of the most vital resources needed for the survival of humanity: clean air, potable water and oil alone, we are in for definite even irreparable trouble. It means if this happens, and all statistics and developmental tendencies point in this direction, then we will have resources-wise no planet left to live on! And why should the rest of the world not try to live like we do?

Alternate sources of energy have to be tapped into. That major players in the oil business like T. Boone Pickens have promoted wind power, and that George W. Bush has owned that we *do* have a greenhouse effect – no president, after all who can be accused of pandering to ecologists! – quite frankly underscores we *do* have a problem on a national and global scale. Oil prices of $145 a barrel are not sustainable for world trade, they are not sustainable for world travel, unless major and drastic changes are made air lines shall collapse or greatly consolidate, shipping shall have largely to go back to sails; it is safe to predict that all wars of the future shall be fought over natural resources and they shall be fierce – make no mistake about it; the Oil Age and the world as we know it shall come to an end before the present generation leaving college shall reach retirement age. And if we are to survive globally we shall have to come up with a viable Plan B real fast.

The man who at least in theory held a monopoly against this kind of global economic calamity, who (in Dostoyevsky's words) consistently rooted for the underdog, "the insulted and the injured" worldwide, and who stood for a more equitable distribution of wealth and for a greater degree of social justice was Karl Marx. For a century and a half since the publication of the *Communist Manifesto* in 1848, a good part of the world went Communist. In the heyday of the Cold War it looked like nearly one-half of the world, indeed, was under the sphere of Soviet influence and the so-called "non-aligned nations" were teetering in this direction. Unfortunately, Soviet-style Communism with its command-style economics had a remedy for the world that would, in effect, kill the patient before any healing could take place - not to mention the gulags with its millions of victims it engendered along the way!

The man who foresaw the collapse of the Iron Curtain and the collapse of Soviet world Communism to the month by a good decade, and who challenged that system from the inside was Hermann von Berg. Professor von Berg is a rare combination of a genuinely original, first-rate mind paired with unusual practical drive and ability and an uncanny amount of sheer, raw physical and ethical courage. He is one of the world's leading authorities on the historical origins and literary sources of Marxism and Communism. In his double academic capacity as historian and economist, he has the deep-focus view necessary to put economic theory into a larger perspective. And in this double-edged political capacity as one of the leaders of the brain-trust behind the East German Communist heads of state and as a high-level clandestine diplomat in the 1960s and 1970s during the crucial period of *rapprochement* between the two Germanys - Capitalist and Communist - prior to reunification, working closely with West German Chancellor Willy Brandt and East German Prime Minister Willi Stoph, he not only saw world history in the making, he became, so to speak, symbolically single-handedly and single-mindedly the deluge that would bring down the Curtain and the Berlin Wall and that would open the Brandenburg Gate. No floodgates of whatever magnitude can reverse what happened. Von Berg is literally the David who took on an Empire armed with no more than an old-fashioned, badly-functioning typewriter that became more powerful than a slingshot and that would bring down the proverbial Soviet Goliath with clay feet! The Stalinist functionaries who wished him dead are legion, post-Stalinists who are still working on his downfall as yet abound. They are ruthless and to this very day they don't shrink from even subverting the most impartial wheels of Justice to their retrograde ends.

The fact that von Berg survived the fray and the past several decades is nothing less than a consummate miracle! Given the highly-precarious world situation and given renewed confrontations with Russia - a direct clash between the superpowers has been arduously avoided even by the staunchest hardliners during the entire period of the Cold War, one "idiot hour that may destroy what centuries made" - the first English edition of this classic iconoclastic work of economics and social science that is in itself a philosophic and literary cataclysm does not come a moment too early! This book challenging Marxist orthodoxy and the orthodoxy of Classical Economics giving a blue-print for a third way beyond Capitalism and Communism, belongs to a mere dozen books that changed my life, a life I may add, not short on outstanding works in world literature and social and economic philosophy.

You may read it with equal benefit.

Cay Hehner, Ph. D.,
Director of Education,
Henry George School of Social Science,
Murray Hill, New York, August 2010

Preface:
Goal, Scope and Method of this Work

Who shuns polemics should not touch this work.

The subject matter of which it treats does not bear a cool, factual, reserved academic procedure. I have composed other works in this manner.

This subject matter screams for protest. It virtually demands sarcasm and irony, as well as partial excess, because the facts that are being brought to discussion and the political consequences that ensue are equally atrocious. And further, facts have to remain facts, just because of this incessant half-German/half-Russian machine-gun fire of a pseudological ideology and policy which serves its Eastern side to continue to paint a hateful picture of antagonism of Germans against Germans in the name of eternal peace! The instructional films of the National People's Army demonstrate this very well: Take heed! Federal German tanks, Type Leopard! Prepare to destroy! Marksman: Take aim – Fire!

How long shall such films continue to be screened? Until they become reality? The eminent German enlightenment philosopher Herder has warned: "Pit patriots against patriots in a fight to the death that is the worst barbarism!"

Shall the Germans of today surpass yesteryear's barbarism of Hitler?

For that reason this work does not undertake to spread esoteric fragrances of a philosophic and literary kind, but it deals with hard historical and economic facts that, in and of themselves, will serve as the coarsest of bludgeons. These are the general characteristics of historical-economic realities as opposed to philosophic-literary ones.

We are, hence, not talking about the Convention of Telgte or about a tête-à-tête in the Hotel of the City of Berlin. What solely matters is to speak the truth for truth's and for survival's sake, the truth about the Marxist-Leninist ideology which is inimical to peace, human and civil rights, to speak the truth about its sources and its current interpretation, as imprudent and life-threatening many a friend and comrade may find this aspiration. Partial exaggeration is, therefore, necessary, to break through decades as well as day-to-day stupefaction, to startle the general lethargy of thought into action. Some evils may be cured only by shock therapy.

Nobody shall think that in this trite and banal heap of straw called Marxism-Leninism there is no grain of new insight, not at all. Even the apparently most known, most simple, most lucid facts serve under critical scrutiny the greatest opportunities for surprising new discoveries.

And further: In the face of lies, spite, disdain of all things human, substandard measures, sarcasm alone may serve as an adequate response. The bitter spite of the *ersatz*-religion of the Communist Party of the German Democratic Republic, which calls itself timidly and with genuine untruthfulness Socialist Unity Party of Germany, and whose 40th anniversary takes place in April 1986: The Party is now forty years old, it is fighting again and still, domestically and internationally, its fight against Social Democracy, although the 'Great' Erich Honecker, General Secretary of the Party and Chairman of the G.D.R. State Council, according to the East German wire service ADN meanwhile in private entertains "very cordial relations" with 'Uncle' Herbert Wehner, Party Secretary of the West German Social Democrats: Behold these remarkable German-German biographies.

In the following I will draw the most essential conclusions of my life, theoretically as well as politically. Perhaps that shall serve young people to avoid the errors which I had to undergo from my earliest youth, grace of my pseudo-instructors, that Marxism-Leninism was a theory and a science with societal and social consequences that could lend credence to life and give it significance.

For the researching university scholar there are three possibilities, once he recognizes that his prior academic and social perspectives do not correspond to the truth:

The first being the one most recommended by friends, comrades and colleagues with a certain melancholy nonchalance:

- Keep your trap shut and enjoy the ample pork, privileges and possessions that come with your position
- The second being to follow the customs of prominent men of the cloth during the French *ancien regime:* Write down your revelations and don't allow them to be published until after the last unction
- The third and most difficult being: To take account with oneself objectively and critically, examine one's conscience before which one has to prevail always, because one would have to give oneself up as a human being entirely otherwise and bear the consequences, which any dictatorship – be it fascist or communist – then octroyates: Incarceration, escape, exile. Here we East Germans have some good fortune in this ill fortune: we do not need to go into exile in another country.

What are my cogent reasons to decide for the third option? Has the West not always been saying that Marxism-Leninism is a false ideology, so what is new and different in the statement of my study of this problem?

Certainly, various people in the West are saying that, but with the ideologically over drilled and pig-headed cadres in our so-called real-existing socialism this will fall on deaf ears, because for them, here the class enemy is speaking. They do not heed the revisionist, Trotskyite, Euro-communist, reformist, liberal and conservative critics of Marxism-Leninism, and a group of youthful enthusiasts within "real" socialism sees it likewise: From those are recruited the leading cadres and my own error continues forevermore. Everyone swears by the classic ideologues, Marx-Engels-Lenin and the Party resolutions.

I will, indeed, answer them with those classics and with the resolutions of the Party. This they will understand. They may be able to verify this without taking recourse to forbidden literature. That is not a language difficult for them; on the contrary, it is their own. They will see with their very own eyes and take in with their very own minds what stupid, nonsensical yada – yada – yada this Marxism-Leninism actually is, given new and hitherto undiscovered facts from the historical and economic sources. So far, the literature in question has not been banished here, but that will soon happen.

Here they will get the explanation for the unbearable contradictions between ideal and reality, which is giving them so much trouble on a day-to-day basis and that is the precondition for all necessary reforms, whose representation matures in their minds and that will have to be realized in their deeds.

Therefore, I shall expect that the cadres will read the classics. What will then happen? I will be accused of the direst transgressions and the greatest ideological subversions. Well, I may, thus, put both hands in the fire: I have quoted all those classic works and Party sources correctly. This will then become a very interesting trial.

Our young, Marx-oriented people in all of Germany have to know the truth about the real tradition and theories of the workers and Socialism if they and our fatherland are to have a future worth living.

Of course, that is especially important for East Germany – the German Democratic Republic or G.D.R. – because this region of the country shall have to be made habitable again for those who think critically. Those men and women shall not have to lose their home and homeland again, for the price of winning an intellectually, spiritually and politically free fatherland.

Do global statistics know of a country that has in mere 40 years lost 25% of its population through emigration? No, even here the German Democratic Republic is at the absolute forefront of things.

What brought me to those findings which I herewith dedicate to paper?

It was the quite painful and penetrating contemplation of what needs to be done to close the rift between constitutional claim and quotidian political reality that is humanly unbearable. As others amongst my comrades, I have held the view over three decades that we are here dealing solely with subjective imperfections which should be annulled through increased activity. Nevertheless, can the subjective factor, can all the Central Committees of all the Communist Parties have been so stupid over so many decades that everything may turn only in circles? Slowly I began to realize that the deciding causes are deeper. They must be of an objective nature. They must be rooted in the system itself.

Therefore, is it not the core of the system, the so-called scientific perspective, "the ideology, the cardinal piece of the party work," to use the jargon of the Socialist Unity Party, the very cause for all those heinous social and economic malfunctionings, for which now the working men are solely held responsible?

I systematically started to examine all essential positions from their sources, both historically and logically, and I reached the conclusion which I herewith make available to the public.

My two academic disciplines, the historical and the economic, both proved to be of advantage as well as a research period of four years in the Chair of the Marx-Engels Faculty at the Academy of Social Sciences of the Central Committee of the Socialist Unity Party. Furthermore, without that glance I was, thus, enabled to take backstage of the party and government apparatus I would have never attained such a critical view. I also owe thanks to my colleagues in the discipline, as well as some natural scientists at Humboldt University and my friends in the Federal Republic of Germany.

Physical survival for Germany and a peaceful solution of the European as well as global issues will be possible only once the peace-menacing ideology of Marxism-Leninism that pseudo-theoretically claims world domination for Soviet Imperialism has been overcome. No socialist, no communist will have to hold onto the Marxist or Leninist version of his faith. Verily, there are better traditions available within the international workers' movement. They need only to be made known within the appropriate forms and structures. It would then become patently clear that Communism in its Marxist variety is neither economically feasible nor politically desirable. And for the Germans it would become apparent, as well, that the egregious cooperation and the following clash of Marxism and anti-Marxism, of Hitler-Fascism and Stalinism for Germany's future political formation may only have one answer and alternative as a lesson from World War II: Dictatorship neither from the left nor from the right!

The persecuted and the injured, the prisoners and exiles of Hitler's dictatorship and the Germans in the Western occupational zones were liberated on May 8, 1945, by the anti-Hitler coalition, but for the people in the Soviet Occupational Zone, the later German Democratic Republic, it was merely the form of dictatorship that changed; the complete disregard of human and civil rights remained even if in a somewhat milder form. The political practice under Stalin came closest to that of Hitler, while it became modified under the regime of neo-Stalinism and the growing political, economic and juridical influence-taking of the West upon the G.D.R., especially upon its leading statesmen, by way of direct intercourse, even though, it clearly remained a dictatorship within the political sphere: Arbitrary, subjectivist, legalistic or formally legal but effectively illegal violence camouflaged by one-size-fits-all rubber paragraphs enforced by the Secret Police on orders of the Polit Bureau of the Central Committee of the Socialist Unity Party of Germany. It is nothing less than tragic that the very group of leaders, through Marxism-Leninism, sworn in on sectarian thinking alienated from reality, really does believe it is serving world revolution, the liberation of the working population, to enforce dictatorship as a necessary transitional stage into Communist paradise.

How does our much honored classical national poet Schiller put it? "... Albeit, the most terrible of terrors is man himself – in his delusion." As a result of this insight the absolute majority of those politically interested in the G.D.R. dream of a pluralistic, constitutional framework of state and society, organized democratically and socially by and large along lines of genuine justice: Free and pluralistic democracy versus dictatorship!

Pluralistic democracy, which enables genuine human and civil rights through political and ideological variety, is thwarted through Marxist-Leninist simple-mindedness or idiocy decreed by the Soviet dictatorship. Russians as well as *ersatz*-Russians nevertheless have a rather correct attitude towards the ideological struggle, which seems to have been abandoned by the West to a large degree. We may agree with the German idealist philosopher Schelling, who has proclaimed long before Marx and the latter's ideological wisdoms: "... as no power or sovereignty on earth, as great or as small as it may be, rules differently than by the force and violence and care of ideas and where within the people the respect for those has been lost ...necessarily the disrespect and disdain will occur, whose respect is only due to the power of those ideas."

After this general exposition of my personal and political motivations let us come to the details and specifics of the following work:

This book deals with the political as well as the economic parts of Marxist ideology and it juxtaposes this ideology with the practice of the Soviet system, which still, for propagandistic purposes, relies on the farsightedness of both Marx and Lenin, which mainly derives from the economic interpretation of the processes of History. This shall be a drop of novelty, of new value within the ocean of the insights of

Social Science. A drop is not much, indeed, but there happens to occur that stage within any spiritual and intellectual evolution where one drop may bring the barrel to overflow, the proverbial straw that breaks the camel's back.

The content of this book is restricted to statements regarding areas in which I have done theoretical research, have taught and have worked practically, in other words, areas in which I am able to pronounce judgment. This tome contains the political result of my economic and historical studies, which I have published separately, as well as my political experiences from three and a half decades of activities in the Youth Movement [Jugendverband], within the Central Authority of Party and State, as well as within adult education [Volksbildung] and the College and University section of the G.D.R. It contains also a political taking-to-account founded upon historical and economic analysis of the theory and practice of so-called "scientific Communism" which forms the base of the implementation of "real" Socialism of the Socialist Unity Party, as well as with the unscientific ideology of "Marxism-Leninism." All the latter concepts may here be understood and used synonymously.

Methodically and from the strictly scientific standpoint a treatment of the subject matter at hand according to the categories of Marxism in logical form would have been the most effective. This kind of party lingo, however, no average human being would be able to understand and I am aiming mainly for a broad effect and not Marxist incest. The latter will be unavoidable no matter what. Therefore, in the following I will proceed as a historical narrative and the theoretical problems are going to be discussed in the context of pertinent temporal processes. This method may not be applied with complete thoroughness, however, as Marx, in his thinking, operates now in the present tense, now in the future, now in the past, and he blends philosophical, economic, sociological and historical aspects continuously. Therefore, if one is to follow the incipience of his ideology, one is held to make equal leaps and bounds which even make repetitions unavoidable. I will, nevertheless, keep them mercifully short. Further unavoidable are a mass of citations and quotes. You cannot attack and refute if you do not previously represent. To save the reader from a deluge of footnotes which will impair readability, I will only restrict them to the absolutely essential. The expert, for instance, will know where to find the quoted letters and lyrical effusions of Marx, namely, in the old *Marx Engels Complete Works* – acronym M.E.G.A. – and therein within the early half-tomes, if he wants to scrutinize the quotes. For the interested layman it may suffice that the text mentions who wrote the given missive to whom and when it was written. I deal likewise with citations from the *Communist Manifesto*. I mention the given sections and where the quoted passages are to be found, I shall refrain, on the other hand, from footnotes with the exact pagination. Given the multitude of editions this later procedure would be rather senseless, anyway. All quotes of historical, economic, or political moment have been correctly identified for the expert. I am here, therefore, aiming for a synthesis of scientific statement in its core and a popular exposition addressed to the general reader.

The circumstances of my life here do not allow me to do scientifically what – given the topic – I would have liked to have done otherwise. I can only urge my colleagues in the discipline to continue to dig or let dig, where I was able only to sketch. My effective proof and deduction that Marx has created new insights and values neither in the fields of materialist historicism, nor in political economy and political theory will have to be elaborated further. This to make it absolutely clear without any remaining shred of a doubt what kind of charlatans the inhabitants of this, our fabled country of poets and thinkers, have fallen prey of and victim to in the 19th and 20th centuries: the megalomaniacal Marx and the equally megalomaniacal anti-Marx Hitler, those ideologues of the red-flagged as well as the brown-shirted dictatorships.

For years the dictum of Kurt Schumacher, the great leader of the German Social Democrats after World War II, has astonished me, who resisted both the Hitlerists in their concentration camps and the Stalinists afterwards, when he said the Communists were nothing else but Nazis in red. Only in recent years has it begun to dawn on me through my own bitter experiences what was meant by that. This true German patriot has pronounced himself correctly both as a resistance fighter and as an anti-Fascist, with regard to both forms of dictatorship, and this not alone because one may and shall well parallel the crimes against humanity of a Stalin to those of a Hitler. In addition, there are Soviet historians today who concur with this very statement and it may be well to let such ideas be published in the West. Surprisingly enough, they are still moving about freely in Moscow. Nobody accuses them of enemy propaganda or rails at them as they are publishing without permission of the State or because they are giving interviews on Western TV. The G.D.R. is in this respect decidedly more Stalinist, regarding the censorship against the Bureau of Copyrighting, the trials against Messrs. Stefan Heym, Robert Havemann and Rudolf Bahro over the past years, as well as other like occurrences and events. But to return to the work here under discussion: On purpose I do not use bourgeois, social-democratic, Trotskyite or like literature to prove things fundamental and essential. My support derives solely from direct sources, party-official documents and the so-called classical works of Marxism-Leninism. The truth is so egregious and atrocious that Marxists will come to believe it only if they are able to verify it from the statements of Marxist Communists themselves. It is especially important in this context to reach the group of Marx-fixated youths in the G.D.R.

With regard to the secondary and critical literature and the various commentaries, I restrict myself to two Marxist historians of unquestionable party-line loyalty, who enjoy, furthermore, a sterling reputation, that is Franz Mehring, the representative of the Marxist wing of the German Social Democratic Party at the end of the 19th Century, as well as co-founder of the German Communist Party, and Dr. Auguste Cornu, a French Communist of the present, who is considered as the nestor-mentor of Marx-Engels-Research in the G.D.R. and who was distinguished for his work from the Polit Bureau of the Central Committee of the Socialist Unity Party of Germany with the Karl-Marx Order of Merit.

With regard to the theorists and equally in contrast to Marx, the real leaders of the workers, I call upon the democratic Labor-Communist, Wilhelm Weitling, prior to Marx, as well as upon the founders of the German Communist Party Rosa Luxemburg and Karl Liebknecht following Marx. I know from bitter firsthand experience in investigative retention how genuinely hostile the Secret Police react with regard to publication of the truth against Marx of just those leaders who were murdered by the extreme right. And that comes as no surprise as the Secret Police derive their orders directly from the Polit Bureau whose First Minister is its permanent member. The death of Liebknecht and Luxemburg, thus, marked the end of democratic Communism in Germany – today we would say the end of reform Communism or Euro Communism – even before it was able to articulate itself fully in theory or organize itself in practice. With Luxemburg and Liebknecht alive the German Communist Party could have never become Stalinist; a common front between Stalinists and Hitlerists for the destruction of the pluralistic democracy of Weimar and of the social-democratic workers movement thus would have never been possible. At times I am unable to avoid fully the party lingo as it is necessary that Marxists-Leninists, those sole and only friends of peace, democratic Communists and pink members of the alternative movement have to understand me, as well. The heretic always has to serve himself of the dogmas just as the Medieval protestant did who dared and was able to take on the Papal Church only in the cloth of religion. Effective criticism of Marxist-Leninist eclecticist ideology can be rendered only in the way, shape, form and with the vocabulary of this *ersatz*-religion that camouflages itself pseudo-theoretically as a science.

One concluding remark: I would have liked to let the finished manuscript sit for about three months, to forget the details, to regain the necessary distance, to give it then a last honing touch, as well as the completion of an index of names and topics, etc., addressed, but, the risk is too high! Every screeching of brakes on the asphalt outside can mean that the head hunters and hatchet men have arrived, to ransack the house again. No! I am sustained by the hope to finish in a second edition what I have been unable to do now. The main work has been achieved and with the manuscript, it is as it is with all works: First things first, then second things and then everything else, and what cannot be done within a given timeframe will have to remain undone.

Hermann von Berg
Schoeneiche/Berlin, August 1985

Part I:

The Political System of Marxism: Perspective and Party

1. The Way towards the *Communist Manifesto*

Karl Marx, "Germany's greatest son," as he is being called according to the official lingo of the G.D.R., founded the "theory and tactics" for the victory of Communism the world over. He developed a "truly scientific perspective of the world" and turned Socialism from a "utopia to science."[1]

Marx gave the reasoning for the "inevitable decline of Capitalism" and this "scientific achievement has no equal in the hundreds of years of the history of the social sciences" as he, thus, discovered "the evolutionary laws of society."

The many communists, socialists and social democrats prior to and contemporaneous to Marx, from which he has in plain English simply plagiarized his findings, are being disqualified as vocal spokesmen of the "spontaneous movement," i.e., of the "unscientific" proto- and non-Marxist international Labor Movement. As opposed to them, Marx were to have founded an "entirely new understanding of History" which would allow the liberation of "all laboring men" from Capitalist exploitation. His "scientific ideology"[2] was to reflect the conformity of interest of the "leaders with the masses." The determining driving force of the Soviet system was, therefore, to be "the unity of a strictly scientific theory with revolutionary practice." That is to say, nothing goes without Marx, be it in theory or in practical politics. This may suffice for the characterizing of the cult about Marx as a *political* agitator. But with regards to the falsification of his *personal* attitude towards life one might still want to listen to the following with an awestruck shudder:

"As a scion of the ruling class he forfeited a brilliant university career ..., condemned himself, his wife and children to a life of perpetual wanderings and destitution, persecution by the police."

Let's start with the last mentioned, let's start with the personal aspect before we get to the professional side. The rabbinical families from which Marx came on his father's as well as his mother's side, would have been quite amazed if they, the Jews perpetually persecuted, found themselves now counted among the ruling class. It would not have been a different experience for Marx's father who, as a lawyer in the German town of Trier/Trèves at the French-German border who, as a dissenter had foresworn his religion, to be able to continue to work in his profession. How should the party hacks in Moscow have known that in 1815 all Jews were excluded from public office and in 1822 they were further excluded from all other business activities?

Thus, this kind of professional blackballing hit Herschel Marx, the father – the representative of the "ruling class" - what lies and crap are we to expect regarding Marx himself?[3]

His parents as well as Marx himself dreamt of a brilliant career, although, his mother correctly felt early that her son was a miserable loser. She had always admonished her son in her halting German that he should regard "order and cleanliness not as secondary virtues" and she wanted to know "whether an economic conduct took main stage"[4] in his own budget management. This is a question that could verily not be put before Marx as he remained on the dole his entire life and, furthermore, lived off the exploitation of others. He proved incapable of sustaining himself and his family through any regular professional activity. And above all, he let himself be sustained by continuous hand-outs from the multinational entrepreneur, Frederick Engels. Then there was money from inheritances or newspaper articles at times published under the name "Marx" although the article was written by Engels. This was the case, for example, with the series *Revolution and Counter-Revolution in Germany* in 19 installments that was published in 1851 by the *New York Tribune*. Marx was even bumming off Engels in the postscript to his condolence letter at the occasion of the passing of the latter's companion … So over the entire length of his life there really was no such thing as a brilliant career, although Marx - if we follow the evaluation of his High School Diploma/College Entrance Exam – did possess "positive qualities" which he unfortunately abused for demagogical agitation alone.

The paternal letters to the student in Bonn and Berlin are brimming with admonitions regarding diligence and order. Marx continued to be lacking these virtues. By and large today, to substantiate the contrary view, mention is made frequently of the mass of papers that Marx has produced. Only, the vast majority of it was not published during his lifetime, and, furthermore, many of these were simply excerpted passages, copied materials and writings meant solely for self-clarification and for a long life without the least professional responsibility. In the existence of a perennial student, this is not much, indeed. Even the euphemistic official party pronouncements make mention of only three works of moment in political theory:

- *The Communist Manifesto*, 1848
- *Das Capital*, Vol. I, 1867
- *The Marginal Notes of the Program of the German Workers' Party*, 1875

Several hundred pages, that is, and we shall see, these works are not voluminous in themselves and they consist of mostly copied materials, nothing new, everything plagiarized.

Marx also wrote little to his much-chagrined parents. He did not even inform them of his arrival at his university. His father reprimanded him severely in a letter, as his mother was undergoing great anxiety on her son's behalf and he added November 8, 1835: "Unfortunately this corroborates only too strongly ... that the prevailing quality of your heart is egotism."[5] If Young Karl wrote at all, so only to ask always for money in order to be able to repay his debts. He got regularly sloshed and was incarcerated for it, but continued even there. Furthermore, he got himself into duels – those were the reasons that caused his father to insist on his leaving the University of Bonn after his freshman year and continue his studies in Berlin. While graduations generally imply a certain state of maturity reached by the candidate little of it is visible in Marx - ethically or otherwise. And the first moral principle that he always stressed, that is, a positive attitude towards work, cannot be found in his own life; our Charlie measured by his own standards appears rather anti-social.

Marx returned to his studies in his sophomore year in Berlin in 1836 and this time he applied himself seriously, if we are to believe his idolaters. He may have been motivated by his engagement to a neighbor's daughter, Jenny of Westphalia, which was kept secret from his parents. At Berlin University his main mentor proved to be Professor Eduard Gans, a friend of Hegel and a teacher of social-democratic persuasions, whom his opponents accused of violent emotionality as well as a frightening agitatorial superficiality in place of a scientific method and procedure. Gans was the man with a regular audience of 600 to 700, not just college-age students, but civil servants and professionals of varying trades, as well. Second place was taken by professors with sixty to seventy students. It is regrettable that the students at Humboldt University today may not elect their professors, and that they have to diddle away their precious time with many long-winded windbags in organized futility. How about using the method applied in other countries that professors are paid according to the number of their students? Would that improve scientific debate? Would that bring back the third-rate Social Science of the G.D.R. to the level?

Gans had escaped the strict orthodoxy of the isolated German Jews, which created "amongst themselves a narrow outlook hostile to culture"[6] and which led them to fall back in bitterness behind the positions of the Enlightenment. He had done so in becoming a protestant like the father of Marx. And this was no exception if we look, e.g., at the great German national poet and Hegel student, Heinrich Heine. Marx, on the other hand, never made that spiritual leap. He never thought much of political, societal and constitutional culture. According to the materialist interpretation of History, which was affirmed by Marx, the environment is to shape man – he, thus, became a victim of these social circumstances. His entire life he aspired ardently to overturn the humanistic positions of the more noble spiritual tradition in Germany – a result of the effort of thought of several thousand years, no less - and to reduce them merely to a small group within the non-possessing proletariat. The interchange and mutual reciprocity of a general Humanism and a concrete political implementation he never grasped. In this respect he remained narrowly orthodox, subject to this negative aspect of the Jewish tradition. This baggage he was never able to let go off, neither as a student nor later. Marx's outlook on life remained narrow-minded and hostile to culture to the end. The practical implementation of his teachings in the so-called "real Socialism" or "real-existing Socialism" (as the present party slogans have it) proves that to be true on a daily basis to a frightening degree. Just to count the heads of those intellectuals exiled through the years and decades, like Gerhard Zwerenz, Wolf Biermann, Rudolf Bahro, etc., etc.

Marx's formative years during his Berlin period display a character contrarian and unreliable in the extreme. His legal studies he undertook, according to his own statements, as minor studies next to philosophy and history. He tried himself as a *littérateur*, as well, without any merit, and he used the same methods that he would use later in his political and economic works, in copying popular examples without giving the work any original or creative turn of his own. His life's aspirations he describes poetically in that period to Jenny that he "in all modesty" would like to destroy the world to live:

> "Among the gods I shall loiter
> Victoriously through their realm of ruins
> Every word be fire and act my bosom will
> Equal only to the bosom of the Creator."

Marx, our Little Charlie, as an *ersatz*-deity for the Good Lord: Excellent! His "divinations" actually did come true in an underhanded, unintended way: Today the Marxist ideology is a complete realm of ruins, in theory as well as in practice! Thus, he had decided futurological gifts. Pregnant with meaning we may also find the following passage:

> "Words I teach, mixed-up in a demoniac confused gear-work. Everyone may think about it as he pleases ... everyone may suck the wisdom's living nectar. I am telling you everything, because I am really telling you nothing."

Read as self-criticism this is really a case of rare unwitting lucidity! No further comment is necessary. It speaks for itself and reveals and classifies itself, as well. Viva the perpetual science of the general-concrete yada - yada - yada! With so many words nothing at all is being said.

No one shall say that these are just tomfooleries of youth that all of us indulged in to a greater or lesser degree! On the contrary, character structures and attitudes are revealed here that have burdened the man all his life and they were carried on by his agit-prop fighting compeers into the Stalinist party system, where they are in effect to this very day.

As Marx had absolutely no sense of responsibility to complete the study of a discipline that he had, after all, chosen for himself, and as he got bored in Berlin after the first semesters as he did before in Bonn, he informed his father that he did not want to become a legal stuffed shirt, but that he had decided to become a professional academic. Life as a university professor appeared to him more glorious than life in a law practice. He intended to get his doctorate in Law, become a professor, go back home, marry Jenny, all of which were mature and virile, good intentions. Furthermore he intended to found a literary magazine – see above as to his capacities in said field – and as if this would not have been enough, he wanted to found a magazine for theater criticism – both magazines he would run as editor-in-chief – and all of this in the gorgeous rose month of July. It becomes apparent that Marx always covered three disciplines as if they were one – never mind only how he or anyone could realistically wing that! Marx never comprehended that the sole virtue of scientific work is concentration, its sole evil fragmentation.

This paranoid-overambitious devising of plans never left him: He announced that he would criticize Hegel in a fundamental way, but he never made it further than an introduction; as far back as in 1845 he meant to have delivered two volumes of Criticism of Political Economy to the Darmstadt publisher Leske, but it actually took him until 1867 to write only the first volume of Capital and that, in spite of the fact that the system of Political Economy had been well worked out.

The eminent classic economic theorist, Prof. Dr. Adam Smith, who had founded the discipline, was connected in many ways with the progressive economical and financial practices of England and had worked on his magnum opus 10 years and the trade practitioner David Ricardo, based on the former's work, completed the system and had his own main work published within two years! The gauche homebody Marx, who was entirely removed from reality, needed fifteen years to complete his Grundrisse alone, a work that is rehashed in the first chapter of the first part of Capital again ten years later. In other words, it took Marx a quarter century to combine the economical analysis of Classical Economics with the socio-historical and economic analysis of Wilhelm Schulz and Lorenz von Stein - what an incredible performance from the standpoint of scientific efficiency!

Marx had the habit of informing his friends about the most amazing plans for publication without ever keeping them. Even where the preparatory work had been achieved he needed a fabulous amount of time as, for example, with the *Communist Manifesto.* He never managed the six volumes of his main work as planned, but only one, and even there he remained well behind the results of Classical Economics with regard to the never- processed content – foreign trade, global market, state. His heirs are considerably burdened by this even to the present. At the end of the year 1851 he let his friend Weydemeyer know that he would publish a second volume against Proudhon – well, thank God, we have been spared that as well as everything else. And as an aside: Proudhon had been sentenced to several years of incarceration at this time because of revolutionary activity on behalf of the French Labor movement. But because of Marx's grandstanding we have gotten ahead of ourselves! Let's see at this point how Father Marx saw the further development of his son.

Father Marx followed his son's studies in Berlin with even greater worries than he had done in Bonn. He saw how Karl frittered away irretrievable time, how he threw away his money foolishly with both hands, and how he in that manner even ran the risk of destroying his health permanently. Marx later often lamented his chronic liver damage. The pain about his son let Herschel Marx worry whether his son had not remained underdeveloped psychologically, without soul, without any ethical orientation on account of a mere intellectual development.

He feared the worst: Was Karl driven and ruled by an "evil demon"? Was his father referring to the megalomania which betrayed itself in the lines of poetry quoted above? He asked about it in a letter dated March 2, 1837, and added ruefully: "Will you ever be able ... to spread well-being and good fortune about in your closest environment?" In such a manner only a father, who has lived mostly for his son, can speak and anticipate the future. A year earlier on March 19, 1836, he had admonished: "Please write openly and truthfully, without reserve." The old man could not stand to be lied to by his own flesh and blood.

Now, if there is anything in life at all that gives meaning then it is the relations to other human beings as comrades, as friends or in love. As the general is comprehensible and existent in the concrete only one may ask with Father Marx, what to think of a chronic world destroyer, who himself was never in the least able to engage in positive relations with his fellow human beings, who never achieved anything positive in the concrete, directly trashed the humanist traditions, the theory of human and civil rights, but who, nevertheless, sounded off all the more so about Humanism in the abstract?

Herschel Marx dealt sternly with his son, feeling the end of his own life close. He reproached him in a letter, dated November 17, 1837, of having neither strength nor virility of character and he increased his criticism shortly thereafter on December 9th of the same year:

"Complete lack of order, dumb weaving around in all parts of knowledge, ... becoming an unkempt savage in a scholarly nightgown, instead of a savage in the tavern over steins of beer, ... forfeiting all decency with respect to the father, ... The art to communicate with the world restricted to one's dirty chambers, ... and here in this workshop of senseless and undirected scholarliness shall ripen the fruits that should nourish you and your love?... I will have to say and must say that you cause your parents many a distress and no or very little joy! As if we were Little Gold Men our dear Mr. Son disposes of 700 *taler* a year while the very rich do not spend 500."

Verily, from his college days to the end of his life, for the entire duration Marx Junior skillfully indulged in the inexpressibly difficult task of spending more money than he made and he wielded it to perfection and his planning and scheming disciples in the Foreign Trade Department of East Germany emulated him in this respect with equal success!

Fighting over money was a constant topic. Even at the beginning of the year 1836 the Father had written the son with regard to the latter's defense: "Your calculation, my dear Karl, is à la Karl without rhyme or reason and without bottom line!" This holds true not only for this small calculation of Young Marx regarding his personal budget which did not add up. This concerns, as well, the calculation of life of the Old Marx which did not add up either: Marx is crap overall, no rhyme or reason and no bottom line!

Father Marx categorically demanded a more orderly conduct of life and he consequently decreased his financial support. Then, not soon thereafter, he died. After that the ties between Karl Marx and his family were torn. The family criticized him, the Father had already addressed the same issues, no more money was to be had - so what should keep him? This much may suffice for the characterizing of Marx. These mean-spirited, lowbrow features of his being did not decrease but increased extremely in later life. Many a reputable researcher and scholar have accounted for that much. One may only note how Marx treated his own illegitimate son in later life. There is nothing to be said against a man who tinkers around to make a little son and there is also nothing to be said if that happens with an attractive maid servant. If they are attracted to each other, so be it. It seems this would not have been the first time that employers acted in such a manner. Nevertheless, what kind of a father is this to deny his own son and let him into the house only through the servant's entry –

that is to treat him as a "lower-class" being?   Is such conduct acceptable?   And, furthermore, acceptable for a person who has officially set out to abolish class arrogance?

So much needs to be said regarding the lies of the near-*fuehrer* of all workingmen. And now something needs to be said about the bitter "relinquishing" of a university career: From 1839 on Marx wanted to become professor not of Law, but of Philosophy! When he, thus, had changed his line of study – what every student at that time was able to do – one would suppose he would have participated with greater alacrity in the development of the Philosophy of Hegel as it was done by the progressive Young Hegelians. But nothing doing! Even the most euphemistic accounting of his life is not able to derive and prove even a fraction of real new-value, which could have been from Marx, unless one would want to count as positive two poems which he contributed to the magazine of the Young Hegelians, which he himself styled as "wild songs," one of which was a simple-minded and moreover tacky imitation of Buerger's *Leonora*. ... Yet better things are still to come. While the Young Hegelians were having it out with the reactionaries, Marx sides with the latter, when he, in 1840, writes a polemic against Theology Professor Hermes who was reprimanded in 1835 by the Pope. It is not possible to act politically in a more stupid and absurd way. Further, Young Marx expected that Bruno Bauer would find him a publisher for that to which the latter responded furiously on July 25, 1840: "You may write in that manner to your washer woman! ..."

Thus scared off, Marx left the thorny field of politics and retired into the saver philosophy of antiquity.

If the corresponding sketches in the old *Marx Engels Complete Works* (M.E.G.A.) are considered, diverse known quantities reappear: e.g., Marx would depict the Epicurean, Stoic and the Skeptical "in their totality and in their complete relationship to the earlier and later Schools of Greek philosophy."   When his excerpts are closely examined it appears that he has not made use of anything except the polemics of Plutarch against Epicure and the listing of the differences between the philosophies of nature of Epicure and Democritus. And this later became his doctoral thesis. Bauer, who was supposed to have provided him with a professorial position in Bonn, admonished him repeatedly to bring his thesis to a conclusion at last. It was only in 1841, after his Mother had completely cut off all funding, that he sent his manuscript to Jena where it was accepted without further examination procedures. Soviet works here finagle a brilliant defense of his thesis at Jena University. The only problem with that version of the story is that Marx never went to Jena.

He had submitted his manuscript via mail to Jena because he did not feel up to the Berlin standards. Such cowardly behavior continued to become a pattern later. He did not side publicly with the Young Hegelians, who made their mark as university lecturers or academic writers, and who congregated in Berlin in the Doctor's Club or in Cologne around the writing staff of the *Rheinische Zeitung* not to jeopardize the expected Chair.

To obtain his professorship he did more work, he changed his dissertation by giving it a new preface and added a footnote directed against Schelling – that was then in print form supposed to be the habilitation thesis of Prof. Dr. Karl Marx! How would such a performance be appraised today, even given the lax socialist exam bylaws and exams? A great academic and scientist: Preface plus footnote = habilitation. Charlie was the Greatest, a world champion of the Social Sciences!

Instead of really concentrating on a habilitation thesis and working it out - which according to German academic tradition would have to excel his doctoral dissertation in quantity and quality several times, at least by the factor three - Marx took seminars in the History of Religion and Art, as he planned to write a longer work about both. At least his fetish theory so much stressed in his later economic writing derives from that period, more specifically from Brosse's work, *The Fetish Gods.*

If one looks at what Marx did after he had finished his studies between April and July one will find two cancelled book projects and half a dozen cancelled articles for which he, in turn, promised a dozen new ones. The net result in reality was a terrific article for Ruge measuring 2 – in words: two – pages that were printed. Its title was: *Luther as Arbitrator between David Frederick Strauss and Ludwig Feuerbach.*

Why this unserious, unreliable manner? Was the well-known laziness from student days responsible for it? At least it was the first bread-and-butter job, his first personal professional achievement after his studies! He could have collaborated like other college mates with the *Rheinische Zeitung* that had begun to appear from January 1842 onward. So it was G. Jung who asked Marx in a letter on May 14, 1842, with no little irony, when he was going to show his true colors and reveal what his political convictions were. Bruno Bauer, in turn, had asked him half a year earlier, why he was not supporting the *Rheinische Zeitung.*

The answer is clear and thence derives the "renunciation of a brilliant academic career" as the official biographies had it. Only after Marx had understood that with such nonsense he would never become a German professor, did he opt to become a political maverick. That meant to work as a journalist and to raise Cain politically. Before, as the Hermes case had demonstrated, he had tried to make nice with the reactionaries in order to become a Prussian civil servant. After twelve

Semesters of University nobody would be that stupid not to know the results of one's actions.

Of course at this point Marx did not yet want to break completely with his Young Hegelian comrades. If they could not help him to become professor at least they should help him to get a position as editor-in-chief. For that reason Marx involved himself in the political debates among leftist cadres with regard to the manning of positions of the *Rheinische Zeitung,* i.e., he was plotting against possible future colleagues. This concerned also the renowned political economist, Friedrich List, who was unable to assume the position of editor-in-chief because of an accident. Through previous publications List had let it be known what would have been his concept: Upon the base of the domestic economic unity to be created by the *Zollverein* [Tariff Association] the political unity of the German empire was to have been formed which would include democracy and freedom. This was the concept of the theoretical and practical application of just that Historical Materialism that was allegedly only later discovered by Marx. Here, in turn, Marx fought against this position of List. For that reason he defended the doctrine that it was impossible "to separate the economic issue from the political one." And in his main work List wrote emphasizing the sentence in underlining it: "The civilization, the political formation and the power of nations are by and large framed by their economic conditions..."[7] In the following Marx - who had no clue about economic realities or their role in history - vituperated against protective tariffs and in a footnote in the *Rheinische Zeitung* from November 22, 1842, he maintained they would turn against the country that employed them. He further had the gall to accuse List of being a reactionary, although the latter had correctly and creatively argued for protective tariffs against the classical economic authorities of the day with regard to the backward and underdeveloped German industry. Engels later silently corrected Marx's position without making a fuss about it. But in the new edition of *Marx Engels Complete Works,*[8] this correction of Marx by Engels is reversed. Against the findings even of today's Marxist economic theory in this "centenary edition" List is being put at fault; Marx and his disciples are made right even if they are patently wrong.

How Marx has not understood at all the complicated mutual feedback system of economics and politics and, therefore, has equally misunderstood the "laws of motion of human society" - which according to Engels in the new *Marx Engels Complete Works* Marx discovered before everyone else - can be garnered from the following excerpts given under the intertitle: "Tariff Crap Association or Tariff Association Crap" And the reasoning for this title goes as follows: "Effect of the Prussian tariff crap upon the joining states. Effect of the extended Prussian tariff crap upon non-joining states. Traffic crap.

Tariff crap. Of the whole crap. About the crapping of Holland on Prussia." The odor may suffice to turn anyone off. The lack of content may do the same. Everything is genuine Marx or crap, that is, everything is genuinely shitty! Marx here displays the same obvious ignorance as does Prince Metternich. For the latter the House of Hapsburg had to pay the bill and Prussia was overcome. For Marx the workers in the so-called real Socialism paid the bill, as its authorities to this very day do not have a scientific relation to global markets.

One should not think that this is water over the dam or an obsolete matter of no current interest. Today and tomorrow the treatment of free trade or protectionism is not for the European Union alone but for all pluralistic Western democracies amongst themselves, as well as in their controversy with the Marxist East of paramount, nay, vital importance.

Therefore, Marx on his scientific level stood not only beneath the classical economists, he stood beneath those "vulgar economists" he so much depreciated! The irony of a real broken leg had it that Marx, instead of List, became the editor-in-chief of the *Rheinische Zeitung* – although only for a short period.

His collaboration there began in the summer of 1842 and Marx apologized to Ruge in a letter on July 9th for his negligence and his broken promises, etc., with the following words, that he had not been able "to work from April 'til now only four weeks and that not even uninterruptedly … the remaining time had been heavily disrupted and disturbed by many a family conflict". He called that "private knaveries" and referred here to the rejection he had encountered in the family of Westphalia; of whom he now meant to marry Jenny with the blessings of the latter's parents.

Furthermore, there were clashes over inheritance with his Mother. The parents had paid for his studies; now Dr. Marx did not return home as would have to be expected to assist the family financially in turn. He did not work and he still expected to draw financial support more even than before, although the Father had died. That was the straw that broke the camel's back. The Mother did not even let him back into the house, so our dear sunny boy was forced to reside in the town inn, so even at this early stage he found himself in his hometown in exile, so to speak.

And that may be the last biographical refutation directed against the mendacious biopicture painted by our Russians and *ersatz*-Russians: When, where and how was Marx, please, persecuted in his British exile? Had he even remotely shared the fate of persecution of the revolutionary workers in the 19th century? Or the lot of Blanqui, the head of the French Communist Party, who could claim in full right that his only permanent residence was prison? No, not at all! Germany's workers had by all means had a harder fate in

34

exile and prison after the aborted revolution of 1848/'49, or even before that then Marx. At least in neither location they would find an impregnable housemaid or a financially-potent capitalist as friends. Marx was able to study, read and write without the least interference. Not even his letters or manuscripts would be checked, controlled or statistically purloined as in today's marvelous Marx-Land and his holiday and health voyages he forgot as little to make to Karlsbad in Bohemia or to Africa, as his journeys into the old homeland of Germany, where one would even print his main work uncensored from where a man supported him financially, who is declared to this very day the arch enemy of all orthodox Communism, Ferdinand Lassalle, and that from inside Prussia that remained at this point quite hostile to the workers' movement. May God provide all the intellectuals of our "real" Socialism with a persecution in this manner!

And what can be said about Marx's "eternal wanderings"? The eternal is quite a critical category, Comrade Forger ... where, please, was Marx "eternally" residing? England's capitalist, pluralist democracy gave its mortal enemy a safe berth and harbor, protection and liberty while he was working at its destruction. Could all the Russians and ersatz-Russians of today not take Marx in British exile as an example with regard to their own dissidents - my God, I dare not ask that for mortal enemies! - especially with regard to the Nobel Peace Prize Laureate Sakharov? The question will at least be permitted, no?

Certainly, the family of Marx had to endure some hardship and he himself had to run around in boxers at home, as Little Leny had to take his trousers to the pawn shop and hock them. But that is not Marx's fault but the fault of British Railways, where Marx, for the first and only time in his life, applied for work. The clerical position that he aspired to was denied him. Reason: illegible handwriting. Even at that early stage he was good for nothing reasonable.

This may suffice to answer for the textual passages quoted above. Let us leave the personal and character side and let us turn towards the other "scientific" lies of the official party propaganda. Here we will have to start with the "birth certificate of scientific Communism": the *Manifesto of the Communist Party*. Let us see what this unscientific document contains with regard to enjoyable passages.

2. The *Communist Manifesto* of 1848
and the Union of Communists

"The *Communist Manifesto* was and is a masterly prognosis of society" and from then on "the scientific prospectus became a characteristic element within the leadership of the Marxist-Leninist Workers' Parties,"[9] that's what East German Communist Party Secretary Ulbricht announced in his heavy Saxon accent in 1967 – a hundred years after the first publication of *Capital* vol. I – to his audience commandeered to the spot of his speech. With the help of this scientific prospectus the Party steered its states masterfully into its systemic crisis, from the uprisings of the workers, peasants and soldiers in Russia in the 1920s, to the uprisings within the G.D.R. in 1953, to Poland and Hungary in 1956, to Czechoslovakia in 1968, to the uprisings in Poland in 1970 and at the beginning of the 1980s, into war, civil war and famine in the mid-'80s in Cambodia and Ethiopia - in short, the general crisis of the Soviet system, whose interior resistance along national colors lurks and breaks out occasionally as a local revolt.[10]

Next to the estimation of the *Manifesto* quoted above other statements are documented that Marx were to have given his two scientific achievements, the foundation of the materialist or economic conception of History in the preface of the *Critique of Political Economy*, that is 1859, as well as in *Capital*, that is 1867, in the latter of which he gave the overall foundation. These alleged discoveries of Marx simultaneously make up the essence of "scientific Socialism." With regard to logical sequence it is fascinating to see that in 1848 - when these "scientific discoveries" of Marx had not even been formulated by him - he nevertheless was already able to endow Communism with a "scientific birth certificate," although the latter had already failed in historical practice. There are, thus, things in existence under the sun that don't exist!

It need not be added that Marx himself never gave his ideology the label "scientific Socialism." This label was only given to it by Engels in his controversy with Eugene Duehring, because leading Social Democrats did consider Rodbertus, Lange and Duehring as the founders of scientific, meaning theoretical, Socialism, but not Marx! This raises the following question:

How far had Marx progressed in 1848 with the preparations of his "discoveries" given in detail at the end of the 1850s and 1860s? Wherefrom does he derive his scientific discoveries, as far as there are any, regarding economic and historical laws? More simply and more cogently put, one would have to ask: When did he understand or copy what from whom? Let's proceed in sequence!

In the fall of 1842 Marx became editor-in-chief of the *Rheinische Zeitung* and he found himself, thus, confronted with problems that had hitherto never interested him. Politically speaking, he held at the time vaguely liberal views, but his collaborators in the paper were socialists and communists and they had a definite theoretical advantage over him in a subject matter that had moved brilliant minds in England, France and Germany from the 18th century onward: How to solve the cardinal problem of the developing European industrial society, the so-called 'social question' of the proletariat, how to give the propertyless masses a meaningful existence in human dignity? The *Augsburger Zeitung* had in this context attacked the *Rheinische Zeitung* on October 11, 1842, of engaging in communist propaganda. The writer, Mevissen, who was a liberal and [mild] socialist had given an exposition in his article that competition and economic crises in England threatened to make the misery of the working class unbearable and that for that reason - unless the State would interfere to abolish unemployment - a proletarian revolution was imminent. This view became the core of the credo of Marx and Engels. Until the end of their lives they expected the increase of material misery caused by economic crises and in the wake of the same they hoped for the victorious proletarian revolution in those countries that had a high concentration of factory workers.

Moses Hess, co-founder of the Democratic Workers' Communism, in the *Rheinische* furthermore had reviewed an article of Wilhelm Weitling, the leading German workers' theorist, in relation with a manifesto of the French Communist Party, and he had reported on an academic conference that had just been convened in Strasburg, where it had been clearly stated that, now, following the fight of the middle class against feudal nobility, the fight of the proletariat against the middle class was the historic order of the day. It also stated with equal clarity that the social revolution was to be expected.

At the time in the French media Capitalism was declared dying; just as in the press of the East bloc countries in the mid-nineteen-eighties was in the "last stage" of Imperialism declared to be dying several times a day. This 19th century of the sociologists sounds decidedly Marxist, long before Marx, especially since this early Communist manifesto of the French demanded peremptorily to socialize land, production and labor, as well as to organize education along communal lines. The French had quite distanced themselves in theory and practice in that conference from the beginnings of their Communism. Instead of following unconditionally the line Blanqui/Babeuf like Marx which had been abandoned after the completely failed revolution of 1848, the Communist credo of Cabet was in high esteem, although that also remained ineffective in practice. The workers did not only turn against Blanqui and Cabet in their national assembly, they also turned against Proudhon. Instead of those stale Communist utopias the proletarians in politically-liberated France put the ideas of social democracy. And that was at a time when Marx was trying to establish the backward and retrograde conceptions of the Communism of Blanqui as a program in backward Germany.

On the other hand, the mass of the German workers organized itself and gained identity in the revolution of 1848/'49 in the General German Workers' Fraternity according to the example and the postulates of their French compeers and not according to the *Communist Manifesto*, the drafting responsibility of which Marx had assumed after two conventions. In 1842 Marx was, as yet, quite removed from a Communist mindset as he countered the attack from the *Augsburgische* with the statement that he "would not even concede theoretical reality to the Communist ideas, but even less wish for their practical realization or even deem that possible."[11]

Simultaneously, Marx announced further polemics against Communists which he wrote after New Year's. Not even Cornu, who is otherwise so thorough in his quotations, quotes this passage. This is simply too embarrassing to be quoted officially! A mere four years after these contributions the boss of the anti-Communists, Marx, would now advance to become the boss of the Communists and he would write the *Communist Manifesto* – what an incredible career! Marx was - as this quote proves - the last from the circle of Young Hegelians to deign even to take notice of socialist and communist issues, although in his paper these had been continuously written about. Marx was the last of the German intellectuals of his period who began to understand the burning need of the Social Question!

But to remain with the Germans: The publisher, Moses Hess, who had contacts to the German workers' movement and their secret societies in France, as well as Wilhelm Weitling, who began to come up with a democratic-communist vision of the future for them, had absorbed and processed all essential socialist-communist teachings from England and from France. They had an advantage over Marx as to the depth and breadth of their knowledge and understanding, but they were for a long time incapable to convince him of their perspective. Even the romantic poet and Hegel student, Heinrich Heine, saw the class struggle between the haves and have-nots, but Marx did not see it. For that reason Marx had sat in on the History lectures of the most eminent Hegel master-student of the time, Gans! St. Simon, Fourier, Owen - the latter of whom, by the way, received money from Ricardo for his communist self-help projects - Babeuf, Blanqui, Cabet, to name only the most eminent representatives of that school who were to become important for Marx later - and one could go back to the Christ, Plato, Campanella and Thomas More in order to demonstrate the origin of the communist idea of equality and social harmony that was to be implemented through the abolition of money - for Marx at this point none of that existed, as the proletariat did not exist for him. As opposed to others, at that point, he had other interests.

In *The Outlaws*, a monthly Paris periodical that was published until 1835 and financed by approximately 200 German workers, Venedey, Maurer and Dr. Schuster published socialist-communist ideas. Ludwig Boerne had already translated Lamenais in 1832. In 1838 Weitling's programmatic writing *Mankind as It Is and as It Should Be* appeared. How it came about the tailor's apprentice describes himself as follows: "For the printing expenses a small number of like-minded comrades made some very touching sacrifices. Some lent their rooms, others worked night shifts as type-setters, printers, or book-binders, again others donated money, some even in lack of money hocked their watches in pawnshops."[12]

These workers did not need elements alien to their class for their intellectual liberation and the political liberation resulting from it. They knew well how to articulate themselves and which rights to demand as human beings, not as laboring animals!

Appropriately, Weitling states in the following: "The year 1844 saw German philosophy fall into Communism and Socialism. First Hess, then Luening, Marx, Engels... Unfortunately, although the latter did serve the common cause with their sharp criticism, self-injury to the movement could not always be avoided."[13]

Weitling's writings had been translated into French and English, into Hungarian as well as Norwegian. He, the worker, and Hess, the intellectual, are the founders of democratic workers' Communism in Germany, a current that would today be called social-democratic, which took up the goals of the French labor movement after the utopias of Communism and Socialism had failed. It is important to prove against Lenin that the worker in the developed European countries did not have to depend upon "the bringing of ideas of scientific Communism" into their midst, as they had allegedly been incapable of coming up with a scientific worldview themselves. Lenin is discombobulating his Russian "barbarians and analphabets," as he himself was still used to call them even after 1917, with the English, French and German workers, who under the influence of public Science and Education - regarding public science lectures, workers' education associations, scientific and academic magazines in reading coffee houses, the daily press - of literature and theater and in communication with highly-educated republicans, such as Boerne and Schuster, had learned to think, speak, write for themselves. One has only to read the disquisitions of workers at the founding conventions of their educational associations, such as those in Hamburg or Hanover, or even check the intellectual quality of their magazines. That is the foundation of their leaders, not the study of Marxist pamphlets!

The European workers wrote their broadsheets in following the principles of *L'Atelier* where it had, in 1840, already been postulated that one would have to be a worker oneself in order to fundamentally understand the situation of the worker. The statutes of the magazine were even more explicit: "The magazine *Atelier* [meaning: workshop] has been founded by workers, who cover its costs. To be accepted as a founder one needs to live by one's own personal labor. Those trained in Science are only accepted as correspondents."[14] And those selfsame, proud, class-conscious workers declared to conduct their mouthpiece in following the "maxim of the fathers": *Liberty, Equality, Fraternity, Unity!"* From their board of editors came the workers Flocon, Carbon and Albert, who we will find again in leading positions in the revolution of 1843. Their positions had been set in 1840 – that was the same period when the alleged inventor of the theory of the labor movement, Marx, fabricated his 'wild songs' of Leonora ...

Weitling had defined "Liberty, Equality and Fraternity" as the goal and the flag in blood crimson as the insignia of the worker union. Thus: the crimson flag with the inscription "Liberty, Equality, Fraternity" and the addition "Union gives strength" can be found again together with the symbol of the hands united in a handshake with the name Ferdinand Lassalle and the date May 23, 1863, in the history of the German Labor Movement.

Ferdinand Lassalle has quite consciously taken up not only this symbolism, but the content of this labor program of the first complete national labor movement of Germany, that had been generated in the 1848 revolution and this General German Workers' Fraternization under the leadership of Stefan Born and Franz Schwenniger gave an adequate reflection of the French labor movement starting with the goals quoted above up to the concrete demands for national workshops, guarantee and organization of Labor. In their press and their literature the German Labor Movement did not even in 1848, the year the *Communist Manifesto* appeared, follow the line of Marx, but the line of democratic workers' communism, that is the line of social democracy. For this very reason up to now the book printer, Stefan Born, as precursor of Lassalle, is being slandered, calumniated and suppressed in Leninist historiography.

If the historical facts are being taken into account, Marx, the ideologue, appears as a marginal figure, as an intellectual alienated from working class consciousness, far apart from the powerful mainstream of the British, French and German work force. His influence amounted at times to include some German labor leaders and a handful of left-wing intellectuals. The Western European Labor Movement formulated and articulated their original and basic values without Marx, autonomous and derived from their own experience. It is well to keep that in mind when thinking of progress today!

Today the principles of the German Social Democracy are Liberty, Justice instead of Equality and Solidarity instead of Fraternity. This linguistic bringing the principles up-to-date does not hide their essential identity. What has remained 'til today is the basic position hostile to freedom and humanitarian concerns, although one is held to honor content and symbolism of the renowned original movement. It may as well be well to remember, the programmatic maxim above Schiller and Beethoven's *Ninth* which was brought into the Union of the Just and that before Marx and Engels pleaded for its abolition:

All men are brothers, all humanity is a fraternity.

Brothers and sisters are, as a general rule, not walled in alive or thrown in a dungeon. Fraternity is a mightier, more sublime goal than class justice and militaristic imprisonment.

Furthermore, on the cover of the contemporary texts of the Commission for Fundamental Values of the German Social Democratic Party the editor, Erhard Eppler, displays the historic flag. That is rather becoming. Until today it remains regrettable, however, that the German Social Democrats don't put Born and Weitling ahead of Lassalle. This would be only historically justified and these brave labor leaders would certainly merit it. And then again, this is the historic truth. The identity of the proto-Marxist Workers' Communism in the first half and the social-democratic mass movement of the second half of the 19th century are quite patent and well established both with respect to programs as well as to personalities. With regard to the future the recollection of contemporary reform Communism to well-established, politically cultivated pre-Marxist positions as to what concerns State, Liberty and Pluralism can make possible a rapprochement to the democratic Socialism of the day, as well as to the Socialist International in perspective, a blending with a social-democratic base.

In relation with the supra-national process of unification of Europe in the E.U. long-term, world-historic changes of an epochal dimension could become possible. The primitive structures of Marxist Stalinism could become completely obsolete and that would be the good fortune of all working men.

It was necessary to venture into this short excursion of world history to clarify which political concept exactly stood at the cradle of the social movements in Europe and, therefore, in Germany: It was *not* the *Communist Manifesto* as drafted, written and redacted by Marx and Engels. We will see further down how German Labor Communists made short shrift of with those "academically advanced fellows." They left them not only outside the Board of Editors like their French colleagues, no! They excluded them entirely from the League of Communists - but more about that in a little while.

First at this point Marx turned himself into a reluctant democrat. In May of 1843 he made the written remark to Ruge that the revolution that was so hotly debated and expected by everybody could be viewed as the work of the intellectuals and the proletariat, as both had to suffer most under the present system. Even Engels valuated the role of the intelligenzia higher at the time than the role of the organized working class.

Whence did Marx now get this idea all of a sudden? Germany's history of ideas is giving the answer. In the general mood of crisis in the seventies and eighties of the 18th century the theoretical head of the German Enlightenment, Herder, had already articulated a democratic critique of society with the nucleus of an evolution theory which he promptly combined with the contradictoriness and regularity of historical processes, just as did Marx one hundred years later. Herder motivated the "Stuermer and Draenger" with this theory and without flinching in any way from the feudal powers and he wrote in 1765: "You, philosopher, and you, plebeian! Form a union to become useful."[15] And Marx wrote in 1844: "As philosophy finds its material weapons in the proletariat, so the proletariat finds in philosophy its intellectual weapons." He wrote this in his introduction to the *Critique of the Hegelian Philosophy of Law*, which was published in the *German-French Annuals* that in reality were only German, as the French Socialists and Communists refused to be mentioned in the same breath with the fanatical hater of religion Marx, not to mention in print. They were not willing to give up positions of a Diderot, a Helvetius, or a Rousseau to follow Marx in falling back behind the achievements of the Age of Enlightenment. And they did not solely object to the latter's Medieval intolerance in matters of faith and conscience. They refused, as well, the idea that "might makes right," that is, that physical preponderance or brutal violence could in any way legitimize a given set of policies. Further, they rejected the idea that conquest in war could lend legitimization to a permanent subjugation of other peoples. Relinquishing the freedom of an individual was as unthinkable to them as the relinquishing of freedom of an entire people. The French President had the good graces during his official visit to the G.D.R. in East Berlin to draw attention to the fact that in France, the homeland of the Rights of Man, this position is still valid and honored today. The really touching solicitude of the Communist Party Chairman, Western statesmen were suffering from the "trauma" of German reunification and would issue in this regard nothing but prevarications, the French Head of State declared unequivocally that France would stand by its duties assumed as one of the Victory Powers of World War II. But let's get back to the French Socialists of the 19th century. They refused cooperation. Thus, another of many projects, like practically all in which Marx had a hand, abruptly and decisively came to nought. But let's continue to quote more, as 99.8% of contemporary Marxism-Leninism consists of the high art of citations, let's thus quote the well-known maxim from Marx's theses on Feuerbach, as those quoting, attribute such genuine original new value to it:

"Philosophers up to now have only interpreted the world; the point is, however, to change it." This maxim is glaring down in gilded letters on a marble background - linguistically slightly updated – from the main building of the Berlin Humboldt University at the exit of my Institute and whenever I have to pass it I have to think of the following: Among the Young Hegelians there was August von Cieszkowsky and the latter had published his work, *Prolegomena of Historiosophy,* in 1838 – a very nice title, almost as nice as Historical Materialism – while Engels had the thesis on Feuerbach published only in 1888 in the appendix to his own work on Feuerbach, after he had found them in Marx's scrapbook listed between 1844 and 1847: "Precious and beyond esteem as the first document in which the brilliant core of the new world conception was laid down," as he commented on them. Now, now, friend Frederick, the seeds came not from Charlie but from August!

Nota bene, Cieszkowsky intellectually overcame the Hegelizing first and he postulated in his work that those Laws of Evolution that Hegel – or Herder, or Luden, or Kant, or Fichte or the German and European intelligentsia in general – had discovered would have to be applied to the future in a revolutionary way. That is, society would have to be changed, turned upside down and in this manner the progress of world history would have to be directed. He demanded a "Philosophy of Practice, a Philosophy of Action" and it was he who actually introduced the central "Marxian" concept of practice first! For that reason, Marx poured such bile on him in his *Manifesto.* Marx always used the same method with those whom he plagiarized, in order to deflect attention. Cieszkowsky asks of philosophy "their effectuation upon life and social conditions at its most concrete in order to mould the future." He sees "the development of truth in concrete action," viz. exactly the "Marxian" interpretation of practice as touchstone and criterion of theory and in that, in the changed, improved and concrete action "the future lot of philosophy" would have to be sought. It was Heinrich Heine, among others, who had the same thoughts before Marx.

Was Marx aware of pages 129 to 132 in Cieszkowsky's work or not?

If not, no awareness of secondary and critical literature, grade F. If yes, what then is Marx exactly? It is a diluted rehash of Fourier, who was so vilified by him as "utopian" and from whom Cieszkowsky had received his inspirations, as well. The role of the conditions of production within History can be found in both sources, which again is something that the quote mongers attribute to Marx as an original discovery. God beware, the French are really mortal and lethal enemies, they take everything away from us!

And what about Feuerbach, whom Marx hegelized when he cremated his idol Hegel in Feuerbach? Shall we forget Feuerbach? Feuerbach as a philosophic materialist thought like the philosophic idealist, Cieszkowsky, which may prove to even the most faithful Marxists-Stalinists that with complete independence of the "fundamental question of philosophy" one may be able to harmonize politically and pass correct judgment! Feuerbach wrote a letter to Ruge in July 1843 that everything in Germany would have to be reformed from the ground upward: "An enormous work of many united powers and forces. No shred shall remain of the old regime. 'New love, new life,' says Goethe, 'new teaching, new life, is our maxim.'"

Ruge and Marx had discussions about everything - even this letter demonstrates in what intellectual milieu Marx resided and how far he had remained behind. Marx was certainly no groundbreaker or trailblazer. He usually just managed, though, to jump on the bandwagon at the last moment!

Marx became a Communist in the French capital only after he acquainted himself with the positions of Blanqui, and which he would accept and take over without any further addition: From the class struggle of the proletariat to "the class dictatorship of the proletariat as the necessary transitional stage for the abolition of class differences" in absolute terms. That was the revolutionary Communism "for which the bourgeoisie itself had invented the name of Blanqui."[16] This, by the way, is the thesis of the dictatorship of the proletariat today in somewhat reduced form. That, again, is not an original conception, but even from its etymological derivation a French formation. Even the concept of the "dictatorship of the worker" Marx quoted in this work as a French battle maxim. For the professional forgers this is the "classic insight" of all insights.

To what extent Marx and Engels identified with Blanqui, can be seen in their translation of the Blanqui address, which the latter had sent to the Banquet of Equals in 1851, an international rally celebrating the anniversary of the French February revolution of 1843. To the address was added a prefatory note which was kept completely in the spirit of Blanqui. Blanqui had called the French Social Democrats traitors and criminals, who depreciate "... violence as the only safe means [of progress]." He reproaches them to have left the corps of military officers as much unscathed as the estate of judges as well as middle-class jurisdiction in general. That has been copied by Marx, as well, as the teaching that one may not take over the machinery of the state, but that it would have to be "smashed." This statement is being declared as the "glorious further development" of the Marxist theory of the state, as the product of generalizing experiences of the French revolution of 1848, published for the first time in the New York magazine *The Revolution* with the title: *The 18th brumaire of Louis Bonaparte.* Double misfortune, Charlie, Blanqui himself simply repeated this glorious further development in 1841. He had articulated it ten years earlier in 1832 in "the trial of the fifteen," in which he was accused, as well. It may be well that from the Communist "revolution" barely anything transpired across the Great Pond, otherwise one would have frontally smacked Marx in the face for this plagiarizing, as well.

Blanqui's conclusions were as follows: "Arms and organization – those are the decisive elements of progress … France studded with armed workers – that is the advent of Socialism."[17] In their prefatory note Marx and Engels called the Central Committee of the European Social Democrats that co-organized the anniversary "miserable crooks," "European hoi polloi," "traitors of the people," a "gang of inferior pretenders." They themselves doubtlessly were superior; Blanqui, on the other hand, was called "the noble martyr of revolutionary Communism."

In order to understand the hatred against the former comrades and co-fighters, one has to bear in mind that the German Labor Communists, who were supported by French and British workers, had by now excluded Marx and Engels from their ranks. For that reason they attacked their opponents in the Communist Association, Willich and Schapper, about both of whom we will have to speak later by name, in their prefatory notes as "chairmen of the central mob." That warrants two important corrections: Allegedly, Marx and Engels got into a conflict with the workers in the federal organization in London after the lost revolution of 1848/'49, because those workers clung to their proletarian revolution, to which they aspired just as ardently as before, while Marx and Engels wanted to have understood (because of scientific insights in the meanwhile), that the proletarian revolution had become impossible at this time and that humanity would have to wait for it for at least thirty, forty, or fifty years. But they still supported Blanqui even in 1851 after their having been thrown out, the same Blanqui who had demanded for the revolution of 1848 to implement the dictatorship of the proletariat!

Therefore, if need be, Marx and Engels would even stump as adventurous putschists, full well in opposition to the objective requirements of the very process of History that they allegedly had so clearly grasped in scientific terms! This anticipation of the year 1851 may be permitted, because it elucidates that the conception of revolution of Marx was foolhardily adventuresome and putschistic, be it before or after the revolution.

What now was the historic truth with which Marx was no doubt familiar? The disciples of Blanqui had ruined the "organization of workers," that is, the national workshops that practiced a workers' unemployment relief for the first time in history. For that reason the Social Democrats managed to gather the workers behind them by the droves, the Communist experiments had been recognized as impracticable and utopian. How proletarian power could have been organized in France in 1843 whereas Lenin, with his New Economic Policy in the 20th century, had declared the erection of State Capitalism in an official party pronunciamento as the result of the "socialistic" revolution in Russia as the remedy of the self-inflicted Communist chaos?

Before Marx nevertheless turn-coated to a Communism of Blanqui's making, he characterized Cabet and Weitling in a letter to Ruge in September 1843 as one-sided dogmatists. He did not differentiate clearly between the concept of Socialism and Communism, although Lorenz von Stein had published a book a year before that letter with the title *Socialism and Communism in Contemporary France*, which had become a bestseller, and brought the Socialist and Communist teachings before the general public as if by lightening. Lorenz von Stein was a serious, highly professional political economist and historian. If one regards his complete works it becomes apparent that it was not he who had copied from Marx, as the latter maintained before the Russian legal and economic historian, Kowalesky,[18] but on the contrary, it was Marx who had plagiarized Stein in the manner already demonstrated. And that fact simply derives from the sequence of their published works, when Stein published his work above quoted in 1842, Marx himself was still completely innocent of any comprehension of the issues analyzed therein; see above the passages on the *Rheinische Zeitung*. Stein, furthermore, published three groundbreaking works in 1849 on the history of social movements in France from 1789 until his days about which we shall still have to talk. With the exception of the *Communist Manifesto*, there was nothing essential or important available from Marx at this time and his "greatest discoveries" after 1849 he copied from Stein, as we shall see later in detailed verbatim comparisons. Probably for this reason Stein is suspect to Marxists even today and he is being slandered as supposedly having been a Prussian police informer, with the alleged order to survey the French Labor Movement. Surely, for that same reason, the Prussian government persecuted Stein and the latter became an important spokesperson against Prussian policies in Schleswig-Holstein. As opposed to Marx, however, the Prussians could not prevent that Stein became a hot ticket for various professorial positions. And one more thing, Comrades Slanderers: don't call the heroic, honorable fighters at the invisible front by the ugly name of informer – one is prone to believe that you had something against Gutter-Jameses or however informers are called! And if you should have been right, that would be all the more reason to be ashamed: Five whole years it took Marx to elevate himself after all that preparatory work, the text-book about Socialism-Communism, to the same level as a "royal-Prussian" police informer.

With Stein's work, suddenly all the educated and intellectuals in Germany were brought up to date. Further, Blanqui introduced the term of the proletariat (previously used by Blanqui and Sismondi) and made it acceptable in polite conversation. Gans himself already had used the term in the 1830s.

As we have seen, Marx became political, after he did not manage to secure a university position, but he still remained a colorless liberal. He became a surrogate democrat actually, at the time when he was being pushed out of the *Rheinische Zeitung.* Socialist he became only after he had been fired from the position of editor-in-chief. Communist then he became when his project of the *German-French Annuals* failed. His personal shocks at the base always revolutionized his superstructure; he drifted from right-wing extremism towards the center, then towards left-wing extremism. But Communist he remained at this time only partly in an abstract and theoretical sense. He did not join a Communist organization. With Engels he still held the opinion that a group organized as a political party was bound to separate itself from the class movement, from the masses, that is, and would isolate itself from them by its own auto-dynamism. This is truly amazing, had he not thought at the time of the "party of a new type" of Comrade Vladimir.

However that may be, the Union of the Just he joined only when he realized that they would need party journalists to draw up political programs. Here he saw his chance to make himself known. Prior to that, however, he already had organized the power struggle in that clandestine organization. Above all, he let loose his literary sympathizers against Wilhelm Weitling whose leadership role he sought to take for himself. Marx, thus, readily provides the template of the career-crazed apparatchik. Rise to the top on the back of the proletariat, live off their account; if crazy for dictatorship, then not in the name of the class, but in the name of the masses, and even then often in the name of the party hierarchy that was isolated from the class – today, moreover, even from its party members.

Before he managed to become "temporary boss of the party," he acquainted himself systematically with the living conditions of the proletariat when he wrote his *Economic-Philosophic Manuscripts* to gain understanding for himself of what he did not know first-hand.

These manuscripts start the phase of his studying and coming to terms with political economy, about the publication of which he signed a contract with the publisher Leske from Darmstadt, a contract that was not honored and not for reasons of censorship as his biography has it.[19] When the editors brought out his early writings in 1932 they made the following remarks about said manuscript: "It contains 49 written pages in folio across mostly written upon on both sides which have been combined to one document in a rather dilettante manner and of which 23 further pages remained uncovered by any writing."[20]

Which author would reasonably cover materials on both sides knowing they would be made ready for publication, so that they cannot be handled appropriately? As usual, these were just carelessly jotted-down notes, nothing at all by way of preparation for publication, things actually ready to be read. That proved to be even advantageous for Marx, otherwise it would have become apparent even in 1844 that his understanding of and insights into economics remained far inferior to the classics, because Ricardo's labor theory of value he rejected strongly in these *Manuscripts.* Twenty-four years later in *Capital* he deduced from that selfsame labor theory of value his (according to Engels) second most important discovery! Even at this point it becomes clear that he had serious problems with the processing of materials in real time and with the quality of his understanding and that not in the politico-philosophical area alone; although he generously slaps himself on the back in the preface that his findings had been brought about "through a wholly empirical analysis based on a thorough critical study of political economy." Well, well, when the neighbors are not at home, then one has no other choice but to praise oneself!

Further therein among other things, he held wrongly that the laborer would become all the poorer the more he produced as he did not here include the historical, moral and statist element in his analysis. That the laboring class in the developed industrial countries one day would be against any kind of Communism, against any kind of revolution, but would remain comparatively content with the continuing social progress was something Marx had never dreamt of. The core of the falsification regarding the scientific new value and new discoveries by Marx rested in his alleged original creativity, in that "completely new view of historical movements," a foundation of a "revolution in historical thought," together with the practice orientation of the 11th thesis on Feuerbach quoted above and the declaration of the material processes, the labor processes, of the economical element within historical cycles.

However, a trace of it may be found in the biography officially sanctioned by the Party which may lead onto the very track of today's forgers, Marx had, one can read there, reproached the Classical

Political Economy for not having been able to understand the historical "context of the movement,"[21] but to presuppose unalterable, eternal, capitalistic - that may be industrial, as well, which is not clear because of the uncertainty and vagueness of Marx's framework of terms - conditions of production, i.e. eternal relationships of commodity - value - money, which would imply an eternal state of exploitation. This view, quoth Marx, would ignore the revolutionary movement and nature of the proletariat, but perhaps it would not exclude an evolutionary movement of the same? Who was here moving what in reality?

Within the period of 1797 to 1860 Wilhelm Schulz lived in Germany, after the revolution - he was member of the state parliament, later member of the left wing of the Frankfurt National Assembly - in Switzerland as a very respected, generally highly-regarded social-democratic writer and publisher and university lecturer of whom not a word is being said anymore in the latest Marx biography or in contemporary G.D.R. publications.[22] In the second quarterly issue of the *Deutsche Vierteljahresschrift* in 1840, Schulz had published a study with the title *The Alterations in the Organization of Labor and their Influence upon Social Conditions*, which he republished in 1843 in a more elaborate form as *The Movement of Production – A Historical-Statistical Treatise for the Foundation of a New Science of State and Society.*[23] And in this new science, honorable reader - you may have divined it already - may I introduce to you: Schulz, Wilhelm, the inventor of Marxism! Marx knew if not the article, then certainly the book by Schulz. In his unpublished notes he often mentions him with praise, in *Capital* Schulz is banished to the footnotes, he is, in fact, mentioned there exactly once.

In his book Schulz realized his intention announced in 1840 after the exposition of the fundamental laws of the production process to describe, as well, the laws of motion of intellectual production. Schulz surpasses Marx by a large margin in the quality of the exposition of world-historical, ethnographic, philosophic, political, legal and other forms of the superstructure, wherein a vivid style and stringent logic make his exposition easy to comprehend. This social democrat, Wilhelm Schulz, has in the final analysis first founded and then at the same time popularized that which today is called the materialist conception of History.

I do not know if before Schulz there had been such an understanding of the subject matter in the corresponding English or French politico-economic literature; in the German literature, however, there was no such precedent. Anyone who knows Marxism even only through vague outlines and the roughest of drafts will come to see quickly how Marx copied Schulz shamelessly. That would still to some extent cut some ice, even if Marx failed to mention the true author, it would, thus, be simple plagiarizing. But that he prides himself in volume I of *Capital* that he himself discovered the "laws of motion" of the modern ways of production is, indeed, hard to take! And Engels, the uncritical or unknowing, toady friend, turns that into the "natural-scientific" lawful foundation of the Marxist, materialist, economic conception of History that would reveal all the secrets of History! Well and good. Let's reveal a little more of Charlie himself! Let's begin with disquisitions of Schulz in the quarter-annual publication *Vierteljahresschrift*.

Schulz therein makes the following telling introductory statements: that in spite of all the difference in world-historic developments, their "unity and connection, like a lawful process" can be clearly made out. This conformity to law would be based on the historically progressive division of the labor processes and that would be pertinent not only for the material processes but the intellectual ones, as well, "so that with the insight into this relation the idea of a progressing social organism of Labor enters consciousness." Schulz considers these labor processes as the primal cause of becoming human in relation with the genesis of speech and even here Engels would remain far behind later, because these labor processes would break up the complete subjugation of human beings to the conditions of nature and would help them on their way to independence and freedom.

In the final analysis Schulz was expecting that the modern forces of production of the industrial age would bring for all humans what bond-slaves and serfs had brought to the ruling class in antiquity and Medieval times, as "the political freedom of the Greeks and Romans had only been based on slavery and that it could not have been otherwise because of the state of the organization of Labor at that time." Modern machinery was supposed to be the slaves and serfs of the future, so that for all humans time could be freed for political philosophy and creative work.

Depending upon in what relation dependence and independence are positioned to each other "we will become aware of lower or higher societal formations." Schulz describes the Gentile order as one "in which material and spiritual work has not as yet been separated" and that there "no special classes or states could be found" in society, as "for the development of public law or the managing of a public ordering power the imperfect societal body has not as yet found expressed the necessary formation of the organs and functions." We will see from the first sentence wrongly copied in the *Communist Manifesto* that Marx from the get-go had not understood Schulz fully.

Schulz here is examining further how the development of "land cultivation," that is cattle raising and farming, forms the primordial form of society, how the increasing separation and specialization of labor develop the artisanship and trade, including special "states and classes, professional guilds and corporations" and how from all three areas capital stock is accumulated to prepare for Capitalism, a process which is greatly enhanced by the "military-feudal element," that is, through violent superstructural processes. The system of feudalism is thus characterized: "Between the two prevalent classes (Schulz refers to nobility and clergy, i.e., the art of war and the production of ideas) the cities became the seat and the location for processing and distributing of agricultural products, that is, retail and trade" and in that manner "the particular class of the patricians, a special branch of the governing state" was created. In this manner even the bourgeoisie or middle class has been introduced. The author proves further that *changes in the process of work for the aim of material production simultaneously and necessarily engenders corresponding changes in the intellectual and political culture."* Herewith, long before Marx the mutual relation of economic base and spiritual-political superstructure is clearly defined. Schulz demonstrates, furthermore, how these bourgeois middleclass forms complete themselves through manufacture into the factory system and he draws the following conclusion regarding future developments: "At this point the series of further evolution of this organism, which will lead to new steps of development, is not yet completed." He defines in this manner the technical and social developments of the future, which will go past the Capitalism of free competition. Here again he sees the problem more clearly than Marx, who wanted free competition to be abolished by means of the proletarian revolution!

"The latter [steps of development]," Schulz continues and he guards himself unlike Marx against empty, meaningless and inappropriate generalizations, "are limited so far only to the European-American lives of peoples and they pertain exclusively to the new times." Historical science has meanwhile corroborated that commodity production, indeed, has developed in Europe and the U.S. only because of inherent laws. The countries with Asian modes of production had it forced upon them from the outside.

Schulz is not glued to or restricted by economic factors in an absolute manner. He describes the end of the Medieval period, the dawn of the New Age of Modernity with a series of great geographical and technical-scientific discoveries. Therein, he highlights particularly the "firearm" as a lethal instrument and the printing press as a mechanical device to copy intellectual production. In this manner a reductionist limiting to local opinions is precluded as, thus, a public opinion is generated. "Thus, the firearm and the press were the first machines which, applied on a large scale, formed social conditions and changed essentially the social and political standing of the respective professional states," he resumes. Marx and Engels repeat this summary later in different variations.

Schulz addresses - next to the extra-economical - the infrastructural, the demographic and the foreign trade rapports of macroeconomic processes, as well - a welcome synthetic view in place of Marx's isolated one. Schulz does not philosophize about this out of the blue, but brings in remarkably clear and cogent statistics from many different countries with respect to agriculture, trade, industry and population, shows causes for different production outputs of agricultural and manufactured production in Europe and abroad, emphasizes intensifying factors of Science and weighs the upsides and downsides of state influence, etc. In short, he reads - in contrast to Marx who never managed such a universal and comprehensive view - like a modern author.

Schulz gives examples for the interconnectedness of Capital that became apparent for the first time in that period in the industry, agriculture and manufacture of England and he already, at that early stage, deduces the blending of interests of all capital-holding factions thereof, a statement that receives the highest accolades today in the teaching of Marxism-Leninism as a pretended Marxian wisdom of the first order, as it were to prove the united front of the Labor movement upon a Communist base against the united front of Capital. Correctly, Schulz demonstrates the output gap between England, France and Germany and assesses with equal correctness "that the actual fabrication is of the newest date and only at the beginning of its development."

The last third of his article on the principles of economics is dedicated to an issue, how the depicted changes in the "organization of Labor" at the base affect the superstructure, i.e., primarily legislation and administration. He sums up that it will have to be "conceded that by and large legislation in its essential features had to follow the changes in the content of society." Marx corrected his theoretical understanding of "society" only much later; at the time Schulz wrote this he was completely captivated by abstruse views of Hegel's State idea. And the latter postulates quite dialectically and materialistically - and this (surprise!) is possible without Marx - that "in all acknowledgement of the relation of mutuality and reciprocity," still "far and wide the facts of the lives of the peoples created the laws and rules rather than that the reverse would have been the case." Now, a more "Marxist" statement would not be possible! And that is not alone Historical Materialism, it is, dialectical Materialism directly.

Schulz emphasizes that objective and subjective, material as well as ideative factors work in mutual reciprocity, work in the historical process and that their simultaneity would always bring about the lawful higher development of societal order. The often "very hostile position of the workers against the capitalists" - following Engels it was Marx alone who coined the terms capitalist and Capitalism - Schulz deduces from the absolute and relative poverty of the proletarian, whereas he makes the interesting point - correctly as opposed to Marx - absolute poverty could be reduced with the simultaneous increase of relative poverty, as with the development of the modes of production needs would increase drastically, as well.

The social democrat deems it of paramount importance to examine the problem of how the capitalist mode of production would affect the "physical and mental health" of the individual worker, "to what extent men work through machines or *as machines.*" Decisive protest Schulz voiced against the intellectual and physical crippling of the working men and, above all, against child labor. We will see later how differently Marx would treat that same point. A farsighted judgment Schulz pronounces on female labor in the industrial sector, as women "would, thus, gain an economically more autonomous position" and, therefore, "both genders would approach each other in their social relations." For that reason future marriages could be based on love relationships liberated from financial considerations of utility; the choice should be made "according to the free inclination of the hearts."

He sees, as well, that element of the factory that is conducive to organization and building of political consciousness, as the proletarians, as opposed to the agricultural producers, "work in manifold communality and are thus able to sustain their mass combinations," so that they are able "to unite more closely in their mutual interests against the master of the factory." Common interests and common work would thus bring about by necessity the association of the workers and their organizations.

Schulz regards the failures and downsides of early underdeveloped Capitalism not as a cause of despair, but views the overcoming of the same through the united forces and efforts of the worker as a real possibility. The citizens' conditions would definitely change for the positive. "For the future of the life of the peoples, the mindless forces of nature that work in the machines will become our slaves and serfs," he reiterates often. And under this precondition, he continues, "can the idea of a general equality of the citizen, as opposed to a shallow leveling" - he was referring to a Communism in the manner of Babeuf - "continue to enter consciousness and life." The social democrat Schulz thus elevates the primitive form of the conception of equality on that basis, for which Marx uses the term scientific Communism - another of Charlie's creative discoveries. Schulz well qualifies these conceptions of equality. Instead of the primitive hatred of the proprietor who has to be clubbed to death and whose property has to be distributed equally, he posits possession as a social parameter. Even that Marx repeats thirty years later in *Capital.* Schulz's attack is not directed against the entrepreneur as personified Capital, but against the social system. That is something the Red Army Faction bandits have not comprehended to this very day. As is well known, even Lenin, after the death sentence of his fraternal terrorists, swore off individual terror.

As a result of Schulz's work which postulates the materialist conception of History that, following Engels' propagandistic lie, was named after Marx, "the changes within the organism of the material production simultaneously will shape the conditions of the spiritual and political culture in an essential manner in both form and content." That sounds much like the balanced treatment of the topic in the letters of Engels written in his old age, while Marx, as usual, exaggerates and skewers brutally.

In this manner Schulz concludes his article, while he articulates in the introduction of the following book his social-democratic credo according to which the distribution of the ideative and material factors of production "would be contradictory and against nature through which all States of civilized Europe would condemn the greatest part of their population to serfdom and dereliction," when one had "robbed those people of the free enjoyment of liberated and joyful creation." As much as politicians were used to "glue over this abysm of misery with arbitrary laws of force, these wounds would rip an ever greater and deeper gap between the proletarian masses and the higher states to an ever more threatening degree." As we can see here the theory of misery in Marxism does not derive from Proudhon alone.

"Will this mutual alienation (even that is a key concept of Marx) escalate to a destructive civil war?" is the question Schulz poses for the future and his answer is the following: "In that manner war has been declared against property ... are not England and France in their coalitions of workers, in temporal cessation from work, in isolated uprisings and assassination attempts, in pillagings and acts of arson, the vanguards of this war?" Schulz regards the causes of this class struggle tied to "a great economic crisis, as it is wont to occur and recur in our society from time to time." That is to say, even the connection of periodic crises and revolutionary preconditions had not been discovered and articulated by Marx first! The latter took a rather long time in England after the revolution of 1848 to find reasons for this well-known connection.

Again, in contrast to Marx who, almost to the end of his life, worshipped and applauded violence as the midwife of the New in over-absolute terms, Schulz stresses from the get-go that the human spirit should not despair "of the possibility of a scientific solution and a peaceful fulfillment of the social task." Even if this possibility came to nought, if "this new teaching has to be whipped with bloody features into the flesh of humanity," so he, the social democrat, would still "side with ever greater courage and confidence with the flag of that party who has that better right on its side, as it has sprung forth out of the living needs of the present and so would have a future."

Regarding Social Science, Schulz remarked that their "new social teachings have originated from the more extreme contradiction between Labor and Capital," as in his view proletarians would also be unpropertied intellectuals, not paid by the State, as well as workers, as both lived by the sale of their labor power. Here we find again the idea of Herder that has been fraudulently attributed to Marx. Schulz recapitulates that those social ideas had developed the class consciousness of the worker, his "proletarian feeling of self," so to say. One has only to think of the French labor magazine L'Atelier! Schulz finds it nonsensical to turn against the "darkly hovering goal of an essentially different formation of production and consumption" and to vituperate against the "ogre of Communism." It would in his view be better to inquire soberly after the material causes of those ideative appearances, as a delusion like Communism would only then become perilous when matched with the truth.

For that reason, Schulz demanded that science should distance itself from philosophical speculation - one may think of philosophy of action and one shall find that this school had more noteworthy adherents - and for that "it should concentrate more awareness than previously upon the examination of problems, which have emerged from the large nations of Western Europe out of their social conditions which are even approached by Germany."

One should not deem it possible without Marxism how completely the entire historical processes, the laws of historical motion, can be correctly grasped and, furthermore, adequately represented, where every crawling baby in the G.D.R. child cradles knows, because it has been inculcated in him with its mother's milk that Marxism-Leninism alone allows scientific insight into the societal processes of development! Schulz militates decisively against the burden of tradition and demands "that every compulsion and every custom be removed from the schools," finally to admit again "all of life as the one and only schoolmaster to attempt whether through all the manifoldedness of its appearances the simple principles of evolution may not be deduced thereof." This paragraph sounds much like the criticism of the XX Party Congress of the Communist Party of the Soviet Union in 1956 of the dogmatism of the Old Marxist-Stalinist School. "Deduced thereof," that is, examine and research continually, Schulz would like to proceed with the evolutionary principles of social processes, not to shout them from the rooftops as eternal truths as Marx would have it and as the East German Socialist Unity Party would have it with him.

According to Schulz the flaws in the treatment of the social question would derive from that fact that one "hitherto had only examined the material side of production and consumption without heeding sufficiently the spiritual creativity and its societal conditions."

"Every particular mode of production" that is - believe it or not - the exact verbatim phrasing of Marx in his formation theory from 1859, "presupposes a particular mode of consumption," in other words production and distribution belong together organically. Here we find methodically the construction of Marx's three volumes of *Capital*: Production, circulation, the integral process; this was to have been overlooked up to now and for that reason "the social significance of individuality" had not been recognized. Now, this is nothing less than the conclusion of Marx's cardinal economic work! To put it into the language we are used to, Schulz postulates to preempt and to guarantee material and spiritual production and appropriation on account of the working human being and for his or her general and all-round development and that is, moreover, through changes of social reform and, if need be, through revolution. In that Schulz turns against capitalist property, which would have an exploitational effect, but he speaks up with emphasis, on the other hand, for personal property. Repeatedly he highlights in that process the "lawful context" of these social relations which would bear an objective character through the division of Labor. Schulz recommends further, one should in contrast to Adam Smith not speak of division or separation of Labor, but of the echeloning or structuring of the labor process, an excellent proposal as it takes immediately into account all the integrative sides of the production process. These echeloned or structured labor processes would allow the insight that production is a living, historically advancing organism, on whose base "the life of a State or the entire political production would have to follow the general processes of production." In the style of Marx that would mean later that the material base would determine the political superstructure and that, thus, the changes in the base would have to follow changes in the superstructure. However, in the case of the current representations of Socialism this particular conception would smack of subjectivism; the proletariat, having become victorious through the Revolution, would have, hence, to create its own economic base. Marx here turns the plagiarized materialist conception of History upside down. From his taking on of power there will again rule arbitrary subjectivism, or proletarian Absolutism.

More decisively and more clearly than in the *Vierteljahresschrift* Schulz here draws conclusions from his theoretical analysis according to which "the idea of a general liberty and equality of the citizen" has to emerge in life as it begins "to realize itself more and more according to the unalterable laws of production." What now, Brother Engels, is this not your "natural-history necessity," the Darwinizing of social processes that you have been praising so much at the gravesite of friend Marx? Schulz makes his conception here even more clear and apparent, it would be baptized "formation theory" later by Marx, when he elaborates that from the most primitive forms of social conditions onward, that is, from the Gentile order so correctly described by him, the primordial Communist society, up to the system of Europe which is becoming capitalist the "same sequence of steps that we may discover chronologically in the age levels of various individual nations" can be proven.

With these amendments Schulz renders his theoretical positions more exact and simultaneously confirms them. Furthermore, he adds a section about the "spiritual-intellectual production" which gives a comprehensive picture of all superstructure processes; he treats therein State and politics, religion and art, literature and law, philosophy and other subjects both in their historical development, as well as in their contemporary significance. He draws attention to the retrograde perspective of the Young Hegelians in that he confronts their views with the political realities in France: "What is achieved by the motion of philosophical thought in a slow manner and with extended detours (the analogous assessment of Weitling may be borne in mind here), the practical sense of the lower classes has attained directly. The need to have a positive religious basis for a new formation of society becomes more and more apparent in Socialist and Communist writings."   Schulz here condemns the arrogance of thinking disconnected from the world "as it is so frequently practiced by youth, who, without having gone through the greater course of experience, try to encompass the whole wealth of life in its abstractions." That could have been meant directly for the Marx of the day who lived at the time in an extreme, naïve disconnect from reality. Schulz, then, made a positive assessment of the pre-Marxian "philosophy of action," if it was held to be "action of a progressive redemption and liberation of Man by Man." Marx had articulated his abstract humanist credo in almost the same words. Schulz demands from the political economists that they put Man and not the profit motive into the center of their reflections. Formally speaking, this is today the main thesis of this surreal Socialism of ours: They shouldn't hold Labor as absolute, but ask for its social significance and sense. Schulz admonishes the State to protect the worker and he turns against a "vain and verbose policy of reflection that does not have the force to comprehend the whole significance of the times from the context of its foremost appearances, in order to make valid predictions, what a policy that would merit its name always would have to be." He postulates further to enrich policies with scientific solutions, so that the concrete truth could be seized and he guards himself strongly against the hollow rhetoric of averages in the later Marx. The necessities of the time, which would be the mother of invention, would need to be harnessed and utilized, in his eyes, in order to master and dominate its social processes. But then again, Schulz never took the stance of the generally omniscient in the concrete rather average and pedestrian quack Marx. Schulz's words sound rather prophetic with regards to the disintegration of the group of Young Hegelians and with regards to the fight of everyone against everyone else organized by Marx: "It so appears that the vain world saviors, young ones and old, would run through all the alleys cheaper by the dozen to preach." And that's what happened for the remainder of the century. The Marxists were one sect among many others who dealt with the (almost) absolute truth. Even more clairvoyant sound the warnings of social democrat Schulz against the "mechanistic unification of divergent principles" which was practiced with such diligence and virtuosity by Marx, viz.: Hegel's idealism stirred up with Feuerbach's materialism, added a spoonful of French Socialism-Communism and a shot of English political economy - here you are with the Marxist potpourri! It could further be spiced with strong Stalinist peppers, so that the eclecticist beggar's stew would become completely indigestible.

As if he really saw what was coming, Schulz admonishes us of the dogmatist's waxing eloquent about the neat order of his things, which would endanger freedom as the real and actual aim of the lawful evolution of humanity on the basis of the general laws of production and intelligence: "Would Thomas More, the martyr of his independent convictions, not have seen prohibited any kind of utterance about government matters by the punishment of death in his utopias. Likewise, in the first Communist doctrines of recent times a tyrannical coercion in matters of media and teaching became apparent in his utopias."

Thus, the G.D.R. reader and Soviet man are aghast, of how could Schulz have known all this so much beforehand? Or had he plainly divined the misery of the German-Russian ideology before it really came about?

Let's summarize:

Schulz, perhaps as the first writer in such clarity, regarded political economy in world-economic and world-historic contexts. With this approach he delivered for Marx not only content-wise but with regards to methodology all the answers, which the latter pretended to have given - according to Engels - in the name of the economic conception of History. With regards to any number of issues Schulz is more mature than Marx, be it scientifically, politically and even from the human perspective. Schulz determines the relation from classless society to one class-governed, he determines the relation of revolution and reform, the mutual reciprocity of misery and alienation in a more balanced and dialectical manner than Marx, who never considered many of these questions at all, and some only towards the end of his life, then forced to do so only at the bidding of the Labor movement. Schulz takes it up with the socialistic school of English economics, that is to say at least with the latter's criticism of classical political economy, as it seems to consider the material-technical as well as the value-related part of economics while not taking sufficient account of the social aspect of production. In face of the retrograde economic conditions in Germany this is an especially honorable achievement for the German Social Science of his day.

It is quite telling in this context that Marx did not manage to attain the level of Schulz; although he did not receive the latter's ideas directly but again indirectly through the intervention of Moses Hess. It may be compared only to what Hess wrote prior to Marx about Labor and alienation: Marx plagiarized Hess to the full, as well. And Hess himself knew the works of Schulz and he is furious about this social democrat who spoofs from a scientific standpoint in a rather brilliant manner the economically ignorant, but, thus, all the more believing Communists, who wanted to have abolished money with Hess and Marx to make humanity happier, because they had neither understood classical economics nor the laws of motion of production and of History - as neither have understood them their successors of today, which is the real reason and deeper explanation for the decisive lagging in labor productivity of our blooming, future-oriented, "real" Socialism behind the dying, putrid, parasitical (and you-name-the-derogatory-epithet) Capitalism.

After Schulz, Marx copied Engels' study of political economy which contained nothing but generally known economical opinions. Engels refused to have it republished again in the 1880s as he found it flawed and sophomoric. For Marx, on the other hand, it remained a "brilliant sketch." Sure, the one-eyed is king among the blind! In this manner we know whence Marxism, this compiled, inorganic "new teaching" without ideas, derives. Marx reproduced the study coherently, with Engels, in the equally then unpublished and unfinished study *The German Ideology* before they went on to work on the *Communist Manifesto*. In the latter they made known to the world the views of Schulz, Hess and Stein in the manner of catchword and catchphrase sketches on the basis of working papers that had been discussed exhaustively in two conventions in London in 1847.

Nevertheless, the topic here under discussion, i.e., the materialist world view, is too important to let it get submerged in the agitational porridge of the *Manifesto* devoid of any rhyme or reason.

There is a study on "Historical Materialism" among the left-wing members of the social democrats written by the publisher and historian, Franz Mehring - who later became part of the Communist Spartacus group - republished in 1950 in Berlin, which was endowed with a preface by the then prevailing economics pundit Oelssner, temporary Polit Bureau member under Ulbricht, that swears to high heaven that above all Lenin and Stalin contributed to the further developments of Historical Materialism. Who else could it otherwise have been, comrades?

The further development of Oelssner consists of the statement that in the execution of the objectively effective laws of Historical Materialism "there exists now no other possibility to realize the socialist revolution in all of Germany by peaceful means," but only through the ukase of the Socialist Unity Party "by way of a revolutionary mass struggle."[24]

But let us pass on Oelssner's brilliant preface, which displays the scientific prevision of Historical Materialism in its true and full colors, because here we are really and primarily concerned with Mehring's text. The text is the older one, but it has not lost any of its brilliance. Professor Brentano has indicated, as Mehring writes, that even the historical school of the Romantics has touched upon the materialist interpretation of History.[25] And Mehring refers further to the "laws of motion and production" of Lavergne-Peguilhen. The full title, which is more indicative, reads as follows: *Foundations of the Social Sciences - Part I* containing *The Laws of Motion and Production - An Essay in the State Sciences,* by M. V. Lavergne-Peguilhen, Koenigsberg, Prussia 1838. The terminology of said work is exceedingly current. In Germany it is Marx, on the contrary, who counts as the founder of the Social Sciences. Mehring does not give the full title, which already gives Lavergne away as a precursor of Schulz, as he doesn't give the early date of publication. He hides further that in a second part the Koenigsberg writer does deal with cultural laws, or in plain speech, that Lavergne already instituted the separation of base and superstructure before Schulz or Marx! Mehring simply libels the unwelcome author, as does Marx in the *German-French Annuals*, as he does with the Romantic School in general, saying that it is scientifically irrelevant and politically reactionary, as it allegedly doesn't want anything else but then the containment of feudal rule. Mehring notes that he has read the study and couldn't agree more with Marx. Period, full stop, case closed! Mehring in this instance is forging that it takes one's breath away!

Lavergne writes - after he has characterized slavery, serfdom and feudalism as lower, Capitalism, on the other hand, as higher forms of the development of society - that the capitalist monied economy would have to prevail, "as only through it could the highest inner freedom be combined with the highest productivity of Labor."[26] But that is not the only comment that needs to be made. Long before Marx Lavergne is using the terminology of the mutual reciprocity of productive forces and conditions of production! Well versed in English Political Economy and Fourier's categorization of the "social formations," he is dealing with the principal and familiar categories of macroeconomics in a perfectly "Marxist" fashion, as well!

As early as the middle of the 1830s our Koenigsberg scholar demands from the intellectuals of his times to assume a materialist and dialectical approach of analysis rather than to engage in fruitless digressions into the Beyond. His colleagues were supposed to concentrate on the here and now, as it were, "complete arrogance ... which does motivate the scholar to engage in the depths of perfectly otiose and futile speculations, to follow the ever incomprehensible needs of an afterlife, while the terrestrial life still brims with a great number of unsolved problems! ... The belief of one's own spiritual superiority, which is more often than not based on delusion, leads to a general loathing of the slaves (he subsumes under this term just like Gans the modern factory-slave that is the proletarian) and serfs, as well as of their productive activities."[27]

Lavergne deems the reversal of the historical development - and such utopias in the sense of a relative protectedness of Medieval systems were championed by certain social reformers such as Professor Windelblech from Cassel, so presented at the artisan and apprentice convention in Frankfurt/Main in the summer of 1848 - impossible, so he writes, as that would ruin society by the older, ineffective modes of production! Our world-removed homebody Marx may have been provoked to his invectives in the *German-French Annuals* by the following passage: "The life of a people, may it be as expressively stated in its national literature, cannot be understood by one concentrated upon himself, without fully comprehending the more or less identical motivational springs of popular life. This kind of study of antiquity and history by mere recluse savants necessarily has to yield abstruse and wrong results."[28] Lavergne makes even stronger statements about those theorists who remain caught forever in the fogs of abstract dogmata.

"I would like to ask any one of our Political Scientists upon his conscience, whether he is familiar with the inner workings of a miner's household, with the conditions of their subsistence, as well as with their sorrows and joys. I would like to ask whether he has made the conditions of existence and production of a small peasant economy object of his studies and whether he has comprehended them?"[29]

A man is talking here who demands empirical research, exact knowledge of the facts, straight analysis of reality, and who throws down the gauntlet to all scholars of the old school. He feels himself in his expression, and rightly so, as the co-founder of a New Social Science. To his honor and quite in contrast to Marx, he also enumerates at the beginning and the end of the book those savants and mentors to whom he owes his knowledge and here he mentions not only the English and the French writers in question but also a number of Germans, among them Friedrich List. At this occasion it may be well to remember that Marx and Engels relinquished their plan first voiced in 1844 to publish a library of eminent socialist writers, a plan curiously never followed up later. For a very good reason: they would have revealed themselves as senseless copyists with no original ideas of their own!

The one great flaw of the German Historical Sciences was it to have left the biographical and conceptual ground-breaking of the works of the German Materialist School in Economics and History to the diligent forgers of the Institute of Marxism-Leninism of the Central Committee of the Communist Party of the Soviet Union and the Socialist Unity Party of Germany who are, thus, extracting capital for the political disorientation of the academic youth.

Lavergne would like to have applied the materialist and dialectical approach to the social sciences, as well, and he postulates to have "method, order and context" established therein. They would have to take heed of the inner and outer principles of life and motion, treat world history as a process of evolution of Man and Society through Labor, division of labor and language. Lavergne demands higher academic standards and he himself lives up to them, as well. He mentions the scientific and technical developments and discoveries – gun powder, the printing press, the loom and the steam engine - as driving productive forces. He comments on the higher demands of industry in education of the workers resulting thereof, defines Labor as a societal necessity and determines correctly the relation between satisfaction of needs and production.

He demands of the State to regulate the economy through legislation of taxation and tariffs and highlights that increasing workers' productivity would serve "all conditions of motion and production."[30]

Increase in productivity would lead to higher levels of culture: Barter instead of coercion, purchase instead of barter. There is no doubt that Lavergne discusses the commodity – value - money relation in 1838 on a higher level than Marx in 1845! He sees the issues of the costs of production, the issues of concentration of money and capital, the negative effects of competition and monopolies, the role of the shareholder company (that will be touched upon very lightly only at the end of the century in volume III of *Capital!*), further the danger of crises and he defines wages not like Marx following Ricardo as price of labor, but more even-handedly as average labor price. In all that he keeps a critical distance to the classical economists. Lavergne attributes physical and intellectual performance, forces of nature and state organization all to the "socially productive forces."[31] On the other hand, he quotes, contrary to Marx, Say correctly, who maintained against Adam Smith, that not Labor alone would create all wealth. This fact helps the Soviet-Marxist greatly up to now. But to go back to our Marx of the theories, the passage about "socially productive force" he liked a lot. According to *Capital* it is the general worker in society who produces the surplus value.

Lavergne correctly explains the theory of the reproduction cost of labor power, as well, and he highlights that pre-capitalist command economies barred a higher evolution of society and that capitalist moneyed economics on the other hand would lead to a "surfeit of misery" and "factory slavery." Capitalism as a whole he regarded as a "new social era."[32]   Whether I say era, epoch or formation was unimportant at the time, it is essential, however, which content the terms have and this new era is now characterized by Lavergne in such a way that one deems to hear textual passages from the *Communist Manifesto* with regards to the boundless development of the productive forces. "It appears as if all the bonds which held the slumbering social forces in fetters were now suddenly loosened." Combinational and labor-divisional processes could be "led to limitless heights". *"To lead a society to higher stages of development,"* educated human beings would have to be brought up *"to institute to that aim as the fundamental condition of social progress"* a *"safe and complete production."* After that Lavergne draws the following conclusion: "That every economic system approaches perfection to the extent to which profit as a measure of the capital invested gains volume on a sustained level and as it furthers the increase of production."[33]

Now, from as far back as the New Economic Policy [N.E.P.] of Lenin up to Andropov's postulate, the Soviet factories should finally make a profit and the official stipulation of "gain" (= profit) in the process of the intensification of macroeconomic procedures within COMECON, this insight, which had been formulated by Marx and was taken above and beyond him, has proven true. Without exploitation a labor-separating society cannot work. The only question remains how high and how bearable this exploitation is, and how good or bad the political, material, and financial living conditions are for the wage earners?

I will have to beg forgiveness of the readers not well versed in economic theory, that those matters are not discussed in more detail, as that would take up too much space. However, the core, I hope, has been clearly exposed. Even the economic lay person can understand what the matter is with Marx in the alleged "new and scientific" interpretation of economic contexts and facts, as well as with their laws of motion. His "science" consists of badly-copied and wrongly-interpreted theories. Verily, today, he cannot even be given the honorific title, as others could, "meritorious plagiarizer of the people." Marx, in fact, did not discover a historical perspective based on materialist and economic laws of motion which would only enable the foundation of a Social Science. His own muddle-headedness and ignorance appeared to him, just like to many a Marxist intellectual of our day, as great theoretical problems and the introduction to the answer that is already known hence would appear as a scientific discovery, although we are here dealing only with an individual monologue. And to close this part let's go back one more time to Mehring. The latter cites our Koenigsbergian writer Lavergne as follows:

"Perhaps social science as such has so far progressed so little, as the *economic forms* have not been distinguished enough, as it has not been understood that they make up the *foundation of the entire social and state organization.* It has not been heeded *that production, productive distribution, culture and cultural distribution, state laws and state forms must derive their content and their development alone from the corresponding economic forms*, that those ever-so-important momentous events of society derive inevitably from the economic forms and their adequate management as the product derives from the engendering and coming together of the germinal forces and *that where social ills become apparent those have their origin as a general rule in the contradiction between the forms of society and state.*"[34]

Marx, so Mehring, "appears ... at first glance to have licked Lavergne with his materialist theory of History."[35]

Did he really? Licked? Copied would be the word in plain English! The predecessors of Lavergne and his successors down to Wilhelm Schulz are the creators and representatives of the materialist interpretation of History in Germany. I do not mean the line of tradition that has come down to us from antiquity or even Western European scholars, but solely the German contemporaries of Karl Marx, who made "his discoveries" decades before he made them. Not Marx, but they have made the "key to historical understanding" with which some but not all of our historical lockboxes may be opened. Marx on the other hand was the key's pickpocket!

Here comes another gag. Mehring writes himself[36] that Marx annihilated the historic-romantic School and its most eminent representative, Lavergne, in the *German-French Annals* with his criticism, plainly, Marx even in the middle of the 1840s had not yet grasped, how far the theoretical reflex of the Western European economic, political and socio-political development in Germany had already gone! We have seen like reactions with regards to Friedrich List.

But the plot thickens dramatically at this point! Mehring found the matter precarious and he tried to get Engels' support when he asked whether he himself or Marx had known the writing in question. Engels answered in a letter from September 28, 1892,[37] he knew the literature of this school "only very superficially" and it remained absolutely "alien to him" and he owed it "absolutely nothing." Marx, moreover, according to Engels, had always loathed this direction of thought. Why actually, one is prone to ask? Had he written his "annihilating criticism" without having read the author? Had he let himself be guided by a political catchword rather than by factual knowledge? Or had he read the texts in question and was simply too stupid to seize what qualitative incision, what incredible factual and methodological enrichment they brought for the Social Sciences? Was he as terminologically obtuse, or, rather, retarded, as in the case of the labor theory of value or Communism? And it is none other than Frederick Engels who reveals the backwardness and incapacity of thinking scientifically in our great "discoverer" Marx, when he continues:

"Had he hit upon those passages, as the one quoted from Lavergne, it could make no impression on him whatsoever at that time, if he even understood what those people meant. Marx then was a Hegelian for whom such a passage was completely heretical, about economics he knew nothing. He could not even conceive of anything with respect to a word like 'economic forms' and so would the passage in question, even if he had known it, have left no trace whatsoever in his memory."[38]

Great, absolutely great! Dr. Marx appears to act like one of my students who when cornered by questions held up both hands and said: Help! Knowledge is pursuing me, but I am faster! Engels telltale comments cannot be relished enough. Both knew nothing, absolutely! Both understood nothing, absolutely! Marx copied without rhyme or reason and, if not from Lavergne, then from his successors Wilhelm Schulz and Lorenz von Stein. There we can prove that he knew those authors! Or did Marx not understand Schulz and Stein, as well? Now, at least it can be ascertained through Engels beyond reasonable doubt what is the "scientific" level of the "scientific birth certificate" of "scientific Socialism," the value itself of the *Communist Manifesto* of 1848, even before we have analyzed one line of it. Marx remained distinctly behind the state of scientific knowledge of the Social Science of his time.

Nevertheless and for understandable reasons, Mehring's question did stir up the Old Engels to an extreme degree, he began to fear exposure! "The passage is really quite strange," he continues, "I don't know the book myself, the writer is known to me, however, as an adherent of the 'historical school.' It is the strangest thing that the right conception of History can be found in the abstract with the very people who abuse it in the concrete the most, theoretically as well as practically."[39]

Engels, who does not know the book and does not have one word to breeze about Schulz or Stein, assumes for Lavergne to "be totally blind ... as far as other forms of economies are concerned such as the bourgeois form of economics and their different political forms which correspond to their economic forms." Here we find not only the sublevel of the "classic writers of Marxism," but, moreover, their complete lack of professionalism. They don't know anything, but they denounce prophylactically everything as incapable that they dislike subjectively! Lavergne was supposedly a doctrinaire defender of the feudal *Junker* (or Prussian yeoman) economics, Engels continues to sound off in his letter to Mehring! Now we know what is meant by "genuine science" in the biography initially quoted. The classic writers don't know anything, they haven't read anything, but they pass judgment galore, Marx in the *Annuals*, Engels in his letter to Mehring!

For crying out loud! Engels doesn't know the book in which the opposite - compare the catchword "the new era" - of what he assumes is stated and Mehring, supported by Engels information, falsifies the history of German Historical Science at this crucial point of the highest significance.

Engels reduces - and that was to be expected - the conception of Lavergne of the "generalization back to its true content ... that a feudal society engenders a feudal order of the State."[40] And when we, Mehring continues, followed Engels' wish "to verify the quotation and found the above-mentioned context in the dug-up book of Lavergne, we could only answer him with the most sincere gratitude for this instructive discussion, as he had been able to reconstruct the entire mastodon from one single bone."[41] It takes your breath away in the face of such "unity in science and party-adherence" to use the jargon of the Socialist Unity Party. That is, Communists have always been like this!

The circumstances of the times may be remembered during which Mehring and Engels conducted themselves in such a manner. The Erfurt Program of the German Social Democratic Party which had been passed in 1891 was the current hot-button issue. It was based on this alleged Marxist conception of History by which Socialism would prevail with the necessity of natural law. What would it have meant to rob the very Party of its program and, therefore, its faith and hope in the future that had just brought down the notorious laws against Socialism? If we regard the decisive weak points which Mehring embellishes in his biography of Marx, in not mentioning them, one will have to doubt Mehring as a historian in the overall. The scientist has to pursue the truth for truth's sake, otherwise he will become a paid liar for the party and that, apparently, was Mehring, as well.

But let's approach the *Communist Manifesto*.

For this reason we will return to names already familiar. Eduard Gans was not only a leading legal scholar who applied Hegel's evolutionary theory to his own field, but he was a political activist, as well. He was active for the liberation of Poland from Russia's yoke, he collected money for persecuted German patriots, such as the Goettinger Seven, and he agitated time and again for social reforms on behalf of the working class. He had already grasped, after the Revolution of 1830 in Paris, that the bourgeois political aspirations, the struggle for the republic, would be blending with and outdone by the social struggles of the proletariat not for political freedom alone, but for economic rights and social security, as well. His impressions he summarized thus: "I had looked once into the abyss of the revolution and made observations about its fiery streams. That the clock could not be turned back to 1793 was certain, for that the social turnover had been too regular, the new middle-class society was too young and the forces of the proletarian were too slight."[42]

This very position he defended in front of his students, among whom sat our Young Marx. Gans' "hereditary law in world-historic evolution" he used as well to prove that objective laws lead the people to ever higher and freer developments, while he was referring to the Prussian State as a "Warden" State. This characterization fits today's Prussia hand in glove. His insights into the conditions of the proletariat Gans derived from the teachings of St. Simon. For him the most essential driving force in History was the contradiction between the wealthy and the proletariat. Let's compare two quotations to understand and admire Marx's "original creativity" once more:

"As formerly Master and Slave, later Patrician and Plebeian, then the feudal lord and his vassal were pitted against each other, so there are now the Idle and the Worker." So says Gans in his lectures that were published while Marx was still his student.[43]

"Freeman and slave, patrician and plebeian, baron and serf, guild burgher and apprentice stood against each other in constant difference. The whole society is split into ... the bourgeoisie and the proletariat." So writes Marx at the beginning of the first section of the Communist Manifesto. One can see clearly and at once how Marx in all his copying remained below Gans. "Feudal lord" is more comprehensive and all-encompassing than "baron," or was it only barons who had serfs? Gans would also not split everything up into bourgeoisie and proletariat. Why? Because then what would become of the peasants, the artisans, the tradesmen, the employees, that is, the masses of the people, who would live off their own labor? The egregious consequences of Stalinist policies in the countries of our "real" Socialism are only too well known. But the true father of all workers and the second greatest fuehrer of all times had relied on Marx to the T: All these intermediary classes and strata have to be annihilated economically, whatever the damage to the economy, let's not even ask about humanitarian transgressions! Cornu[44] reminds us that Marx, among other things, took the distinction between Medieval and modern states in his criticism of Hegel's Philosophy of Law from

Gans – I shall add what Cornu left out without even here quoting the source. And as an aside, in fifty lectures each of which I read with students, correspondence course students and students in professional training the above-quoted passages of Herder, Lavergne, Schulz, Feuerbach, Gans and others and let them be classified historically. The answer each time was the same: Marx, 19th century. There was not one exception! Popular education fulfills its mission in the 16th Soviet Republic at least in this respect with flawless ease.

The Frenchman Cornu, bearer of the Karl Marx Order, surely checked the sources, as well, but he remains by and large on the level of Mehring, he retouches, euphemizes, and interprets according to the party line. Well, but one has to do that; how would one get such an order otherwise? Checking up on sources is a criminal activity! That would lead too close to the truth and to understand the latter and speak it openly would, in turn, lead into the hole of concrete of the Stasi State Security prison. There one would find ample time for undisturbed reflection of the small difference in Marxist-Leninist Social Science as to what is right and what is true.

Gans was fighting for truth. In his students he saw the young generation who he was supposed to prepare for life, not just in their subject matter but also give a political orientation, as well, so that a democratic and socially-conscious future might become possible for them. Without the protection of the Prussian Chancellor Prince Hardenberg he would not have survived the presence of informers in his lectures, but between Gans' father, a reputable banker, and the prince-chancellor there existed not just a business relationship but a personal friendship, as well. Praised be every tenured professor of the Berlin University who had at least one prince behind him!

Gans' radicalism could not pass forever. The History teacher Koeppen is telling the story in Ruge's *Annuals*[45] of the occasion of his presentation at the convention of the Berlin University historians that Gans finally had to cancel such lectures nevertheless at a certain point. Koeppen was the man who - next to Gans - influenced Marx in the subject of History. Social intercourse with each other they had in the so-called "Club of Doctors." If one is to check Koeppen's publications to learn about the state of Historical Science, so one becomes aware that he had not a thread of a notion of the materialist conception of History and, consequently, he could not teach Marx anything in this respect.[46]

For his students Gans sketched the state of the working class and the prospect of their class struggle in the following manner: "One shall visit the factories of England and one shall find there hundreds of men and women who are sacrificing for one person alone their health and their lives' enjoyment. Is it not called slavery when human beings are exploited like animals, and even if they would be free would have to die of starvation? ... The fact that the State has to care for the poorest and most numerous class, that when it wants to work it never be deprived of a meaningful occupation ... is a more profound insight into our time and the following History will, from its side, have to talk about the struggle of the proletarians against the middle classes of society more than once. The Medieval Ages with their guilds had an organic framework for Labor. Those guilds have been destroyed and can never more be reinstituted. But should liberated Labor now be let go from the professional corporation into despotism, from the lordship of the master into the lordship of the factory owner? Is there no way out from this dilemma? Yes, there is. It is the free incorporation, it is socialization."[47]

It may be well to remember that Marx did not even let himself be impressed by this teacher. But later, when he was betting on a career for the labor movement he plagiarized Gans. The "free corporation" he turned into "free association" in the *Manifesto*, certainly a creative linguistic act of at least world-historic significance. "Exploited" [Latinized in the original German] became one of Marx's favorite standard expressions. That should suffice as far as illustrations go regarding the political ideas of Professor Gans in the not quite Gansian *Manifesto* of Marx of the Communist Party. Or to quote (and vary accordingly for the occasion) the popular German folk song of the fox who had stolen a goose [pun on the German goose = Gans] Charlie Crap, you stole a goose and got it cooked, as well!

Who will find this unduly sarcastic may consider that at the beginning of his "serious" period of study Marx took lectures with probably the only teacher whom he revered and who influenced him and Gans, according to accounts of contemporaries, had spoken with a much more radical bent than he displayed in his writing, especially about the class struggles during the revolution of 1789. The personally over-sensitive Marx remained cool as ice about the social issues that occupied and stirred all hearts at the time and that during the student period of his life when one is the most susceptible to new influences! One has only to think back to the letters written by Herschel Marx, the father, in the same period and the picture takes a clearer relief. Cornu described Marx reluctantly as "ignorant of the world." When cold reason told Marx the time for the hot-button issues addressed by Gans had come, he regurgitated them half-digested in his *Manifesto*.

Let's now turn again to Moses Hess whom Engels with Wilhelm Weitling called the founders of German Communism in former times - something he later forgot in favor of Marx and Engels! Hess came from a Jewish middle-class family. His literary output started in 1837 and he tried at first to give the Jewish religion a socialist interpretation. Like Marx, his philosophic mentors were Hegel and Feuerbach. Marx, who took up all essential ideas and the overview of the Communist credo from Hess, according to which the development of society went from a simple primordial communism to a more varied and developed communism of the future, interrupted by the exploitatory social formations of slavery, feudalism and capitalism, fought Hess, at first his admired mentor and teacher, later as a competitor in the basest and meanest of ways. It was Hess, by the way, who brought Engels into the Communist fold.

Hess spoke up for the social revolution, for the abolition of private property and the elimination of hereditary laws. All those positions can be found in the *Communist Manifesto* and in the 17 postulates of the Communist Party of Germany of 1848. In Hess' conceptions the causes of social injustices were supposed to get revoked and a new society founded on equality and harmony. The idea of Hess that the class movements of the proletariats derive in conformity with natural law out of historical developments, that this proletariat would have to fulfill a world-historic mission, brought him into the vanguard of the socialist and communist writers of Germany. Today in the Marxism-Leninism classes all this has to have originated from Charlie, because we are dealing here with nothing more and nothing less than the "scientific" perspective of the decline of all pluralistic Western democracies again in conformity with the law and the world hegemony of all Russians and *ersatz*-Russians. Moses Hess subscribed to the practice philosophy of Cieskowsky and he understood the main task of the social scientist to be to shape social developments in a revolutionary way, not only to interpret it! Here we find only one aspect of the world-historic mission of the proletariat, this alleged so great discovery of Marx. Let's beat the Marx crazies with Marx himself, as the latter wrote in the *Holy Family* in 1844: "When the socialist writers give the proletariat that world-historic role …"[48] Yes, that was it, indeed! The socialist writers had this aspect worked out and written down in black and white way before the communist Marx, namely, all of whom he would later "devastatingly criticize" in his usual blowhard manner. It was Hess who had most clearly worked out these thoughts for the boon of the dispossessed, as the dispossessed may not be confused with Marxists. In the same passage Marx owns how teleological and that is, therefore, how unscientific his conception of History is which he, after all, took from Hess in the first place, which would have to produce paradise sooner or later according to the Jewish faith. Paradise, i.e., the communist table-set-thyself. "It is not a question what this or that proletarian thinks or deems to be the goal or even what the entire proletariat thinks about it. The question is, rather, what it is and will be forced to become in its being according to the laws of History. Its goal and historic action are irrevocably and sensibly pre-designed in their own life situation as in the whole organization of today's bourgeois or middle-class society."[49]

Irrevocably pre-designed, that is teleology at its purest, Comrades Forgers! What the individual thinks or all men think of one class is not relevant, not pertinent, but that is complete non-freedom! No, this rather curious "being" forces us to accept the execution of this secular religion of the Hess-Marxian variety. Glorious, Comrade Crap as the greatest helmsman of world history! What else could we want? Who was it then actually who "pre-designed irrevocably"? What blind automatism forces upon all of us this kind of politics? This doesn't sound much different than the irrevocable and fundamental belief in "*Vorsehung*" [Hitler's belief in predestination] and the *Endsieg*, the "final victory." Brilliant, the red-shirted dictator, Marx, and the brown-shirted dictator, Hitler, united ideologically in final consequence! Would it strike us as amazing that a man of historic standing, of whom we will come to speak later, namely, Karl Liebknecht, the co-founder of the German Communist Party in 1918, has completely and in no uncertain terms rejected this ballyhoo of a philosophy of History?

Furthermore, Marx took from Hess his theory of revolution, which holds that Socialism can be victorious simultaneously only in the industrially and civilizationally highly-developed countries in Europe or not at all! Europe's rebirth could happen only, according to Hess, through the European triarchy, that is, the combined forces of England, France and Germany. Only in this manner would the reactionary power of Russia be kept in check! Marx and Engels' invectives against Russia and the "historically incapable" smaller Slavic states testify to a rather incredible and troublesome tendency toward Greater-German nationalism. And this tendency may not be explained away simply by justifying it as criticism of the feudal state of the czar!

Hess puts his hopes into these three states, precisely, because Germany had started the process of spiritual and intellectual liberation through the Reformation and France had realized this as political freedom in 1789. England, as the most economically developed, was now supposed to provide the kick-off for the social liberation of the proletariat. Following this template Marx and Engels prophesied regularly and wrongly the proletarian revolution first for England, then for France and last for Germany. When they were finished with touting these fallacies they undauntedly recommenced as if nothing had happened. Astoundingly enough, none of the three working classes adhered to the "irrevocably pre-designed" Marx-Engels master plan. A part of the German working class had dared an uprising against the export of the Marxist revolution by the force of arms and tanks and they were railroaded in the name of Marxism by Russian tanks in 1953.

Lenin, now, took the revolutionary theory of Hess, to which Marx had subscribed hook, line and sinker, and turned it totally upside down and inside out in both theory and practice! For that reason, in matters of logic Leninism is fused with Marxism in an inseparable unity, just because Lenin, according to the Marxist conception of revolution, made foolhardy putsches. Lenin called this "modification of the regular sequence,"[50] and the recently deceased General Secretary of the Communist Party of the Soviet Union Chernenko reminded us of that. His contribution was virtually hidden in the Party's theoretical publication *Unity*, quite contrary to the usual customs, neither outwardly nor inwardly in any way remarkable or distinguishable. Here, Chernenko confirmed earlier theses of Ulbricht about Socialism, which precipitated East German Party Secretary Ulbricht's fall as he declared against the thesis of Marx and Engels of a short transitional stage, meaning that developed Socialism had the character of an "epoch" in Ulbricht's usage, a relatively autonomous formation that is. In plain English, all the stupid slogans that the West be economically surpassed by the East by 1980 - strictly logical slogan of the Socialist Unity Party of Germany: Surpass without getting even! - had failed; the end of misery in "real" Socialism cannot be foreseen. The attainment of Communism is being put off in the revised Party Program of the Communist Party of the Soviet Union until, literally, Kingdom Come. Chernenko confesses, moreover, "Some of our present-day problems and difficulties have been historically connected that so far not all the tasks that were engendered by the modification of the "regular sequence" have been solved in a satisfactory manner." In plain speech, Lenin should not have made a putsch in the most retrograde agricultural land of Europe, isolated without industry and proletariat - by 1920 four million workers had been reduced to one million! He should have let develop political and economically more mature conditions in democratic Russia with 140 million peasants after the February Revolution in 1917! In his own way Lenin was just as much a doctrinaire ideologue light years removed from reality as was Marx. On the other hand, he did not shy away from doing exactly the opposite while constantly quoting Marx. How out of touch Lenin really was Clara Zetkin describes in her reminiscences which were printed during the period of the Weimar Republic. In the East German edition these passages have been carefully deleted. Zetkin tells the story of how Lenin apologized to Radek after the routing of the Red Army in front of Warsaw. The latter had warned of the offensive saying that the Polish workers with their traditional hatred of the Russians would fight the Red Army bitterly and would ultimately defeat it. And that is exactly what happened! Lenin, on the contrary, had predicted his army would be hailed as liberators with jubilation and open arms - not in Poland alone, but in all of Western Europe. He was serious about World Revolution. It's instructive to read Lenin's telegram to the German workers in the revolution of November of 1918: "Vote Liebknecht for President!" This is, by the way, quite an interference with another people's affairs. I'm just quoting this to demonstrate the gap between this rather curious "being" and "having to do" of the workers in Poland and in Germany.

Only those who have lived through it can fathom the intellectual incest of those teleological fanatics of History whose theoretical limitations correspond to their political fanaticism and their paranoid saboteur-reactionary-spioteur-agent craze! And with regards to the permanent falsifications of History: Forward to more deeds, Comrades Professional-Swindlers! However, in this way Communism cannot learn from its mistakes which will accelerate its doom. Today the Russians have reached the point of the Romans in the 4th century A.D. and they have declined, even without cooking the history books, as every world empire before them and after them.

After this short excursion into the analysis of the application of Marxist theory let's go back to its history: What Marx introduces as "scientific Communism" is nothing more or less than the insights of the Communists Weitling and Hess and of the anti-Communist von Stein, who had already summarized as follows in 1842: The Capitalist economy precipitates the class struggle of the proletariat and is engendering Communist ideas in the process. As a scholar and scientist, Stein proved back then what today has practically become common knowledge among Communists: Communism is a failure in practice! Society with its division of labor and, therefore, its commodity production and money cannot be abolished and neither can economic performance structures. In order to build the society of the free and equal another way has to be found. In direct contradiction of Marx and Engels all Soviet Communists postulate that the role of the Party and the State and, therefore, a dictatorship of a minority, i.e., societal unfreedom grow and grow and grow like a cancer!

Hess had proven the processes of concentration in production and trade as well as the social fallout for the worker when he influenced Marx ideologically, and even formulated those distribution principles of a Communist mode of production which Marx only made his own in 1875: work according to one's abilities, consumption according to one's needs. Of course, neither Hess nor Marx pronounce themselves in concrete terms on what needs actually are: for everybody the MacMansion complete with butler from the Secret Service, sauna, swimming pool, etc., for everyone Western luxury motor vehicle, sailing yacht and hunting forests, helicopter, government hospital, Western pharmaceutical drugs, West travels, dollars and convertible Forum checks? Friends in Moscow are telling me that with one's needs one should always take the family circles of the socially most advanced hoary old men in government as bellwether and benchmark and every Romanov should be able to eat from golden plates engraved with "Romanov" in golden lettering. Let's just hope that the plates will survive, since as we know the late Romanovs didn't!

But even Hess, the anti-Marxist, thought in "Marxist" terms, that the enormously increased productive forces should make up the basis for the satisfaction of material needs under Communism. He himself had copied that from the social democrat Schulz and Engels again copied Hess in his sketch of Political Economy, which our genius Marx incorporated without much ado into his economic-philosophical manuscripts. In such an intricate and convoluted manner, Comrades, Patriots, Friends of the People, at times the intellectual reproduction process progresses: accumulation, concentration, centralization! Hess even condensed the well-known conception of the misery of alienation, turned against the separation of producer and product and reiterates that Capitalist competition is the root of all evil. The solution according to Hess would lie in the future not in nostalgia for the Middle Ages.

Hess, who published the first German magazine *Gesellschaftsspiegel* or "Mirror of Society," which would devote itself exclusively to workers' problems, thought solely the proletariat capable of social change. His studies about Capital and money contained passages that, coupled with the Socialist School of English Political Economy, gave Marx the definition of the commodity "labor power," which by the way was called that directly by Lorenz von Stein long before Marx. Hess defines "money" as "social blood" within the societal organism, "Mr. Moneybags" as the law-maker of the modern State, unchecked competition as war of all against all. The accumulation of less Capital would thrust the masses into the deepest of misery, soon the bell would toll, then the timepiece of the money machinery would have run out, etc., etc., one can hear it Marxing and crapping even as a work in progress: Communism is the absolute finality of the genesis of society.

It appears most interesting that Marx took the proposals for solutions of social issues from Hess directly, not solely the perspective on things, viz., abolition of money as the expression of the exploitatory capitalist conditions, product barter rather than purchases and sales. Infuriated, Hess takes exception with Schulz who had written correctly that the abolition of money would be an illusion equivalent to a command to world history to return back into the womb and he, consequently, calls him a "literary jester."[51] The religiously faithful cannot take it that economic realities do not brook terrestrial paradises. The "genuine" Socialist Hess, as well as the "genuine" Communist Marx, has been refuted by the "literary jesters" Schulz and Stein in their own time theoretically through the evidence and results from Classical Political Economy and practically by the isolated failed Communist experiments in Europe and in the U.S. The full and definitive refutation brought Lenin's comprehensive state experiment in the 20th century and the practice of "real" Socialism, but we will hear more about that later. Hess, as well as Marx, is a teleological utopian whereas Marx has glued onto his unprovable speculations the label "scientific." He is refuting himself with his materialist view taken on from others. According to the latter, the way to scientific knowledge leads from sensual perception to abstraction, which will, in turn, be corroborated by practice. Now, where can we find the empirical facts of Communism so that they could be taken and generalized into a theory? Answer: Nowhere. Nowhere, not even in theory! There is no such thing as a scientifically-founded theory or a scientifically-implemented practice in the Soviet Communist countries. They cannot be found even with the Maoists; one may compare the economic performance of the blossoming "Western" oasis Taiwan where Chinese are living also in contrast to that of the People's Republic. Here it is becoming evident why Marxism has become obsolete in Asia as well as in Europe. Island states may contain an explosive social potency and force: whether they may be called Taiwan, Hong Kong, Singapore, or West Berlin.

What can be found in all Communists and Socialists, in Germany especially in Hess, Weitling and Marx, is a futurologist expectation of the future, a working hypothesis at best, but not a "genuinely scientific world view." Taken in and by itself, a science has to be true already, but a true truth, like Marxism-Leninism, has to be truer, especially if that is written in a biography authorized by the Central Committee.

Let us now look more closely at the *Manifesto of the Communist Party* and let us look especially at it as a political-futurologist resume of the development of the very "Marxism" roughly sketched here above. To depict Marx's role within the first Communist Party of Germany means to explode the person and personality cult of "real" Socialism, as the terrestrial cult is based on the one around the heavenly General Secretary Comrade Crap. The alleged infallibility of the theorist and short-term Party Chairman, Marx guarantees the infallibility of the Party, which as it is expressed so nicely and wrongly in the Party song, "is always right" and her popes and pundits, the stand-ins and representatives of Comrade Crap down here on earth. In classic Absolutism matters were far simpler. There the authorities were "by God's Grace, WE." Today the Communist gods, Marx and Lenin, are ruling by quotations and their falsifications, really socialistic "by Moscow's Grace, WE." Criticism of the system of our unreal Socialism has to begin with the criticism of the person and the ideology of Marx himself! Historically, as we have seen, the Marxist world view in ideology and politics and in its concept of Humanism has fallen behind both the Classic era and the Age of Enlightenment. Economically speaking, it projects the future constitution of the

Medieval Age into Modern Times. Everything economic is planned: labor power, production and distribution - plain everything! Free Market and competition are abolished: and above and beyond that, worse than in the Middle Ages, money is abolished. The given national or domestic economy as well as the global economy is thrown back to direct product exchange and, therefore, back into an economic Stone Age and that being for the sole illusion of attaining a paradisiacal cornucopia in that manner. In this system probably not even our modern day Marco Polos, Marcus Wolff and Beitz, would be able to undiscombobulate and orient themselves unless they would diligently study the classified section of the *Berliner Zeitung*: Will barter marinated herring for single wool sock!

All this together then brings the full development of men through an unlimited freedom in the superstructure and the relinquishing of classes, parties, police, secret police like the State Security [Stasi], et al. That is, according to the teaching embodied in the *Communist Manifesto* that Marx was ordered to summarize and finally edit on behalf of the second Convention of the Union of Communists. Said text is celebrated as the first document of "scientific Communism" whose economic nonsense will be later spread large in *Capital.* Nota bene: I do not target here the criticism of the first Capitalist development phase of free competition, that is, the underdeveloped early Capitalism of Europe, whose infirmities can be readily perceived in the developing countries even today. This criticism, nevertheless, had been rendered for workers by others more easily, more scientifically and more clearly prior to Marx. I am targeting here more precisely the completely off-the-wall deductions from the *Manifesto* and from *Capital* with regards to the formation of the socialist future society.

Historically speaking, the composition of the *Manifesto* was brought about as follows:

On January 25, 1848, the Central Authority of the Union of Communists commissioned their branch office in Brussels "to indicate to said K. Marx that if the *Manifesto* of the Communist Party, whose draft he had undertaken at the last Congress, not be finished and delivered in London by Tuesday, February 1, of said year, then further measures against him would be undertaken. In the event that said K. Marx would not draft the *Manifesto*, then the Central Authority would demand imperatively and instantaneously the remission of the documents put previously at his disposal."[52] Marx as usual had a hard time to compose the thin pamphlet. If the sources are consulted it becomes evident that the *Manifesto* - above and beyond the intellectual theft of the given writers already quoted - is only a compilation of what workers had brought up and elaborated upon in their unions, newspapers, educational associations and their correspondences, as well as in the pre-drafts for said Congress.[53] The First Congress of the Union of Communists had accepted the draft of a Communist Credo on June 9, 1847, from which, following renewed discussion in the state congregations - meaning the local support groups of the Congress - the final *Manifesto* emerged during the Second Congress at the end of the same year. In the first section of the introduction Marx states that the whole process of History would be impacted by class struggle. The thought of class struggle was not alien to anyone, but, for instance, W. Schulz and M. Hess had correctly excluded it from the Gentile Order. Again, Marx here was not up to the height of the latest research results of his science. Even his attention-grabbing journalistic scoop was wrong. And in like manner everything else continued with equal brilliance as long as it was he who actually contributed. And for us only those passages are of interest here. After class he comes to talk about the State and that shows the poverty of his historic-political views. He, who as a pure Hegelian saw in the State the incorporation of the ethical idea and who expected all weal from it, now states, again in over-absolute terms, exactly the contrary: "The modern power of the State is only a committee that manages the common affairs of the bourgeois class." Marx here sees alone the constitutional, not the administrative side. This oversimplification of the role of the bourgeois or middle class and the Communist State - because what is good for the one is just as well for the other - bears down on us to this very day. This passage explains the intolerance, the willed uncertainty of Law. One need only look at the amendment of the one-size-fits-all paragraph of the G.D.R. Penal Law Code of the year 1979, published in the Law dossier, Part I, Nr. 17, as of July 2, according to which every harmless conversation with a German from the other side may lead to the clink as the taking up of "connections" and the handing over of "news not subject to censorship" would be punishable even in the attempt. This Medieval conception of the acolytes of Marx signifies that for Soviet citizens there is no equality before the Law, but only arbitrary decisions by bureaucrats. One may travel into foreign Western countries, another may not; one may read literature of the class enemy, another may not; one may receive relatives from Western countries, another may not; one may emigrate, another may not; one may phone and correspond, another may not. And that is so not because what is right rules, but what is decreed is legal and here again not what is written in the Law Code, but what is being decreed by ukase through the internal channels of the Party and State bureaucracy. That is just what the "dictatorship of the proletariat" amounts to! As far as I know even here in our land the proletarians can be found in the factories and on the fields. They must give their terrorist orders after sundown, otherwise how else could our system of a Sundowner dictatorship function?

The conditions are absolutely schizophrenic. In the entire Soviet system the Party chief is equally the head of State. As party chief he has to force mercilessly the ideological uprooting of religious hereticism. As "father of the country" he has to further his Christians. As party chief he has to annihilate Social Democratism, pluralism, etc., mercilessly down to the physical annihilation of those who profess it, even all those who profess oppositional thoughts. As father of the country he has to safeguard the freedom of conscience that is constitutionally guaranteed. How shall a normally disposed, average human being be capable of doing both? The theoretical misconstructions of Marx are a permanently bubbling source of the dissent of the majority of its adherents fed by its own inner contradictions. For that reason elsewhere, like in Russia, the nationalist glue proves to be much more potent than the Marxist one. East Germany here is the exception as the nationalist glue in this case does not glue but divide. For that reason the Marxist glue has to do double duty here, which is not to say that the G.D.R. citizens are not divided - see introduction.

One shall not say, as social-democratic authors are used to doing, that in Marx's life time the State had not as yet been a social State, i.e., one with a social net of health care and retirement benefits, etc.; Schulz, Hess, Stein, Weitling, et al., well saw the issue of the constitution, viz., the question of power as well as the issue of the administration, i.e., the possibility of reform through the extension of the function of the State. The real issue here, though, is a much deeper one: the peoples have fought, suffered and bled for centuries and their most outstanding representatives were crucified and burnt at the stake in order to break the power of the uncontrolled ruling class, the power of Absolutism. The revolutions in the Netherlands, in England, in France, in the U.S. have shown the backward Germans that democratic rights and liberties, human and civil rights of the citizens may well be instituted. The Enlightenment, the period of *Sturm und Drang*, [literally "storm and stress," a pre-romantic literary movement in Germany with the early Goethe and Schiller as its most distinguished members] the German classic writers, the workers in their secret societies have endorsed these civil rights concepts unanimously and they have combined these with postulates of an economic foundation of these political freedoms which are still current and valid today. Marx on the other hand is denying all of that! He does not find any words at all for that progress of political culture that needs to be extended which has been achieved in the classic tri-partition of powers. His recipe is: Abolition of the historic progress through dictatorship. The "dialectical Eulenspiegel"[54] Marx, as Bakunin called him, has "by character as well as a German national" always aimed for absolute forms of rulership. Marx reflects the backwardness of the German political conditions. He wants to replace feudal Absolutism by proletarian Absolutism. The most paradigmatic perpetrator of this aspiration became Stalin. Stalin became the Marx of the 20th century, a totally sinister, not even vaguely enlightened despot following the classic feudal maxim: one king, one faith, one law.

Stalin, who dogmatized everything, even the smallest trifles, into unwieldy absolutes lived intellectually from the bequest of the super-oversimplifying Marx and his concept of the proletariat. Truth is always concrete, there is, thus, no such thing as "the proletariat." At the time there were master artisans working independently, journeymen, apprentices, then the agricultural and industrial proletariat. This proletariat was not equal either in economic or in social terms and, least of all, did it have politically unified Marxist views. The interests and aims of the proletariat diverge as much as their perspectives. There are materialists and idealists, revolutionaries and reformers, Christians, Moslems, Buddhists, Atheists, etc. All this did not concern the teleological futurologist Marx in the least, because his proletariat, whatever its own aspirations, is going to have to do what according to its Being it is coerced to!

This cavalier Marxist style of thinking in this country corresponds to the communication of his ideology, which enrages or bores our students to tears. So they read during the sermons reasonable books, write letters, talk or engrave in their desk-boards: "Proletarians of all countries, forgive me! Charlie Crap."

Marx exaggerates and sets as overly absolute the concept of the proletariat - and that methodologically speaking in science is always wrong - in face of the continuing and increasingly dominant organization of factories. He used the term for the numerically at the time drastically increasing, today decreasing, group of predominantly unskilled and untrained industrial workers, whose men who, replaced by wives and children, became "mere paraphernalia of machinery." Marx set as absolute what was only a transitory stage within the industrial development. He does not see early Capitalism as a passing period, but defines the workers, who, after all, are thinking, sentient beings "as a commodity like all other commodities" as if they were fatalistically subject to the social excrescence of the underdeveloped Capitalist production mode of the day. After class and state comes the concept of the party for Marx which today has assumed first place over third, who here transfixes the standpoint of the worker that was then the end result of the contemporary discussion: "Organization of the proletarian into a class and, thus, into a political party." Lenin's definition of the "party of the new order" bears testimony to what extent Lenin, in matters of revolution theory, broke decisively with the Marxian concept of party. Lenin's definition, in fact, is a direct slap in the face of Marx's.   And it has remained like that to this very day, as for Marx class and party are identical, while the "professional revolutionaries," i.e., the official apparatchiks are always found in contradiction to the party rank and file: otherwise the crises of "real" Socialism would be unthinkable and, thanks to Soviet Social Science, we may say that today, as well. And I may add from personal experience: The party is not only a pile of paid surveillers and bosses separated from the worker, but it dissociates itself, as well, into lower, middle and higher ranks of which most are permanently preoccupied with that peculiar form of class warfare of endeavoring to increase their own incomes.

Following his party concept, Marx comes to talk about his conceptions of democracy: "All movements up to now have been movements of minorities or in the interest of minorities."   How interesting! The slave revolts of antiquity, the peasant wars of the Medieval period, the wars of national liberation in the 18th and 19th century, they were all minorities? This discovery beats even the barely discovered Historical Materialism! The struggles which Europe waged against the hordes of Ghenges Khan, against the Turks, against Napoleon – these were not all democratic movements to save the national culture and independence? Would there have been, for example, under the rule of the Turks the same modern commodity production in Europe and would historical progress have prevailed?

Marx here appears at his most elitist, his constructs at their most devoid of rhyme or reason. No destiny of a people interests him. He is interested in the movers and shakers, the powerful, that particular group of the ruling class to whom he himself would love to belong. This in his entire attitude, style, appearance, not excluding the monocle, which in this country symbolizes the facetious illustration of the arrogant presumptions of a highly decadent group of noblemen, and, not to forget, his entry into the registry of a hotel: "Man of independent means." There we have it; he was no mere journalist at the time, but a man who could afford to live off the work of others!

To bow to the plebeian becomes obviously indispensable for reasons of deception when he is needed as a stepping stone in one's own career. Marx was the erstwhile party apparatchik: bow down to the top and kick below. Verbally and formally speaking, the popular masses are for him the driving forces of history. This he took from Gans. But they are that for him only in the sense that they provide the material base of the movers and shakers. In this manner matters are handled here to this very day. There is, thus, the *lumpenproletariat* not alone in the sense in which Marx defines it: "as the passive rotting away of the lower classes of the old social system."   That *lumpenproletariat* existed, as well, ethically depraved in the upper echelons of the old society. The leaders of the General German Workers' Fraternization expressed that clearly in 1848 in their party media. The savvy and streetwise workers had no illusions in this respect. What would they have to say about today's *lumpenproletarier* in the upper echelons of the Socialists Unity Party?

I would like to demonstrate that briefly in giving the context in my own working environment: There exists in the Department of Political Economy a professor who is called "Dumbbell" everywhere in Berlin; the spelling of his real name is actually somewhat similar. This very man has fraudulently acquired a Chair in a revolting, at least half-criminal manner and adorned it with fantastic and histrionic titles that include World Economics and Global Trade, academic disciplines actually that he has neither studied nor done any research work in at all, much less know them in practice. His lectures consist of cut-and-repasted economic bulletins of the East German Wire Services; the only problem is that he has difficulties with correctly repasting them. Thank God, barely a soul at the university knows about these bulletins! He creates a workshop, lets experts discuss "confidential proposals" therein, puts these discussions in writing and publishes them partially in his own name, suppressing the origin of such 'research.' He takes talented students, say, the daughter of the present ambassador from Finland and has them compile interesting material in other languages that he can neither read nor translate and he publishes them under his name, suppressing the name of the girl. His lecturing duty is 30 hours, not weekly or monthly hours, mind you, but annual hours! What would the G.D.R. workers think, if they received 42,000 marks a year for thirty annual hours of work in their Workers' and Peasants' State just as a token of appreciation of theoretical propaganda to illustrate the Socialist performance principle and that as a legal salary, especially considering the fact that they receive 350 marks for 44 hours of weekly work? Considering further that according to all official appraisals, views of the Youth group representatives, as well as all colleagues, the lectures of said man have no quality whatsoever. On top of that, considering that a tenured professor - and I speak from experience - may effortlessly make an extra 1,000 marks on the side, with 72 weeks of full sick leave salary recompense, the worker by comparison receives 6 weeks' compensation, heavens, our man is certainly living like the lords before the revolution!

Why would such an anti-social derelict cheapskate – as one would ask not only in East Germany – not be replaced, demoted, repositioned, given more tasks? Now, his critics have tried that. What then happens? This man is being protected by the Party secretary in house. The latter does not want the party education of the basic organization to be disregarded or depreciated - professors, of course, are always party comrades - that would only fall back on himself. And the latter again assumes the function of party secretary only in order to become professor himself, as he lets it be known with some self-satisfaction at regular round table discussions in the local bar, professor by way of the local county party organization. For that reason everything has to be honky-dory in the basic organization. To that end, he engages in groundbreaking scientific work. He plagiarizes anything and everything exclusively about the domestic budget from *Neues Deutschland [N.D.]* and lets the paper circulate with the stamp "Highly Confidential" in house. He seeks approval from his higher-ups and when there are no objections he carries this "collective opinion" into the classroom: the collective opinion of *N.D.* and of the head section of the Ministry. That even disgusts the most aloof dogmatists among the professors in the Economics Department, those who do nothing else but turn and twist phrases from *Capital*. They look at the paper and point their fingers at it: Have you ever seen such an arsehole as this Burian - this blowhard - *N.D.* material exclusively, all clippings and that "Highly Confidential"? And these selfsame professors who say in private sarcastically that they do not consider one deduction from *Capital* correct regarding the construction of Communism, flunk every student during an exam of the Economics Department who does not quote the last comma of a Marx quote correctly. Poor students, but they take revenge through lethargy like the Russian kolchose peasants: Grade average is a C in the Marx subject.

Why is it possible that the "Dumbbells" and the "Burians"[55] manage to hold on at all levels? It's the Russian system that does it and Dumbbell is permanently anchored as the most colossal producer of nonsense in the Central House for the much touted German-Soviet Friendship [D.S.F.]. Burian is protecting him for that reason and because he is giving him possibilities to publish in various press organs through his polygamy; and publish you have to in order to become a professor otherwise you'll not just proverbially perish! By now he has reached his goal. And both will be protected from harm by the chairman of the control commission of the party, Hay or Stray, (it's obviously not necessary to remember names of that kind), who reports proudly that he has fought long and hard on the invisible front and that he continues to fight there. Thus, in the same breath he threatens any critics to throw them into the clink if they dare to criticize. To the sheer outrage of the students at the historical Institute he also arranged that a kleptomaniac would not be excluded from the party ranks, as her husband, a Chekist and *ersatz*-Russian works for *State Security* [Stasi], while another comrade likewise caught in the act in the Big Store is excluded from the party without such protection. What redeeming features has this not passively - as Marx thinks - but actively rotting *lumpenproletariat* to show for? Thus, all candidates who passed the exam - after all historians and ideologues of the Party - refuse categorically in face of such examples to do research projects in East German History or to publish on it. There are no more than two correspondence students who have agreed to work on history up to the year 1949, but no further. Added to that is the pressure from the Ministry of Colleges and Universities upon the faculty: You must qualify your instructors better, the courses in History and Political Science at the schools are scandalous, it creates the reverse effect of what is intended in the students with regards to Party and East German History! How strange. Hadn't the two Government Ministers in charge declared exactly the reverse just the day previous in *Neues Deutschland?*

Is it possible under such dignity-defying, honor-insulting circumstances to remain an East German professor? My life experience has taught me that that cannot be changed. Against a wagon-load of manure, a Mecklenburg farmer friend of mine is always telling me, if I lose my temper, you cannot win a reeking contest. So adieu ideological Crapland! But let's continue to look at the *Manifesto:*

"The proletarian movement is the self-contained movement of the overwhelming majority in the interest of the overwhelming majority." One would think that this is a tautology and that it is clear that the majority cannot represent the interests of a minority, but what of it: When, please, and where exactly was the industrial proletariat the overwhelming majority in the 19th century? Didn't Marx know how many inhabitants Germany did have at the time and what percentage of them exactly were peasants, artisans, or proletarians? Well, France, economically speaking, was better developed. Why, on the other hand, was Communist party boss Blanqui, after initially enthusiastically supporting the new election laws for the National Assembly, suddenly against those elections the closer the date came? Simply because he clearly saw the landslide victory in the elections of the landowning peasants! For that very reason Blanqui meant to prevent free elections by all means as the non-owners were the minority among the population. The foolhardy misconception, however, of the majority of that minority led in 1848 in France to the bloody carnage against the Communist workers in France, and in 1918 to the revolution in Germany, brought again a repetition of the same experience. Along more revolting lines this was repeated in 1933. From the Nazi Party you heard "Heil Hitler!," from the Communist Party you heard "Hail Moscow!"[56] Crushed out between the Marxists on the left and the anti-Marxists on the right, the social democracy of the Social Democratic Party and the middle-class democratic Republic of Weimar was annihilated by the dictatorship of the brown-shirts. The dictatorship of the Soviets came to be victorious only later.

The overwhelming majority of working men in today's Germany stands behind the Social Democrats [S.P.D.] and not behind "Hail Moscow." In the history of our people there were factions that shouted

"Hail France." We know what happened to them and their republic. In the long run nobody will survive who puts himself against the people and the nation. The popular masses in the last analysis do not only make their own economic history, they make their political history, as well. And it is not true that the Germans are a nation devoid of dignity, who do not stand for their own proper union and their own proper honor, that their subservience under the knout of the Russians becomes a political sado-masochistic pleasure. That may be true for *ersatz*-Russians; it is not true for the German people as a whole.

The Communists were, are and will remain in Germany the party of the absolute minority. Up until today they don't even have the courage to show their true colors and give their true name: Communist Party of the Democratic Republic of Germany. They are calling themselves demagogically German Socialists and their Party organ, with delusions of imperialist grandeur *Neues Deutschland* or "New Germany," whereas, in reality, their leadership is anti-national down to the bone and marrow! Furthermore, where are today the incredible majorities of the proletariat in Afghanistan, Kampuchea, Angola, Nicaragua, i.e., in all those places in which the leaders derive their authority from Marxist teachings? The Marxist ideology is the cape of camouflage for the claim of world hegemony of the most brutal kind, nothing more and nothing less. Nobody in Moscow would be ready to draw these conclusions, although it is as plain as daylight that the premature births of History languish in the incubator with severe brain and heart damage: War, epidemics, famines ... same old, same old, just like the in the East much condemned Capitalism. And what happens where the incredible majority of the workers is able to voice its desires like the 11 million members of *Solidarnocz* in Poland? Now Comrades, we learn, the entire Polish people - not their working class alone - consist of counter-revolutionaries! Which brings us back to Brecht's commentary of the uprising of June 17, 1953: Would it not be better, if the government dismissed the People and elected a new one?

The material oversimplification in Marx runs parallel to the spiritual one. For the proletariat he decrees morals and religion to be "bourgeois prejudices." Should he not, rather, leave it to the workers themselves which ethical standards they would like to choose? Should he not, rather, honor freedom of religion and conscience? Have the inquisitions and witch hunts been overcome to put in place of crucibles the GULAG with bedlams and labor camps? Why Solshenyzhin was first allowed to write about that in Moscow and then he was exiled?

My students are telling me that their own experiences with ethical standards are as follows: The best and most performing in the extended high schools [E.O.S.], the most decent of character, who does not camouflage his true political opinion, or one for whom religion provides certain standards, those will not be admitted to college and university nor will they find work. Who carries a Christian cross around the neck, the slogan "swords into plowshares" as a button, or even worse, the black-red-gold of the German flag on his lapel is called a traitor in the Free German Youth, the youth organization of the Communist Party, which is led by official Party apparatchiks and he or she is exposed to reprisals, pressures, even organized physical beatings.

"We of the Church," declared Bishop Dr. Hempel, "desire for certain areas of our social life manageable guidelines for the further realization of equal rights and equal honoring even of Christian citizens."[57] - "Trust between you and us," he told the Secretary of the Communist Party, "will grow to that extent to which it can be experienced by the people at the base of society."[58] What a shame for crying out loud! The Bishop manages to say this 35 years after the foundation of the State. And how many people outside of the Church wish to have manageable guidelines for a more humane treatment at the base of society? It is remarkable that such insights have finally made it into the Party organ, *N.D.* This truly honors General Secretary Honecker! Maybe one day this insight will even filter down to Secret Police Chief Mielke, that with the differentiation between ideological adversaries whom one may fight with intellectual means and acting enemies who need to be locked up, one fares better not only for one's own society but also one's own State, than with the primitive oversimplification of Marx and the sanctifying of violence, arbitrary abuse of terror and power. Has our ruling class never comprehended that a Frederick the Great or a Catherine the Great have successfully made use of the halo of the Enlightenment? Have they never read the paeans of Western freethinkers about this Russia and this Prussia? Who is hindering them to make such a step with Moscow from Absolutism to enlightened Absolutism? The G.D.R. is not so weak that it could not stomach such measures and the same holds for Moscow. So Comrades, listen carefully and pay attention when it happens, Party Chief Erich Honecker may tell Stasi Chief Erich Mielke, I'll have to explain to you a new system ... and much later the clerks of History will be able to announce: Both Erichs were the greatest. We only wished that came true. Then, our "real" Socialism would come into its own after all.

But let's go back from the clouds of fantasy land into the real world of the last quoted thesis of the *Manifesto:* This thesis displays an incredible measure of presumption and arrogance, which should tell all wage-earners a lesson in rising above this nonsense of Marxism-Leninism. By the way, this arrogance explains Marx and Engels later exclusion from the Communist Party. The democratic Labor Communists excluded Marx and Engels unanimously and categorically. Engels, for example, speaks to Marx of those "asses who believe to be in one party with us" when he passes on the information that at the beginning of the 1848 revolution the workers in Germany had begun to form coalitions, but just that was quite contrary to Marx-Engels' intentions.[59] That further explains, why - barring a group of left-wing intellectuals - nobody cared for Marx's theory. When Marxism, that is the Schulz-Weitling-Hessism to be exact, became written in stone at the end of the 19th century in the so-called Erfurt Program the Social Democratic Party had taken Bernstein's course and it had remained on that course, thank God, to this day.

Julius Vahlteich, one of the most impressive leaders of the Social Democrats, has expressed that rather dryly and succinctly: "As said, our understanding of Political Economy was scant. We did not have the slightest idea of constant capital or variable capital, i.e., of the terminology of Marx. But that Capital *per se* was our enemy we were exceedingly well aware of and we knew equally well that we could overcome it only through deployment of power and through organization. We had no clue about relative surplus and a thousand other economic categories ... but we were completely certain in our conviction that we were being cheated and robbed by the entrepreneurs and that laws were passed to sanction this kind of action."[60]

Steinberg's question, what exactly a worker would need a theory for - an ideology I would say in contrast to him - might be added here. Verily, the working class did not need hundreds of economic categories in the over-Hegelian, for them incomprehensible, linguistic usage of Marx, in order to grasp their class interests! And that it had done long before him both in theory and in practice. The working class that had developed from the serfdom of the petty peasants had known from time immemorial that exploitation was unpaid labor for the masters: three days of serfdom for the lords, three days on their own land for themselves – and in the factory that was merely continued.

Which brings us to the last item of Section I: "The worker becomes a pauper and pauperism develops even faster than population or wealth." That is the anticipation of the theory of miseration from *Capital.* All so-called scientific, i.e., economically, founded theories in Marx have been anticipated politically. That, however, makes them by no means more correct. One need only compare the standard of living of the Soviet working class and the American working class to see what is really going on. Or one may ask how many hours a West German or an East German worker has to work for a high-quality consumer commodity and one understands the principle of pauperism in the spirit of Marx. Hess and Marx surely would sing high praises of the average standard of living of today's

Western European industrial workers and would deem it over-fulfilled Super-Communism.

The democratic Labor Communist Weitling, by the way, saw the Communist workers' paradise/utopia in much more realistic terms. Thus, he wrote: "Nothing is perfect under the sun! Never a form of social organization shall be found that will be the best immutably and for all times, because this would presuppose a standstill of the intellectual capacities of Man, a standstill of progress, which is unthinkable. But given that nothing is perfect ... the necessity of continuous progress arises."[61]

This was written by a German worker in 1849, one year after the *Communist Manifesto*, who did not have the leisure to read the dialectic Hegel for six years at university! And Weitling continues in a jab against Marx: "Progress is a law of nature and to promote progress is a concern for all of us, not just for the privileged class."[62]

Verily, these proud and autonomous German workers needed the intellectualizing Marx gang as little as their French counterparts of *L'atelier!* And, furthermore, in stark contrast to Marx, who proceeded without intellectual or moral scruples whatsoever in his plagiarizing, Weitling says that he was plagued by doubts, but that colleagues encouraged him: "You share our opinions, they said, you know of our yearnings and desires, we are giving you the opportunity, so onward, be up and about and do the work as long as you still feel the power within you to do so ... They worked for me, I worked for them, had I not done the work hundreds of others would have been glad to in my stead ... *The work at hand in consequence is not my work but our work, as without the support of others I would not have been able to achieve it.*"[63]

Weitling concludes his preface with programmatic sentences and one may heed the sequence: "We are human beings, we are Germans, we are democrats, but we are also communists. By this word we describe a state in which all members of society share justly all the burdens and joys of life. We indicate with it, as well, that we are willing to aspire to this highest, never fully-attainable consequence of this state and even are willing to share the joys and sorrows engendered on the way when this possibility is realized."[64] On the front piece of the first volume of his work appears a picture with a flag at a popular gathering with the following inscription: *Democratic-Communist Family Association.* Here they were and that's what they wanted, the democratic Labor Communists! The roots of democratic Communism, of today's reform Communism or Euro Communism even in Germany reach back before Marx and that is, in fact, a tradition which directly runs counter to Marx, a socially and democratically-shaped concept of Party, State and Society, the anticipation, actually, of Bernstein's "the goal is nothing the movement is everything."

Bernstein later retracted that statement, to avoid the misunderstanding that Socialism meant nothing to him, but he is right all the same.

The first part of the *Manifesto* is imbued with the idea of the evolutionary nature and temporality of the social order, ideas which had been developed, made more precise and elaborated by the German and European intelligentsia before and after the French Revolution of 1789. Completely in contrast to Marx, the whole European and German intelligentsia rejected the one-sided terrorist principle of the Jacobin regime – excepting Forster in Mayence who failed in his attempt to appease the French occupying forces of the Mayence Republic - they strongly rejected arbitrary, terrorist and lawless violence! Anyone can live in an arbitrary manner; the intellectuals postulated with Goethe, those honorable aspire to order and law: i.e., due process of law, the honoring of human rights they demanded instead of terror. Marx places himself completely outside of this German spiritual, intellectual and ethical tradition. It is an incredible lie of Lenin to maintain the Marxists were standing on the shoulders of all the great writers of world history. Marx can neither claim for himself the tradition of the German democratic Labor Communists, nor the tradition of the German intelligentsia. Everyone of repute in the European world of the Spirit was affirmative of the progressive perfectibility of Humanity, the idea of a development of society from lower to higher forms, that should proceed as much as possible in peace, without civil war and war in social conditions safeguarded by law, in liberty and in respecting all human and civil rights. The German intelligentsia as well as that of other countries fought for freedom of religion, conscience, speech, press and the freedom of congregation; and in the assessment of the economists these freedoms were to be brought about by social and economic progress and through the unification of Germany.

Unity and Liberty, Liberty through Unity, these were the battle-slogans liberals, democrats and the labor movement held in common. Looking at today these slogans still apply and considering that back then one had to unify three dozen Germanys, while today the job has to be done prospectively for only two plus the quartered Berlin - who would now doubt the march of History? And why not keep the old battle-slogan of the Socialist Unity Party: the German labor movement will unify what imperialism has put asunder! We will just have to come to an understanding that red imperialism was what is meant here.

And now the question in reverse: What is there that is new in the *Manifesto?* Answer: Nothing! It has not even attained the level of knowledge and research of its times. On the contrary, it has fallen back behind the German Classic movement, behind the Enlightenment, behind the Classical Political Economy of Great Britain and behind the level of understanding of social movements in France.

Furthermore, the *Manifesto* is destroying the classical conception of Humanism. It posits contrary to it the lethal conception that middle-class or bourgeois democracy is a formal democracy or democracy in name only! At the behest of Stalin, Thaelmann organized to have the Weimar Republic be destroyed by the Communists. That simply cleared the path for Hitler. It was, furthermore, the first step toward World War II. Stalin himself destroyed the middle-class democracy of Poland in cahoots with Hitler and then they shared the loot. Stalin made his Pact with Hitler to keep his back free in the East so the latter could thrust his troops on what was meant to become the destruction of Western democracies. The ideology of Marxism and of anti-Marxism, although ideologically incompatible, blended seamlessly in politics. This would once again prove the "scientific character" of Soviet Communist and *ersatz*-Russian politics.

The destruction of "formal" middle-class democracy, of the "class dictatorship of the bourgeoisie" formed an integral part of the Stalinist credo. With good reason they quoted Marx. Lenin had warned as early as 1920, after his experiences following 1917, against this kind of sectioneering of left-wing extremists. Just previously during the founding Convention of the German Communist Party at the end of 1918, deputy Radek - who was illegally present - had supported just this kind of extremist politics in the fight against the German Social Democrats. Lenin, as opposed to the orthodox Marxist, Stalin, was open to a learning experience. The first German democracy which had been won duly by the workers during the November revolution, was supposed to get annihilated on behalf of a brown-shirt or red-flag dictatorship. And that program worked beyond anyone's wildest expectations. After it was too late, in 1935, the seventh World Convention of the COMINTERN condemned this foolhardy policy of the German Communist Party as a case of "left-wing deviation." But that was not the case. Those "Hail-Moscow" callers in Germany were simply following Stalin's orders in a religious manner. These were based on calamitous misapprehensions and they do not exactly strengthen the confidence in today's Soviet assessments which are equally calamitously wrong, as they are based on the same foundations and they are produced by the same apparatus.

Let's listen to Stalin as to what he had to say, according to the stenographical protocol in front of the Central Committee in April 1929: "The development of the working class toward the left" would testify "that in the countries of Capitalism the elements of a new revolutionary surge are ripening." For that reason the task, he continued, "to intensify the fight against Social Democracy as the left wing of Capitalism and especially against their 'left' wing ... therefore, the maxim of the cleansing of the Communist Party from the social-democratic tradition."[65] Is that enough to unmask the egregious lie of the Central Committee of the Socialist Unity Party of Germany, the Social Democrats had fought against the Communist Party of Germany and, thus, helped Hitler come to power? This Communist Party had "cleansed" those who were reasonable from their own ranks to make room for Hitler and they slandered the German Social Democratic Party as social Fascism. If that is not enough, let's continue where Stalin underlines with emphasis that the "new revolutionary surge would not be possible without the decisive licking of the Social Democrats." One may continue to read Stalin, how he governs the German Communist Party externally, in putting the demoted Thaelmann back into power and how he "cleansed," in turn, the "crappy" Brandler and Thalheimer, who wanted a common anti-fascist action with the German Social Democrats; how he emphatically demands "the cleansing of the German and the Czechoslovakian Communist Parties of Social Democratic elements and traditions."[66] We know now from the XX Party Congress of the Communist Party of the Soviet Union in 1956, how these "cleansings" were put into effect by the Secret Police.

The Socialist Unity Party of Germany has taken up the fight against the so-called Social Democratism and its "cleansing" accordingly. God protect the Social Democrats and Germany of their "potential Grotewohls,"[67] as they are smugly and cynically called by East German apparatchiks, upon which the hopes of the Socialist Unity Party rests to annihilate for the third and last time the free German labor movement. Is Hermann Weber publishing absolutely for nought, as well, who has hit the Socialist Unity forgers with his sources publications lethally? In this country nobody - not a soul! – even dares to mention Weber, the former lecturer at the Party College of the Socialist Unity Party, who knows his shop inside out and knows exactly where to place a hit! Weber proves with German Communist sources, how the German Communist Party fulfilled Stalin's directives and thus helped to bring Hitler to power!

The Stalinized German Communists let themselves be guided by Marx's thesis, that the crisis – and above all the Great Depression! – would intensify the misery of the proletariat to unbearable proportions and that it would, thus, bring about the proletarian Revolution, for that matter "Hail Moscow," for that reason the maxim: Soviet Germany, Berlin – the German Moscow, for that reason the symbolism of Hammer and Sickle rather than unity, liberty, fraternity! The German Communist Party followed the COMINTERN and the latter followed the "materialist" conception of History, which is characterized exactly by a one-sided, dogmatic setting of dynamic economic processes as absolute. The "scientific" policy that was borne out from Marx's "thesis" led directly to German Fascism. Germany is confronted today with the consequences of this policy. We have survived the ideology of the brown shirts thanks to the anti-Hitlerian coalition. What coalition do we need to survive the ideology of the red flag?

Stalin was hoping to erect his world empire upon the ruins of the Western democracies after Hitler, which he did succeed in doing, at least partly, with regard to Germany. Not the materialist perspective of History, but war launched Marxism in Europe and in Asia on a broad basis. In peaceful emulation the Marxist model is doomed.

By the way, Germany had had some good experiences with the rightful application of the materialist conception of History when it was handled dialectically by the Democrats and not dogmatically by the Communists. The Prussian reformers and liberal civil servants practiced what Lavergne and Schulz had previously reflected in theory. Since 1818, the Liberals tended strongly towards a German Customs Union [Zollverein] under Prussian aegis, to reach German political unity through that common market. Even today this conception is linked not to a narrow national, but a larger European template of the same. Prince Metternich did not understand this development! He forgot that History by and by takes place outside of diplomatic intrigues in the absence of Chancellery notes of governments and in this manner Prussia could rise to become the leading power in the German Union [Deutscher Bund] and the House of Hapsburg was suspended from the business of German government and relegated to Austria.

Friedrich List found support with just those Prussian civil servants, whose world view had been shaped by the progressive University of Goettingen, where Britain's classic writers of Political Economy were highly regarded. One may look at the memoranda of the Prussian Ministers, e.g., that of Minister of Finance von Motz from June 1829, which stipulated: "Political unit – necessary consequence of the commercial unity." This missive can be recommended to certain people who would like to put the brakes on the process of the European Union today. But Motz does not stand alone. Minister Count Bernsdorf declares in a memorandum from February 1831, how the economical treaties and agreements of Prussia led to greater political influence. Minister of State Buelow, the brothers Humboldt, Baron von Stein and even Field Marshall Gneisenau drove the economic unifications of the middle class forward based on these insights, which included industrial espionage in England. In that endeavor they were actively supported by unusually talented civil servants like Secretary of State Beuth, who led the respective department from 1818 'til 1845.

Now, brothers and sisters, what did our Karl Marx do in these years, as whose grandchildren nevertheless East Germany's Communist Youth see themselves after all? He followed the path from his diapers to his scientific existence as a suckling, called the

Philosophic-Economic Manuscripts, while the above-mentioned men alongside many others drove German history forward upon the basis of an economic conception of History. It is quite astounding, that world history moved at all without the Marxist, scientific interpretation, isn't it? Perhaps an *ukase* should be decreed that it did not start until the publication of *Capital*, volume I? Now we know, the true Prussians had done more - before Marx even learned that there is such a thing as Political Economy and a materialist conception of History - for it, as all Communists put together until today. This would prove that the entire *Manifesto of the Communist Party* is nothing but unscientific crap.

This Prussian matter is actually quite striking in theory: the feudal apparatus of power, which, according to Marx, is arch-reactionary, is promoting by all means possible its ideological and material arch-enemy, the *bourgeoisie*. What a terrific class struggle, indeed! And from this ornery sublevel Marx postulates in the second section of the *Manifesto*, that he and through him by now the Communists until the end of the earth before all other men "had the theoretical insight into the conditions, the process and the general results of the proletarian movement." Here we have finally got a scientifically endowed clairvoyant! There is now finally someone, who knows - and on what high horse of rhetoric - about the conditions, the course and the goal of a historical development before this movement even came into existence! And this is the same writer, who, in a drive of philosophical inspiration of his eclectically registering brain that is without equal, brings up the equally true formula that real knowledge may proceed only from the study of empirical facts, because truth is always concrete. Consequently, Marxists are always concrete-in-the-abstract. Now, as the "rest of the masses," the non-Communists that is, from that orthodox Marxist perspective are seen as stupid and don't know at all what will happen, they will not catch this process, or will they? For the things to come there is a restricted elite, the Soviet functionaries, the professional revolutionaries, the apparatchiks. They know what's up, they know the course of things, they know, for sure, what is to come. This is because they have a direct wire to Marx and to the Kremlin. Engels in his old age was somewhat more skeptical in this respect: "Because what every individual wants is being thwarted by every other individual, the outcome will be something that nobody wanted."[68] This is what he says having become older and wiser.

This is a very good description of a constructive policy built on compromise and it is a remarkable qualification, as well, of the ex-revolutionist Engels at the end of his days. In Marx we do not find such a maturation process. He was too calcified in the head too early to be able to continue to learn!

Nevertheless, let's, for once, give Marx his due! Let's suppose the "general insights" were established. Now, who will translate these general laws, who will translate them into the sphere of the concrete, the applicable; who will check that the translation will not be wrong, who then is in the possession of the absolute wisdom, which will correspond to the course of History – not absolutely Marxist, see the warnings of 1933!?! No response, comrades? Well, no answer is an answer, as well. The general conformity of History to law is revealed as a historic nightmare, nourished by the divine-economic omnipotence of prevision, which will steer the proletariat to the height of political power or into the abyss of Fascism, of war, into the ecological and demographic catastrophe of Germany, or into all those things put together? If there be always different possibilities which one will become reality?

Or, to put more concretely: Who will steer, when, where, how and whereto? Not the proletariat, per se, but the Communists, as has previously become apparent. Who are those Communists? The Party! Who is the Party? The heavenly Party Secretary Charlie Crap and his Central Committee secretaries on earth, amen. Personal claim to power covered and guaranteed by historical infallibility. Therefore, checks and balances of this power are not necessary and further, therefore, the abuse of power down to and including genocide becomes possible. Furthermore, an abject and egregious cult of personality becomes possible, down to hereditary succession, proletarian Absolutism at its best.

But no effect remains without its counter-effect. This very cult of personality and this very abuse of power have stimulated the forces of resistance within the labor movement, Marxism was split into Leninism, Maoism, reform Communism. Class struggle continues within the Communist movement, forgotten is fraternity. Fraternally the Communist powers of the Soviet Union and China stand against each other, fraternally their rockets of peace are targeting each other, while the dogs in the manger in Kampuchea lovingly tear open each other's throats. The outcome is something that nobody wanted ... the outcome is what Marx called in his favorite quotation "the same old crap." That is the Marxist summary of its theory and practice in the 20th century!

In the second section Marx speaks up again of bourgeois liberties, which he reduces to a mere economic quantity, viz., free competition. That only confirms his reductionist understanding of democracy, which we have already examined, his barbarian unhistorical thinking. He speaks up for the "Communist abolition of haggling," but he is silent about what should take its place. How should the trade streams of raw materials, of investment and consumption commodities be guided? How should incentives for production, which presuppose a will to perform, be kept when money is abolished? How shall Communist surplus be produced so that underproduction and atrocious scarcity - centrally managed, mind you - will not take the place of that surplus paradise?

We are hitting here upon a fundamental problem that Marx did not solve ideologically either in the *Manifesto* or in *Capital*, simply because it is unsolvable. Here the utopian character of Communism of all colors becomes apparent, as the globally still increasing division of labor, the necessary planning of microeconomic and macroeconomic processes would never allow to abscond from a planning according to value and that is money. Very well, one may siphon off money, the social blood, as Hess calls it, from the organism of society. Then the Communist revolt operation will have succeeded, but the patient will be dead by that time - see N.E.P. and the following experiments about which there will be more to be said later.

The whole world knows the uneven position of the COMECON countries with regards to money. How strange, since they have at their full disposition the "truly scientific Science" of Marx as demonstrated in his main work! Every COMECON country engages in its own national economic and financial policy. One is for, one is against the International Monetary Fund, with regards to membership, that is, one is for and one is against convertibility, one is for a unified, one is for a split convertibility, one is for and one is against a unified world market, one is for two world markets, the Capitalist on the one hand, the Communist on the other, etc., etc. Since everything that will determine the action of human beings has to pass through their concrete heads first, the explanation of this organized chaos happens on the basis of the unified Marxism in the discombobulation of the chaotic concrete head of Marx himself. He, who barely ever made his own money, had a thoroughly irrational conception of gold and money.

In his early studies he describes it following verses of Goethe and Shakespeare, which he translates into prose without rhyme – a great economic method! Twenty years later he treats of it again in *Capital* - and there money is the root of all evil! According to him Communism stands for the abolition of the monetary system, as, thus, it stands with all Communist ideologues. It apparently never occurred to Marx and his disciples that money, not entirely by accident, is an ancient phenomenon. Even Alexander the Great already used it brilliantly for his banking system within his empire. In ancient Lydia coins were struck as early as 700 years B.C.E. and in the third and second millennia B.C.E. Babylonians and Egyptians utilized silver and gold in the shape of bullions for that purpose. That means here we have quite an ancient Capitalism, if Capitalism is to mean plutocracy or the rule of money.

Money is an irreplaceable equivalent in all societies based on the division of labor, i.e., in the past, present and future, as the Marxist proposition, as well as that of all Communists, to measure value in terms of time instead of money, is a complete and utter nonsense. But we will deal with that issue in more detail later.

From the science of Political Economy that is not quite kosher to him - he even gives a wrong definition of the wages of labor - Marx in the second section jumps back to ideology and so I have to jump with him, although the exposition is, thus, repeated: "The workers have no fatherland." Why was it, then, that of all classes the working class had fought most bitterly against the alien rule of Napoleon? That had happened just three decades earlier, or did our young man have no interest in the most recent history of Germany, or what exactly he did view as his fatherland? Oh, not to forget, as an *ersatz*-proletarian he did not have one! Why then have the German workers fought so bitterly for the constitution of the unity of their fatherland in the 19th century, on the barricades of the revolution, in the struggles for the constitution of the empire, in the wars of the unity of the empire?

The disdainful valuation of the land of the fathers is matched only by the scornful verdict of the fate of the German nation. In both cases one would have to say that the Socialist Unity Party of Germany surpassed Marx in their policy against the fatherland, against the nation, against Germany. Unique in world history it has cast in concrete the brilliance and flexibility of its genuine Marxism - and that really has significance in the verdict of all times and peoples. With the Berlin Wall it demonstrates its creative capacity to solve problems of and by the German people *against* the people! The Wall through Berlin and the Iron Curtain through Germany is the most singular, the greatest monument for the greatest son of the German people, as the Central Committee has baptized Marx.

In the *Manifesto* he expressed himself in the following manner: That the "national particularities and contradictions" would disappear in his global system. For that reason it seems while the last borders are falling within the European Community, the borders between the G.D.R. and Poland, that had been opened of late, have been closed again! Following his insights into the conformity to the laws of world history it could be predicted that this would not turn out well. Why had they been opened in the first place?

And what about the fate of the following prophecy: "With the antagonism of the classes amongst themselves within the nation, the antagonism of nation against nation will fall as well." Of course! That is the explanation for the shots at the Ussuri[69] and elsewhere. Either the *Manifesto* is completely wrong or our superpower is anti-Marxist. Who would have ever thought that things turned out the way they did?

At the turn of the 20th century Bernstein vanquished Marx on the intellectual battlefield. In the Socialist International the right wing and the centrists consequently stood against the Marxist left wing, represented by Rosa Luxemburg, Karl Liebknecht and Lenin. When Lenin started in 1917 to translate the left-wing Marxist ideology into practice in Russia, the theoretical head of the German left, the co-founder of the German Communist Party, Rosa Luxemburg, stood decidedly against Lenin, quite in keeping with the tradition of the democratic Communism. Luxemburg's texts unmasked the demagogy of "scientific Communism," this ominous "manual to action" using the example of Lenin, and its familiar precept that practice is the decisive criterion to evaluate theory! The blistering criticism of Rosa Luxemburg notwithstanding, the propaganda of the Socialist Unity Party hammers home incessantly that the Leninist views based on Marx should be the way into the future for the Labor movement even in Germany. Rosa Luxemburg wrote in complete contradiction to today's Marx cult. She was published in East Germany for the sole reason that the West quoted its writings before the Socialist Unity Party, who fought long against the "Luxemburgism," which explains why even in the eight volumes *History of the Workers' Movement* of 1966 Luxemburg's picture in the row of ancestors is missing in the first volume.

She wrote:[70]

"The silent and implicit presupposition of the theory of dictatorship in the sense of Lenin and Trotsky is that the Socialist revolution is a matter solved by a recipe in the pocket of the revolutionary party that is only waiting to be realized with decision. Unfortunately – or fortunately, depending – that is not so. To be far removed from being a sum of applicable rules the practical realization of Socialism as an economic, social and legal system is a matter still completely engulfed by the mists of the future. What we possess in our program are a few broad signposts showing the way in which the measures have to be sought ... by and large they are of a negative character. ... Of what kind and nature the thousand practical and concrete, small and large measures are – and which have to be taken step by step - to implement socialist principles in economics, in law and in all social relations no Socialist party program, no Socialist textbook will be able to inform us. The negative aspect, the deconstruction, can be decreed, the positive aspect, the construction, cannot be decreed. This is a new world and there are a thousand issues and problems. Only experience will be able to tell, to correct and to open new ways. Only unfettered, foaming life will come up with a thousand new forms, improvisations, will receive creative force, will itself correct all missteps. The public life of States with its limited freedom is for that reason so poor, so niggardly, so schematic, and so sterile, as it cuts itself off from all the living sources of spiritual freedom and progress through the barring off of democracy. The whole popular mass has to participate, otherwise Socialism will be decreed and octroyated in back rooms by a dozen intellectuals.

Public control is indispensable; otherwise the exchange of experiences is confined to the closed circles of the civil servants of the new government. In that case, corruption will be unavoidable. Nobody knows that better and describes this more perseveringly than Lenin. Only he is mistaken completely as to the means. Ukase, dictatorial power of the factory foremen, draconian penalties, a reign of terror, all these are just palliatives! The only way to rebirth is the following: the school of public life itself, unbridled democracy on the broadest base, public opinion. Just the reign of terror demoralizes completely ... without general elections, without freedom of press and of congregation, the open emulation of opinions withers away life in all public institutions, it becomes a sham, in which bureaucracy remains the last active element. Public life becomes dormant by and by, a few dozen party bosses full of indefatigable energy and a boundless idealism direct and govern; among them in reality just a dozen prominent minds reign, an elite of workers is called to assemblies from time to time to provide applause to the speeches of the bosses, to confirm prearranged resolutions unanimously. At heart this is an oligarchy, a dictatorship, indeed, but not a dictatorship of the proletariat, but a dictatorship of a handful of politicians, i.e., a dictatorship in the banal bourgeois sense, in the sense of the regime of the Jacobins (the postponement of the Soviet assemblies from three months to six months!). And all the more so, such conditions must engender a brutalizing of public life: assassinations, shooting of hostages, etc. This is an overwhelming, objective law which no party can escape.

The basic flaw of the theory according to Lenin and Trotsky is just this, that they juxtapose dictatorship, just like Kautsky, to democracy. ... "As Marxists we were never idol worshippers of formal democracy," writes Trotsky. Absolutely, we never were idol worshippers of formal democracy. We also never were idol worshippers of Socialism or Marxism. ... It is the historic mission of the proletariat, once it has attained power, to create a socialist democracy instead of a bourgeois democracy; it is not its mission to abolish all democracy. ... Socialist democracy begins simultaneously with the deconstruction of class rule and the construction of Socialism. It begins with the attainment of power of the Socialist Party. This is nothing but synonymous with dictatorship of the proletariat.

Yes dictatorship! But this dictatorship consists of realizing democracy, not abolishing it ... this dictatorship has to be the work of the working class, not that of a small minority in the name of that class, i.e., it has to derive step by step out of the active participation of the masses, it has to be put under its immediate influence, it has to be subjected to the control of the entire public..." Here it becomes absolutely clear, what democratic Labor Communism is and what dictatorship against the proletariat! Democratic Labor Communism from Weitling and Luxemburg to today's reform Communists is characterized – in contrast to the ideology of Marx – by the safeguarding of the humanist tradition and the guarantee of human and civil rights. The focus of this understanding of a social democracy is the freedom of the individual:

"Freedom only for the servants of government, of the members of a certain party – as numerous as that may be – is no freedom. Freedom is always the freedom of those who think differently. Not because of the fanaticism of 'justice,' but because everything invigorating, everything wholesome and clarifying of political freedom is connected to this essence, its effect comes to nought when this 'freedom' becomes privilege."[71]

This is the famous passage that Herbert Wehner quoted in his speech before the German parliament *Bundestag* Oct. 21, 1949,[72] and who added that a Soviet military court had condemned four young Berliners, members of the Socialist youth group *Falcons*, as usual to 25 years of confinement as they had distributed copies of this utterance by Rosa Luxemburg. As we can see, the Germans were not only liberated from Hitler, they were liberated from the leading thinkers of the Communist Party of Germany, as well. The youths were again, as usual, tried and convicted without having been able to contact their parents or legal counsel.[73] Had the Communist German Youth organization or the Socialist Unity Party ever tried to establish that such youths should be allowed to affirm the views of the co-founder of the Communist Party? We all know how it was and how it is. How would the Berlin citizens react during the annual commemoration of Luxemburg and Liebknecht if "Karl's grandchildren" would bring them hand-outs of the writings of Luxemburg?

The criticism of Rosa Luxemburg after the splitting up into three wings led to the further splitting of the left wing of the Party. For that reason, she is of paramount historical importance and her work has been amply documented and publicized. Had Rosa Luxemburg survived the murderous commandos of the reactionary German troops, she would have inevitably, like other German Communists - whose names could not be mentioned for decades - have fallen prey to the murderous commandos of Stalin, become victim of his ideological "cleansing"! Today the criticism of Rosa Luxemburg carries not just abstract-theoretical significance, but it carries world-political and practical meaning. That increases her weight.

98

From the study of History we know about the disintegrating processes of all ideologies. Luther had barely smashed the uniformity of Catholicism, when he was attacked by Calvin and Zwingli. Bernstein had smashed Marxism, Lenin and the reform Communists continued his work. The progress of knowledge cannot be stopped and, thus, it holds that change alone is permanent. No founder of religion could thwart the further splitting of his teaching through his successors. Those ideological fanatics achieve gargantuan things: the torturers of the Shah leave, the torturers of Khomeini come. We got rid of the Gestapo; the Stasi is at our throats! From the Crusades onward ideologies have brought only blood and death, suffering and misery upon the Europeans. In the final analysis, the ideologies of Marxism and anti-Marxism have led only to Fascist and Stalinist dictatorships and have, thus, led to World War II! Shall the misery of the half-German half-Russian now lead us into World War III? Have the East Germans not been preached to since toddler stage to develop "hatred towards the class enemy"? Have we not being preached to incessantly to "identify the enemy Federal Republic of Germany"? Does Marxist class craze lead to anything different from the anti-Marxist race craze? Is it possible in a climate of trust and measures that inspire trust to safeguard peace in Europe with lies, hatred and the constant slandering of anything and anyone other?

Is it possible to effectuate the dissolution of the military blocs of the Cold War and have atomic, biological and chemical weapons be banned from German territories with the daily hateful propaganda of the decline of Western imperialism proven by Marx and Lenin, accelerated by the worldwide Socialist system? Who actually does believe that and consequently: What do the Russians really want: Unity and peace in Germany and in Europe or splitting-up and war in Germany and Europe? Shall the Afghanistan of today become the training grounds and the killing fields for men and weapons for the last of all wars, just as Spain in the Thirties became the template and scrimmage for World War II? Can the ideological delusion, which lies at the bottom of the political imbecility of the continuing hyper-armament not even be stopped in face of the looming total destruction of Humanity? Can the *homo sovieticus* and the Soviet system not reform themselves autonomously, begin to respect human and civil rights, honor the rights of the peoples for self-determination, those of one's own people as much as those of alien peoples outside of Soviet borders? Would that not be, hence, the most promising way towards disarmament and peace?

If hatred and enemy propaganda were to cease, one could be certain that the material foundations of peace would not be waiting long in the wings! It could be like that, but it will not be like that, because the Marxist ideology is not capable of reform, such as the system that goes with it isn't, either. The failed experiment of the XX Party Congress of the Communist Party of the Soviet Union proves that. Politically there is but one choice: The Soviets have to be forced to keep the peace through superior military might. There is no other way to attain disarmament and détente. There is no other way to guarantee the survival of the Germans. Whosoever thinks differently about homeland and nation than does Marx may never forget that.

After the sullying of homeland and nation Marx goes on to sully human dignity in its most profound core as he continues to write in section II: "The ideas of freedom of conscience and religion only express the rule of free competition in the realm of conscience." How many human beings through the ages have chosen to die for their freedom of faith and conscience? For how many victims the Inquisition, the Fascist Gestapo, the Stalinist Secret Service can be held responsible? Thus, let's abolish free competition; let's return straight to the most sinister of Medieval ages, as: what is a valid pang of conscience is decreed by the Communist Party and the Secret Service guarantees that every one has a squeaky-clean conscience.

Just consider: The most sinister Absolutism still allowed the Enlightenment. It even endowed the *encyclopédistes* with paper and a printing license, something that would be thwarted in the G.D.R. under any circumstances as our proletarian Absolutism makes no such allowances! Since its implementation through the Russians it was decreed that magazines and books from the West should be barred, just like the German landed gentry was wont to proceed close to the French border after the revolution of 1789: absolutely no Western ideology was allowed; those who would spread anything like it would find themselves behind bars, directly. And Bautzen is not the only high-security prison on German soil.

Whence this incredible, indelible funk of the spiritual heritage of Humanity? Whence this *angst* of empirical facts, contexts, critical annotations, other ways of life? The answer is truly easy: The core of the Marxist ideology is a lie and a sham in theory and in practice! It can be sustained only as long as the slightest notion of truth is kept out. We are dealing with that mentality of Absolutism so prevalent in Russia for the past so many centuries, its insane *angst* of the progressive ideas of the West. The dunderheaded funk of the ruling class is even well founded; their defense, on the other hand, nevertheless, is pathetic and futile. The tide of modern mass communication cannot be stemmed. Scientific and technological progress works on all sides against the ideological Medieval age of the Russians and *ersatz*-Russians.

Nothing will abet or escape that: not the joint antennas on the same blocks, not the blackballing of Stasi officials, policemen, members of the army, etc., given the case that it can be proven that they are, in fact, watching West TV. The "cleansing" of libraries will help as little as the attempt to confiscate the private stock of Western literature held by scholars for their research. At the push of a button everyone can access the desired political information from the West. Scientific information which makes literature indispensable is being barred even for College and University lecturers. This explains why the real-existent Socialism always lags ten years behind the West in Research and Technology. The system is completely schizophrenic!

Nevertheless, according to Lenin "Marxism is almighty, because it is true." It doesn't seem to be the real thing after all. At least that must be the position of the authorities who prohibit their most faithful adherents to catch contagion through Western contacts. If the latter engage in those anyway, they get politically decapitated. Death heals all ills and evils! At least on Opera Square in front of Humboldt University no more books are burned as they were burned under Hitler. Those who are on the Communist index merely go into the shredder. The authors are no longer burned at the stake, either. There are more subtle methods to turn their lives into a burning hell. Nobody is considered worse than the criminal merely thinking thoughts, when he, thus, becomes a breaker of ideologies and we Germans always had trouble with freedom of thought and freedom of conscience and with the true faith.

Our ancient forebears slugged it out in the wake of the Reformation ostensibly for the best ideology for three whole decades during the Thirty Years' War (1618 – 1648). They literally and mutually clubbed each other to death with the assistance of the then prevailing super-powers. Then an ideological peace was negotiated. Does any Protestant or Catholic understand today what the ideological cavils of the past were? And now a remark regarding the freedom of conscience and religion as "product of free competition." That is not only cynical; it is, historically speaking, an imbecility!

When did free competition become apparent in Europe and when, exactly, did it become prevalent? Let us take the Dutch Revolution as its incipience and the completion of the German Revolution at the end of the 19th century through Bismarck as its end-point. In between we have the English and the French Revolution. It becomes immediately clear at this point that the period of Capitalism in free competition falls between 1789 and 1871, when the Capitalist production of commodities in Europe finally prevailed over feudalism. And Marx, in his diligent academic dilettantism and his present interpreters as well have to be reminded that the Europeans and among them especially the Germans negotiated successfully the religious peace of Augsburg in 1555, that is, in the depth of Feudalism and a century later they negotiated the peace of Muenster and Osnabrueck in the year 1648.

The Peace of Westphalia solved above all the religious and ideological problems within the Holy Roman Empire of the German Nation; there was, thus, freedom of faith and conscience long before the epoch of free competition!

For the predominantly feudal Europe - the Netherlands and Switzerland had left the Imperial Federation in 1648, for which Young Engels wanted to see them punished because of their "betrayal of the Empire" at the beginning of his period as a journalist - the era of Absolutism began in which the bourgeois or middle-class ideology was at least tolerated. When will the so-called Eastern Community of States in Europe elevate itself in the political and ideological sense to the height and standing of the wisdom of statesmen of the European principalities of the waning Middle Ages? This may not be expected of the Russians. They have not managed to reform their orthodox creed in more than 1,000 years; consequently, they will not reform or modernize their Marxist-Leninist secular religion.

When will "real" Socialism make its religious peace? When will the General Secretaries of the Communist Parties rise up to the human height of the level of decency of centuries ago and let any subject, who does not swear by the credo of his or her father of the country, emigrate without discriminatory harassment or torment? And emigrate precisely in a manner in which one was used to be able to among civilized people in the Medieval Ages, after a quiet arrangement of one's affairs, after the sale of one's possessions, following fixed legal principles and not after harassment and arbitrary confinement that would extend to the imperiling of one's very physical existence? Not after years of waiting in uncertainty, or after forced resettlement within the borders of the G.D.R., or after eviction within hours, etc., etc., but emigration according to the rules and regulations which have been practiced in Germany for four-hundred years! Raise yourself up, Comrades, have the guts finally to stand on the shoulders of the best German tradition! Upon whose example did the Chekists in East Germany model their barbarian practices? Certainly not from any other German template! When will such human rights of political self-determination of a new global era - which have been written down and ratified almost half a millennium ago by the Mecklenburgians and the Brandenburgians and the Thueringians and the Saxons - be accorded to the last and remotest of tribes on the remotest and least accessible parts of the globe? Or shall we endure the practices of Russian serfdom for the rest of eternity?

Thus, Comrade Crap, tell it your very own at the next general assembly: even the most fanatical counter-reformationists respected the freedom of faith and of conscience as yet still in the Medieval Ages. When they were trying to recatholicize the workers of the imperial *Salzkammergut* by force during the counter-reformation,

Austria, in the summer of 1600 - and 90% of the inhabitants of that county were affected by the measure - the imperial order was given that either one had to become catholic again, or one would be free to leave. Either/or, at least that would be a decision!

The so-called *Neues Deutschland* or "New Germany," world-historically unique Party organ of the Socialist Unity Party, at times publishes historical items. On February 2 and 3, 1985, it commented on the Augsburg religious peace with the following words: *Cuius region, eius religio*, i.e., each region its religion. Our journalistic quotation mongers did not deem it necessary to add anything further. Our historians, on the other hand, at least had to clear their throat, even if not completely historical, with regard to all modalities of the freedom of faith and conscience and the right to emigrate: "Free choice of religion was meant - with regard to the ratification of the imperial assembly of religious peace from August 25, 1555 - only for imperial states, while their subjects had to go along with the decision of the respective father of the land or emigrate."[74]

That is, thus, in fact, the very German tradition, which Marx completely ignored! And that explains, as well, why Lenin, the Russian, in this matter, did not correct Marx, but found the doctrines fully compatible without any necessity of "further development." That as opposed to other parts of Marx's ideology: Marx's thinking is undemocratic; it is absolutist, retrograde, czarist thinking. Russians never took on the Humanist ideas of the Enlightenment in their applied form. For that reason Lenin and Stalin found Marx completely of one mind with them. The neo-Stalinists in the G.D.R. do so to this very day. How fortunate we are that according to the *Manifesto* the ruling ideas of the times are never the "ideas of the ruling class"!

This statement is absolutely imbecilic; nothing could be more unhistorical. Let's just take the times of Marx himself. The ruling nobility takes up the cause of the Liberals in opposition, regarding *Zollverein*, regarding Bismarck's unification of the empire! And how did the opposition get founded in France prior to 1789? And how is it that the working population of East Germany today thinks so differently in terms of ideology than the unproductive class of the Party functionaries, secret service bureaucrats, so that the latter do not only erect the Wall of Concrete, but they erect the juridical Wall of more severe penalties and then they wield the big lethal bludgeon of "ideological diversion" against Germans in East and West? And they want even more: A third Wall is to be erected, the Wall of international Law, the abolition of the right in West Germany or Federal Republic of Germany [F.R.G.] of general citizenship. It is to become the third dividing line to effect and complete the final splitting of our nation. None shall say that they have had no prior knowledge of this, regarding *Neues Deutschland* of January 30, 1985, page 5, the

Foreign Policy Section: "The Execution of the Personal Sovereignty of a State ..." Slowly but surely the Socialist Unity Party is dropping the rest of its national masquerade! Had the *ersatz*-Russians not sworn in front of Stalin, the Hitlers would come and go, but the German State would remain? Had they not declared in a high and holy manner, the Russians had at various times guaranteed German Unity in international Treaties, last in Potsdam in 1945, without any whens, buts and ifs? At that time, at least, the found themselves still, ideologically speaking, in unison with the people as far as the national issue was concerned. Today there is absolutely no more talk of this. The remainder of common ground held between the ruling and the ruled has been broken in East Germany; the seeds are sown for increasing conflicts with those who govern!

Marx concludes his second section of the *Manifesto* with the remark that those who act politically "had to concentrate all instruments of production in the hands of the State, i.e., in the proletariat that is to be organized as the ruling class." The G.D.R. worker recounts in reaction to this passage, which he knows inside out from Party schooling sessions: Now, my U.S.-American colleague gets up at five in the morning, makes himself an omelet with six eggs, drives his huge car into the factory and lets himself be exploited. My West-German colleague makes himself an omelet of four eggs, drives his smaller car to the factory and lets himself be exploited. I myself in East Germany make myself an omelet of two eggs, jump on my cycle, work up a sweat pedaling to the factory and, thus, I co-govern! That is the most fitting illustration of the central Social Unity Party maxim: Co-plan, co-govern! The great abstractionist Marx here really gets hit by a very concrete case, nowhere he makes it clear: How is the State, how is the "class" organized? How does who govern, in fact, who selects those who govern, who controls those who govern, who will replace them? Is it the people who determine or is it the Party apparatus? Are there to be free and unfettered discussions, criticism, elections, or is everything drowned out and pseudo-sanctioned in waves of fake applause?

But then again at the end of the *Manifesto* Marx almost becomes really concrete. He collapses his political concept about the future turning-of-society-upside-down in a list of ten talking points. Let's just take up one item to see whether, after all that theoretical nonsense, Marx might finally have some tangible political ideas. How would he have liked to see the peasants treated - the main force of the up-and-coming, anti-feudal revolution - also the absolute majority of the population of Germany?

First of all, he does not treat them under one heading, but all over the place. Let's garner together as to what is his intent.

"Expropriation of landed property and utilization of land rent for State expenses."

What does that mean, exactly? Expropriation of everybody? Is the intent to drive the small peasants, peasants with middle-sized landholdings and large-estate farmers up onto the barricades? How off his rocker someone has to be to think that the peasants and farmers would risk their life, limb and property not to safeguard and retain their fields and ground, but to lose them? Why does he not take up the legitimate concerns of the peasants and demand a revolutionary measure on their behalf, a radical bringing-to-an-end of the Prussian reforms, the redemption of the repayment of the serf's ransom, etc., something that the landsman will understand to be his very own interest, for instance, the sharing and partition of the large-landed estates on behalf of the peasants? Lenin classically broke with even this thesis of Marxism, the so-called association policy with the peasants. He did not take his peasant program from Marx, but from the populists and the social reformers. Stalin, on the other hand, took up Marx's concept again and executed it with the prompt result that because of the constant performance boycott of the Russian peasant of Red Imperialism, nobody is able to survive up to now without the yellow-golden wheat of Western imperialism.

Perhaps Marx guaranteed property rights for the peasants? On the contrary, he decrees: "Abolition of the right of inheritance." Again, a very catching slogan, especially for the sons of all peasants as well as for the elders who have to subsist without Social Security on their shoals during the sunset years of their lives. "Cultivation and improvement of the lands according to a communal program." Does that mean syndicalist and unionized production? "Erection of industrial armies, especially for the cultivation of the lands." Does that mean agricultural wage laborers as property of the State? In East Germany the attitude with regard to the most nonsensical and imbecile slogans and activities is always: Well, our Comrades in the Central Party Committee will have thought real hard about that one. With regard to Marx this should be triply true, as he was certainly right with the industrial armies: Meaning the utilization of all college, university and high school students and of all elderly inhabitants of the G.D.R. for the turnip harvest year in, year out.

Even that is a classic, because the maxim of the "army" is clearly: "Equal compulsion to work for all." Who, now, is really decreeing this wholesome compulsion? The Central Authority! It does the essential work, coerces everyone and orwellizes the shop. These are the most primitive, barbaric ideas not even of Blanqui but of Blanqui's predecessors. But then again, Marx does not, like these, demand the abolition of the cities as the centers of power, money and vice; he, thus, demonstrates his true commitment to progress.

Marx's political representations of the core issues of the revolution can only be called extremely hazardous and foolhardy. He was simply what he liked to call his opponents, a "twaddling blowhard." His conceptions were not only alien to the people, they were hostile to them! Next to the imbecility of a policy that was not unionizing but inimical to the peasants, his idea of industrializing agriculture was one of his most catastrophic theoretical mistakes. The Communists and Socialists who came before him had already regarded the factory as inhuman, but Marx pleaded for a senseless destruction of a way of production and life that was given by nature, which precisely and thank God, doesn't make man just an appendix of the machine.

Where would we be today if Stalin had not destroyed the family-based agricultural economies of Russia by force, but had only endowed them with the necessary technical gear? The Soviet Union had a surplus of nutrition and leisure products like the European Community and would not have been dependent on their subsidized export. The S.U. could have easily nourished its starving allies in Ethiopia and elsewhere. Where would we be today with the disastrous ecological conditions in our "real" Socialism if every peasant would not ruin the soil with over-cumbersome Russian technology but were able to use his patch with the due proper and natural care? More than half of the soil in East Germany is polluted by toxic substances. This results in diminishing agricultural returns of 10 – 40%! Furthermore, because of this grains have to be imported against hard foreign currency. The technology that is adapted to the needs of soil and plant has to be exported to the Soviet Union. Thus, again, the people are made to pay double. Would the glorious Party through its insight into the "development in conformity with the law" not have been able to see that every nation needs the peasant of the future as the preserver of nature, as the guardian of the earth, of water and forest? Have all those wise General Secretaries of the Communist Parties in the East Bloc States not understood that there are definite differences between a social overturning of the status quo and the scientific-technological development? Could that mean that Marx did not get his definitions straight from the outset? As, for example, social tensions create class struggle, but class struggle, in turn, does not create scientific-technological progress, that latter state is caused by a scientific-technical-economic state of competition, by factors, in other words, that are eliminated by the social revolution to its own detriment? What drives a society forward are its inner contradictions. "Real" Socialism has eliminated them through the change of proprietorial conditions and it has put outward administrative pressure in its place. After the mistreatment of Science this was the second decisive flaw in the system; flaws that explain the permanent scientific-technical and productive disadvantage towards the Capitalist industrialized nations.

Marxist dogmata hold the pulsating life of the economy in iron fetters, damage the working men by many billions in monetary value and act like the religion of Islam as an extreme brake to progress.

Nevertheless, there are Western diplomats and publishers who found themselves impressed by East German agriculture. Have they asked themselves, what the cost was to the great distress of the entire macroeconomy, the industrialization, the stable technologies, the silos, the infrastructure facilities, in short: How overly expensive and how senseless this over-centralization really is? Have they really and truly looked around outside of the exhibition and prestige objects? Have they seen how acid creeks of manure contaminate the groundwater deposits? How this contaminated manure, in turn, contaminates the pastures, so that no grass, weed, no flowers grow there anymore, just reedlike blades, which, cut and processed, become cattle fodder and, in turn, reduce meat and milk production? In the dairy farms a large percentage of the milk supplied is getting spoiled, assortments of quality cheese cannot be produced anymore because of the low-quality milk.

Enormous losses ensue through the large-area monocultures, through overly long ways of transportation, through so-called modern technology that is not all that modern. The few harvesting machine drivers of the E 512, which by now have an onboard computer, are saving per harvest four to five tons of grain that would otherwise be lost! One may multiply this and compare it to the amounts of imported fodder grain!

In former times the peasants in Mecklenburg said the "forework" swallows the revenue. "Forework" in the vernacular of the region meant approximately two miles of work and transportation ways with a wagon and a team of horses. Today the peasants are bussed around about 30 miles through the countryside, they lose precious time and then they may in total disinterest plow, sow and harvest on foreign lands. Marx called this the reduction of the contradiction between city and country. Separation of animal and plant production by way of specialization is what it is called today by the Central Office. To separate the animal from the plant – how smart! How about separating the Central Office from their fodder trough?

This system give the peasants work in three shifts including the "rolling shift" on the weekends. What an advantage against the former tradition of a heightened concentration of forces in the summer and a comparative quiet in the half year of the cold season! What, in effect, *really* is the background of the failure of the agricultural policies in the COMECON countries? It is, again and again, the ideology of Comrade Crap. Russians and Bulgarians are experimenting with "new ways towards Communism." The peasants in the G.D.R. who have been sufficiently long suffering and battered by Lyssenko and Mishurin with their cattle stables and square net planting methods, etc., etc., are again fighting for nought. The specialization process was carried out at all costs for none but ideological reasons and a certain innate obsequiousness. The result: now after unspeakable losses the course is changed again to status quo ante. The quality staple of the Socialist Unity Party has forever been: Now tackle the potato, now drop the potato, now you see it, now you don't!

Our *Neues Deutschland* has by now rediscovered a fact known for centuries – after the Central Committee had researched and decided on it – that the planting of willows on creek and river shores would reduce the damage during flooding and that simple weirs or locks could well serve to irrigate pastures, because the grass would grow better in such a manner!

In former times peasants knew that water makes grass grow, they even knew that the mug of a cow could be the cheapest and sharpest scythe. In our "real" Socialism all cattle remain tied down in the stable: a Soviet experience! They are made to devour silage, dearly produced with high tech and high energy, instead of grass and hay: a Soviet experience! The become sick and sterile, never mind, they'll get an antibiotic syringe for health, so that one may buy meat from now on only on prescription: what shalls? It's all Soviet experience! Who actually is forcing the East German functionaries and bureaucrats to adapt their methods and technologies from the agriculture with the weakest performance level in the world including, thus, all the root causes of the ensuing catastrophes? Would it not be better to send our peasants to the annual Agricultural Fair in West Berlin, where they can study what is truly state-of-the-art and cutting edge? This project may have failed in the past as I was recently told, because peasants wouldn't know how to use the L-train. By the way: Because through the O.P.E.C. and the S.U. there is not enough diesel to be had in the G.D.R., cattle are again let out to pasture. That's how contradictory the economy works, because of the large quantities of oil that are moved at bargain prices from the Soviets, the genuine horn-oxen are regaining their much-deserved freedom.

East Germany would have saved itself billions and billions in investments and it would have been spared an ecological disaster of the worst magnitude if it had engaged in the development of family farming like the European Community, with a technology that is appropriate for plant and soil, which would lead to the production of high surpluses of qualitatively-impeccable products. It could have vastly improved the miserable infrastructure of its region or done other sensible things with those gargantuan means that were wasted in wrong agricultural policies. The same holds for the industrial sector: Since the global economic crisis and the switch to intensive reproduction are forcing the party functionaries to ascertain that materials and energies are used more sparingly, startled East Germans are learning that their increase in the national income is made up by half of reductions. Let's take the - certainly falsified - statistics seriously: Who then is responsible for the billions of intensive economic strategy that have been wasted year after year to the detriment of the working population? How high, actually, is the damage that has been engendered against the people by the crappy economic policy of the Socialist Unity Party? And this holds not only for the agricultural and the industrial sector, it holds for all other sectors, as well. In agriculture the mismanagement is more patently obvious, when you look at the productivity gap between state, syndicalist-unionist and individual economy.

If COMECON continues to pursue the maxim of Marx as before: "unification of the agricultural and industrial units" and the "abolition of the contradiction between city and country" the crisis of "real" Socialism will grow rapidly worse. One may ask: What will the Soviets do, when they will lack foreign currency in the foreseeable future, as Western Europe is developing alternative sources of energy? How will they pay for their future grain imports? How will they deal with the coming rebels in the famine areas? Will they just cut all lines of communication as in the Twenties? Will they then let fifty million starve instead of five? During the last COMECOM summit it was for the first time decreed that the smaller and weaker East Bloc nations had to deliver nutritional goods to the S.U. But these smaller nations have to import their goods, in turn! But perhaps here again the super-weapons of Comrade Lyssenko will help: Blades of grain as strong as telegraph poles and as far apart as those, as well.

But let us recapitulate our analysis: The *Communist Manifesto* is a foolhardy putsch program, without even the thread of a notion of understanding of the real situation in the 19th century and, moreover, directed against the absolute majority of the German people: the peasants! Furthermore, it is a perfect manual to achieve practical ruin for agriculture in our "real" Socialism. To round off the characterization of the political quality of Marx's thinking, it may be added that a short time after the ten points of the *Manifesto* the Communist Party published seventeen postulates which were drafted more realistically under the influence of the workers within the Central Committee, but not at all in a manner that they would have activated the peasants. Not only is Marx a loser in theory; Marx as a politician is a complete loser, as well, an ideological home front crasher of the first order. Here it becomes unequivocally clear that he had not the foggiest notion of the "scientific perspective of History," his alleged own discovery. How could he have otherwise proposed socialist measures for middle-class-democratic revolutions in Germany? How could he have otherwise postulated tenets that would revolt the class-related main force and thrust of the revolution that is the middle class and the peasants? This man, Marx, had no relationship whatsoever to even one class of the German people! He had no clue what workers, peasants and democrats were thinking, feeling and wanting to do, even though, all had their full and finished, already published, specific programs. Marx was a splenetic, aloof intellectual without home or fatherland; completely consumed by his hatred for Jews and Germans, apt and fit only for destruction, an element alien to any class, "half-educated," as the democratic Labor Communists would call him, when they excluded him from the Communist Party.

The political program for the German revolution, the seventeen postulates that is, he seemed to have formulated with Engels in premature anticipation of a victory, when he saw himself as emperor of Vienna and Engels as king of Prussia, as the news from Germany were promising the complete victory for the revolution. More disconnected can the discrepancy between assumed scientific insight into the objective laws of the historical process and the tactical-political action not be demonstrated as it was done in the 10 items of the *Manifesto* and the 17 postulates of the Party program.[75]

It goes without saying that Marx-Engels, the sons of the bourgeoisie, were not ready to put their lives on the line for these ideas! They remained in the Rhineland under the protection of bourgeois law, under the protection of the class dictatorship of the exploiters, and they tried to obtain a position as editors of the *Neue Rheinische Zeitung*, in material and ideative terms, although they knew that the fate of the revolution would be decided in Berlin and Vienna. These historical processes we will examine later when we regard the development of the Association of Democratic Communists. For now we still have to take a look at the third section of the *Communist Manifesto*.

Here Marx is making comments about his ideological predecessors, whom he accuses summarily of being incapable "to grasp the march of modern History." How brilliantly he himself had seized this march we have just seen regarding his concept of the revolution. Then Marx makes a prognostication against his antagonists, whom he regards as petty-bourgeois ideologues, which has had disastrous effects both economically as well as ideologically to this very day! He prophesies again with extreme dogmatism that the petty bourgeoisie that is peasants, artisans, tradesmen, innkeepers and the service sector in general, will "completely disappear" and simultaneously with them their ideological representatives. The eradication of just this intermediate strata of society that has been customary in our "real" Socialism and the concomitant annihilation of a sound infrastructure that has grown organically is the source of abiding economic and political troubles, difficulties and economic losses of the largest dimension, which at the bottom line of the strife of the systems have a markedly negative impact.

The Capitalist concerns know full well why they keep a broad stratum of deliverers. The middle-class State knows full well why it keeps and furthers artisans, tradesmen, small and middle-class enterprises. They are the indispensable drops of oil in the giant machinery of macroeconomics. Their economic, ecologic and social utility cannot be overestimated. Marx and his brain-dead imitators don't know that! At present, after decades of destruction of the high-end, high-performance sector of the skilled workmen and service industry for reasons of ideological stupidity and economic imbecility, now that the situation has become clearly and unmistakably unbearable, these bearers of the economic micro-infrastructure are being slowly revived. On the side the small gardeners who have been scolded and defamed for decades as petty bourgeois and anti-revolutionary are now being revalued, deservedly, as patriots of the people. Necessity does not only break iron bars it may even break Marxist ideology: There is cause for hope!

In the interim we would like to state the following: Marx had in his *Manifesto* and its "manual to [revolutionary] action" neither a macroeconomic, an infrastructural, nor a microeconomic concept that would have been realistic and useful in the 19th century. Economically, if we may cite Engels again, he knew absolutely nothing! For that very reason the economy of our surreal Socialism is not only for nought, but less than that.

And again Lenin's layers of interest coincide with the one of Marx: Czarist Russia did not have a microeconomic structure, just as little as the Soviet Union today does not have it. The ideological imbecility of Marx could serve there from the get-go as high theory for the camouflage of a deeply-flawed economic practice. That is the entire "inseparable unity of Marxism-Leninism." Russia's economy consisted mainly of self-sufficient peasant farms prior to the rule of Marxism. In this manner, Lenin, following Marx, could propagate that the petty-bourgeoisie needed to be annihilated, as the small productive unit was supposed to engender Capitalism on a daily basis and that it was supposed to menace the fledging Socialism both economically as well as mentality-wise.

The economic damage in the quantity of billions which this manner of thinking has caused, everyone in the G.D.R. can testify for himself or herself. Every third rooftop here needs mending, as the magazine *Junge Welt* [Young World] states, everywhere the apartments fall apart in the upper stories, ground floor stores and magazine fronts are rotting to this day. The projects are rotting even worse in the true sense of the word, for thirty years there neither a roof gutter nor a broken chimney was repaired. The rents are P.R.

material; for this kind of income no one can do any maintenance. With penny increases precious living space and utility space could be kept up. They are not to be had! After penny amounts have turned into damages of millions, for billion in costs new multiple-storey concrete projects are being set up right smack on the acres where precious cattle fodder should actually be growing. Who pays? The State pays. And from where does it take the money? From the worker and the peasant! What they save in rent they spent again macroeconomically by the tenfold and by the hundredfold as they are the sole proprietors under Communism. This is the most efficacious efficacy.

The housing calamity paired with the misery in the service sector, the maintenance sector and the spare parts sector makes the population latently rebellious and the pressure from the Stasi brings large parts of the population close to the boiling point. Everything considered, a chronic hemorrhage by way of flight from the republic ensues. How about letting the Stasi and the military border guards - instead of going on their manhunts - produce spare parts and construction materials and letting them be employed in service repairs for the republic? After this (almost) first discovery of Marx being, as a philosophic category in this case, would be positively changed and, thus, all negative reactions in consciousness would become moot, no? Capitalist West Germans would migrate in droves to Socialist East Germany; the second most powerful Capitalism in the world would break down, even the carnival revelers in the Elector's castle in Mayence would chime in "Hail Moscow!" rather than their customary carnival slogans and nobody could say anymore "poor Germany," because we would all be rich!

I wish the Hungarians success, as they have the courage to try other ways, even though these are also not without their own problems. And I wish the same for the Chinese, who announced St. Nicolas Day of 1984 in their Party paper that the economic theory of the cultural revolutionary, Marx, would need to be put into indefinite storage and that a modern society could not be run upon dogmatic lines, but that a modern macroeconomy would have to be led in a modern manner. How would natural scientists look at us if we demanded their science should be based on the insight of an alchemist, who was spouting Medieval truisms in the 19th century?

Fifty years of macroeconomic disorientation ensuing in the abolition of industrial production of commodities, fifty years of microeconomic disorientation ensuing in the abolition of the agricultural and artisanal small commodities production, fifty years of disorientation resulting in a complete neglect in upkeep of the infrastructure mainly have led to the fact that both the Soviet Union and the East Bloc States have not been able to attain the performance level of developed Capitalism. Marx personally, as well as his blindly faithful followers, have to bear the responsibility for that. Notoriety and honor to all crap-producing ideologues! As life consists of a million details and on the other hand much of little ends up making much, for those readers who live in another world altogether some abstract things may be made concrete and understandable as follows: A hometown craftsman goes across the street to tighten a bolt of a washing machine. Our "real," completely disorganized Socialism needs for that a number of phone calls during office hours or written order slips. That goes for restaurants, as well. Impossible, you say? Then please cast a glance into the restaurant next to the Trade College at the Railway Station Friedrichstrasse, East Berlin! Not that you, dear West German or denizen of the Western hemisphere, could have the spontaneous idea to reserve a table for yourself and your playmate tomorrow night for dinner, good riddance to such practices, you live in a completely planned out society: Fixed times for everything!

Within the framework of those fixed times now the craftsman arrives, not on an hourly but, instead, on a daily basis: Wednesday *or* Friday between 7 a.m. and 7 p.m. Thus, the paying customer takes a vacation. With some luck only the vacation is wasted. Should the craftsman arrive, he will have driven for 100 miles with highly toxic-emission gasoline, as low-emission gas is not to be had in the country of True Progress. If he has used up his gas allotment he does not come at all. In that case one has to take vacation twice. But then again the working class is never shy to find impromptu solutions. The craftsmen buy gas on the side and account for it as overtime. In this way it is proven that the government-official economizing of gas has been achieved through the given government bureaucracy unit. For this the government pays high premiums. In this way everybody gets to govern some, better a dictatorship of the proletariat than no order at all!

Another example: as one is not supposed to do transports or taxi fares across county or district borders to save gas, a smart driving instructor is paid handsomely and, thus, an instructional ride serves to bring one's brother-in-law the remaining construction materials for his nursery. All those glorious working men who lead the heavily planning bureaucrats by the nose on a daily basis and, thus, make it possible that life continues to function at all in spite of the functionaries are saying to themselves: Stupid we may be, but we nevertheless know how to get on in a fix!

In another current case telegrams arrive, three, four, or five at a time with different dates, each for the delivery of chalk-sand bricks during the night shift. In this manner someone spends four completely futile nights on the construction site. The eight thousand bricks finally arrive unannounced in broad daylight, when nobody is there and they are dumped not on the site, but on the street. Nothing better to increase productivity! Whoever has devised the name "planned economy" for this kind of dysfunctional economy deserves a real laurel leaf. Nothing at all can be planned in this system. An adherent and debutant of black humor must have been at the origin of this! Or, let's say, the media picks up the topic of tardy execution of work as, for instance, in the Eastern *Berliner Zeitung* of February 16th and 17th in 1985. Wolf Biermann, [the singer] who went into compulsory exile years ago has been accused and discriminated against repeatedly in *Neues Deutschland* that he had defamed workers as being lazy. Today everybody reads what humongous and real problems there are with labor discipline in the Western *Berliner Zeitung.* What is not being reported is that the workers are called for only half-day service and, in fact, are playing cards the other half because materials are not available. How shall the worker care for minutes if management and the system waste days and weeks? There is nothing more irresistible than organized chaos! Someone is waiting for copper, someone else for mortar, another worker for boards to contain the cast of concrete, one is waiting for cables and power cords and one is waiting for the proper technology, another for gas, and so on! Labor cannot be applied and that in a society that allegedly doesn't have a sufficient quantity of labor force!

So, for example, the technician arrives and looks around and says, Well, I cannot repair the stove at this time; there are no hot plates to be had right now. Nothing beats the economic conception of History, indeed, for two pounds of ideology alone no stove can be repaired!

But management is working away doggedly at improvements and, indeed, they exist, at least that is reported in the papers year in and year out. Twenty years ago I could go to the local tram depot and say, 300 yards behind my plot there are some of your tracks rotting away, I need a few yards as support. No problem, would say the colleagues. Pay us and we'll cut them for you and deliver them. Today things are done differently. To get a piece of rusty metal for construction I have to drive 100 miles to Fuerstenwalde or to Frankfurt/Oder. There are the central scrap metal depots. Here everything goes according to plan. What has not been provisioned by the plan is the possibility of getting some scrap iron locally and just sending the receipt to the central depot as proof that the plan has been fulfilled and the premium has, thus, been secured. That would be paper pushing, Comrades, hence it would be bureaucracy! Thus, the plan needs to be fulfilled for the sake of the individual premium! Doesn't matter if the wrong stuff is delivered altogether! That creates another obstacle for the construction site, but the premium for the party secretary and the party contractor would still have been fulfilled. No problem if the unwritten typewriter paper goes into the shredder, as long as the premium is o.k.! In former times truck drivers, as long as they got paid according to mileage per ton of gasoline, they let the diesel disappear into the ground, following the Russian example, as they had read their fiction bestsellers and, thus, knew how to do it! In the municipal forest of East Berlin each year and at all seasons much self-cut wood is rotting away, the maxim is to buy timber from Scandinavia.

All this reckless slovenliness really amounts to systemic economic crimes which are being paid first and foremost by the worker, peasant and craftsman. And this is not a matter of isolated cases and negligible individual problems. If the Russians are not delivering spare parts for the given technology and half the vehicles on the construction site remain stationary, how then shall continuous production be possible? From millions of macroeconomic veins the wealth of the working population vanishes on a daily basis into the swamp of an incapable Party and State bureaucracy that conducts the affairs of the people according to ideological dogma. This ideological dogma, the promulgation of the teachings of Marx, is "the heart and centerpiece of the work of the Party." Here may be found the deeper reasons and causes of the race between hare and hedgehog of Capitalism and Communism. But this very fact may not be stated, as truth is inimical to the Party. And as this is forbidden to be expressed, it cannot be changed. So for these deeper intrinsic reasons of the slovenliness and incapacity, superficial outer reasons have to serve as stopgap excuses, sabogents and spioteurs have be brought on. And here comes in the Stasi State Security that has to protect our Eastern heroes from those Western villains! And the G.D.R. working class superheroes make good for everything. Through overtime, weekend work; with extra shifts and special premiums, more production and cost intensive, inflation intensive, but furthering our Socialism no end. These methods of economic suicide engender political imbalances and against those the only help is the dictatorship of the Stasi *against* the proletariat. This becomes a truly vicious circle as the only remedy against the Stasi is the flight from the republic.

But let's return to the true petty-bourgeois Socialists from the *Manifesto*, which Marx appraises as follows: "This Socialism dissects with great perspicacity the contradictions within the modern conditions of production. It unmasks the deceptive euphemisms of the economist. It proved irrefutably the destructive effects of machinery and of the division of labor, of concentration of capitals and of landed estates, of overproduction, of crises, the necessary decline of the petty bourgeois or lower middle class and the peasant, the misery of the proletariat, the anarchic modes of production, the screaming gaps in the distribution of wealth, the industrial war to the death between the nations, the dissolution of the old mores and customs, of the old family ties and the old nationalities."

If this Socialism has achieved all this already, one could ask, what then is the new quality in the critique of Capitalism of Marx?

Right after this passage Marx makes short shrift of the German Socialists. He does not have one good word to say about his national competition, all these "beautiful spirits and demi-philosophers." He could have written Plintscher at this point directly. Let's have a look at some of these humanist and early Socialist ideas as Marx gives the impression that there had been no progressive elements in Germany prior to him: As far back as the Early Enlightenment, Edelmann, for example, a precursor of Lessing, developed a conception in the Social Sciences, "whose archetype he found in the early Christian communities where goods were held in common, as well as where grassroots democracy was practiced."[76] Frederick II granted asylum to Edelmann in Berlin, who had gathered middle-class and peasant-plebeian forces in his oppositional circles around himself, while his books were burnt upon clerical edict in Frankfurt/Main in 1750. The Association of the Outlawed and the Just, who were the precursors of the Association of Communists, were strongly influenced by this kind of German Socialism; their groups were called "congregations."

Lessing, another humanist, in following Edelmann developed with Gellert and others the image of a virtuous, diligent, compassionate human being in protest against the class arrogance and the mendacious double standards of the ruling class. The humanitarian idea that was so spitefully treated by Marx does not just include the socialist tendencies of his contemporaries, which he plagiarized, he does not just mention the "philosophy of action," he also mentions and emphasizes the German "philosophers and literati"!

Lessing, as well as other enlightenment philosophers in contrast to Marx, put general humanitarian norms in the center of his work, most clearly visible in his tragedy *Miss Sarah Sampson*. Klopstock's *Messiah* embodied, years prior to the postulates of the Communist Party, the claim for the indivisible German Republic as a national epic of all Germans. One may compare the spiritual and intellectual poverty of Marx with the wealth of spiritual and political ideas of the writers of the *Sturm und Drang* period, with whom the Enlightenment took general German and national features for the first time. This movement around Herder and Goethe, as well as around the group of Goettingen aimed to have pre-revolutionary and populist effects.

It was Herder who first took the thought of evolution from natural to social processes; he articulated laws and contradictions within the historical process long before Hegel and certainly much longer before Marx. From there stems his citation quoted above about the linking up of philosophy and the proletariat. This was not mere "literature" but analysis and representation of real societal interests. Here the people received a voice: its needs, its dreams, its intentions were articulated here. And in opposition to Marx, the German people in spite of all its proverbial poets and thinkers were never made up of just one class and one of the classes was never made up of just one faction! Here no anti-humanist deficit of democracy was demonstrated, nor a state-terrorist dictatorship of minorities!

Schiller strongly insisted that it would have to be the popular masses to sweep away the feudal conditions. Marx then made the role of the popular masses the pivotal point of the political interpretations of this so-called Historical Materialism. This is and was Marx's fundamental discovery up to now: He had not read Schiller's main social dramas, *The Brigands* and *Cabal and Love*, prior to writing just by sheer happenstance and coincidence?

Kant demanded - writing from Koenigsberg in the preparatory scrimmage of the middle-class revolution - to come around to have a just, rationally arranged human order as an association of equal and free individuals. He anticipated Weitling and Bernstein's criticism of Marx's utopian brand of Communism, as he saw the state of the ideal just as an orientational parameter not as a state of the real. "The approximation of the ideal is all that nature demands of us."[77] Kant articulated in the same spirit the hope of a "general cosmopolitical state."

Following him, Hegel saw this state mature in the face of the "splendid dawn" of the French Revolution in 1789 and he gave the evolution idea its full form in the face of these momentous historic events: Nature, History, Spirit were engaged in constant change, development and flux and that held true for the entire development of humanity. Goethe's *Faust*, as well, was breathing this kind of optimism and faith in progress, because, in spite of all individual tragedy an optimistic expectation of the future for humanity and the philosophy of Humanism was clearly drawn up. This same attitude determined Goethe's faith in the future of Germany, in the unification of the Germans to become a nation, to the institution of the unity of the fatherland in spite of all disparity and division on the State level and in spite of all interference from foreign lands. Thus, Goethe wrote on December 13, 1813, to Heinrich Luden: "For us as individuals all that is left is to endorse everyone according to his or her talents, inclinations and status, to further and strengthen the education of the people and in this manner to spread and increase the same on all sides, downward, as well as preferably, upward, so that it may not fall behind the other peoples, so that it may at least stand in front in this respect, so that the spirit would not wither and remain fresh and joyous, so that it may not lose faith and courage, not become petty-minded, but would remain ready to undertake any kind of grand deed at hand, when the day of Glory would break."

Russians and *ersatz*-Russians may well be asked to remember that a man who is today largely forgotten, Karl-Friedrich Dahrdt, the head of the secret society *Deutsche Union* that was spread all over Germany, wrote in 1787 in his writing *On the Freedom of the Press and its Limits:* Human rights come *before* feudal rights, a position that is very current and cutting edge in the struggle against the proletarian Absolutism.

Marx, of course, knew about these traditions and he knew further in what great esteem they were held by the labor movement. Engels later, strangely enough, drew attention to the fact that these "demi-philosophers" should be regarded as a source of Marxism. Germans, philosophers as well as labor philosophers, were not mentioned in any positive way at all in the *Manifesto*. Even the author of the first programmatic writing of the Association of the Just, Weitling, is missing and that, although Owen, Fourier and St. Simon are mentioned emphatically as "critical and utopian Socialists and Communists". This much is certain: Marx eliminated the democratic Labor Communist Weitling in the 19th century from their gallery of forebears and Ulbricht did the same with Rosa Luxemburg in the 20th century. Marx, nevertheless, has to concede in the relevant passages of the *Manifesto* that these "utopians" had given a full picture of his later ideology "about the future of society, i.e., the abolition of the contradiction between city and country, of the family, of private property, of wage labor; the announcement of social harmony, the transformation of the State into a mere administration of production - all these sentences express merely the falling away of class differences." His predecessors, hence, achieved not only the criticism of the old order, but the illustration of the new order, as well. Is there a better way of unmasking oneself as a plagiarizer?

What else is Marx saying?

At times he reduces the fanciful depictions of the future to a few sparse abstractions, nailed down thought-bones without flesh or marrow which would not bring a dog back from behind an oven, not realizing that these illustrations are necessary to interest and captivate the worker and concentrate his will. The cornucopia elements of the proto-Marxist image of Communism, thus, fulfilled a tangible propagandistic and organizational goal. Marx, however, dresses them down as "utopian." Nevertheless, what those utopians were preaching, writing, propagating, was lapped up with eagerness and, in parts, even practiced experimentally! No proletarian took notice of Marx's miserable philosophy and philosophic misery, just as later no one took notice of *Capital*; and the leaders of the German Social Democratic movement filed away his third deed of glory, the *Marginal*

Notes to the Program of Gotha - that was the actual influence of Marx, one sectarian among many sectarians.

Section IV of the *Manifesto* is at last dedicated to political action: "The main attention of the Communists is directed towards Germany, as Germany finds itself at the eve of a middle-class revolution and ... because the German revolution can only be the antecedent of a proletarian revolution." That was the definite summit of the historic height to which Marx's "scientific conception" of History had reached: He discombobulated the socio-economic conditions and the political possibilities completely. The leaders of the proletarian revolution, that could only be Marx-Engels; why else would they have joined the association of Communists and why else would they have rallied?

Historizing dilettantism, delusions of grandeur and subjectivism could not be overlooked. Marx and Engels as the spearhead of several hundred members of the Association against the three dozen German States with their just about three dozen million inhabitants, to establish the Communist revolution of the absolute minorities by way of violence and terror. The events took the following course: the foolhardy, politically as well as theoretically hare-brained concept of revolution of Marx lost out completely in the middle-class revolution of 1848/'49. Nowhere did it even come to bear. The Association of Communists was nowhere taken seriously with this concept; it was simply submerged in the surge of the revolution. Marx recognized this and simply dissolved the first Marxist Party. He held the view that the revolution had attained freedom of the press, it would no longer be necessary to have a secret propaganda society. He could care less about the Party of the proletariat as it had not made him emperor of Germany! As editor-in-chief he felt, furthermore, that his material position was now secure. Marx and Engels were sitting in Cologne as professional journalists, isolated from the proletarian mass movement and opposed all proclamations of the Association. When the General German Labor Fraternity constituted itself in August of 1848 as a national labor organization, they were again seeking contact. Political opportunists like Marx and Engels always managed to ride on horses that were saddled by others.

The German workers then constituted a new Central Authority of the Association of Communists against Marx and Engels in London in September of 1848. They strove to keep their organizational autonomy. But their emissaries did not manage to reorganize the Association on German soil. A year later, after the revolution had been beaten down, and Marx was back in London, the management of the renewed central authority was put again in Marx's hands. As late as March of 1850, Marx and Engels drafted an address for the Association in which they repeated the declaration of the final part of the *Communist Manifesto*: The proletarian revolution would be the instant follow-up of the middle-class one in Germany - they wrote that, be it well noticed, in 1850 after the popular democratic movement had been beaten to shreds and no revolutionary force could be discerned anywhere far and wide! In spite of all the setbacks they had learned nothing.

Between March and November of 1850 six magazines appeared, published by Marx and Engels in Hamburg as the *Neue Rheinische Zeitung – Politisch-Oekonomische Revue* [New Rhenish Times – Political-Economic Review]. These magazines propagated for the first time the concept of "permanent revolution," as well as the central category of "class dictatorship of the proletariat." But even this concept was not Marx's.[78] In his review Marx quotes the French Socialists and Communists with their revolutionary maxims: "The red republic means dictatorship" and "Bring down the bourgeoisie! Dictatorship of the working class!" This term was used publicly everywhere. Marx describes Blanqui's conceptions of Communism as "class-dictatorship of the proletariat."[79] Suffice it here to state that the Blanquistes were united with the Chartists in the "world society," to have it corroborated by Marx once again that the "Marxist" terminology even in its key term of revolutionary theory did not derive from Marx. Had he at least conceived of this term, it would have had to be used in the *Manifesto.*

The short formula, which is being used everywhere in Marxism-Leninism today, "dictatorship of the proletariat," does not appear in Marx's *Review*, as this is disingenuously and incorrectly maintained in the preface of the Marx Engels Works [M.E.W.], by the Institute of Marxism-Leninism of the Central Committee of the Socialist Unity Party of Germany. There everything is represented as if Marx had coined and defined that term which is so essential today, as well as the determination of the term of the policy of alliances [Buendnispolitik], which Marx has also taken, according to his own testimony, from French pamphlets. Now, let's make sure from another source: In the series of articles about the class warfare in France published initially in the *Review* the historical task of the proletariat had been expressed for the first time in a "rigorous scientific formula" according to Engels. He refers to the "dictatorship of the proletariat." Does Engels really not know from where Marx has copied it? Has the French revolution happened before or after the publication of the *Review?* Or had Marx written the history of the French class warfare as a clairvoyant, before it even entered the historical stage?

Engels makes these observations in an introduction of a reprint of the *Class Warfare* from 1895, where we may also read that in the scientific birth certificate of Marxism, i.e., the *Manifesto*, this theory had only been drafted in the roughest of outlines[!] So we are not only satisfied, we are literally over-satisfied or, in plain English, completely fed up.

Given these facts it becomes clear why the workers in the Association stated when they excluded Marx-Engels that there were no substantial theoretical differences of opinion, but only tactical differences. Marx is corroborating this involuntarily when he writes in his *Revelations about the Communist Convention in Cologne* in 1853 that in France "the onslaught on the existing government concurred simultaneously and directly with the onslaught on the bourgeoisie." He had again transferred his expectations about the revolution geographically, but had not given it up at all. After all, he had preached to the German workers for years the "thundering of the rooster of Gaul" would initiate the proletarian revolution in Germany.

From the summer of 1850 onward, Marx-Engels understood that their revolutionary war games amounted to nonsense. They began to present this insight to the members of the Association rather timidly. Those workers now comprehended nothing anymore that their great *fuehrer* was telling them. Did he have the "great insight into the march of matters" or was he simply a charlatan? After all, Marx-Engels had not only preached permanent revolution in the March address of the Association, they had done the same for the "global society of Communists". When the Blanqui-adherents, that is, exemplary Communists for Marx, in the later strengthened their German comrades of the Association in the belief that it had been right to fire Marx-Engels, Marx disbanded the "global society," as he had done previously with the Association in Germany. He understood the art of government, of dissolution and of founding, in that respect he was really creative and almost a democrat. Who did not comply was disbanded or "cleansed," to use the jargon of our later signature democrat Joseph Vissarionovich.

The absolute majority of the German democratic Labor Communists in London gave the following reasons for the exclusion of Marx-Engels in their address of October 1, 1850, in the context of the development after the 1848 revolution:

> "From the Central Authority to the managing circle.
> Brothers!
> We deem it necessary to inform you about events which have happened in our Association and although they may appear highly unpleasant at the moment we are fully convinced that they will be of great advantage with regard to the strong organization of the proletarian Party in the future. Following the revolution of 1848 the leaders of the popular Party showed a partial incapacity to further the interest of the people, to another part they committed an open betrayal of our cause and that in

spite of the fact that hitherto they had been trusted completely and the workers had obeyed them wholeheartedly – they were eliminated. The Communist Party, now - after it had understood the necessity of a strong organization - did not believe it was possible or even right to follow the lead of strong party bosses as this was done previously. The people have to become autonomous in every respect in order to emancipate themselves fully. This insight, however, was contradicted by a certain number of people - journalists and the half-educated - whose intention was aimed at the assumption of the position of the dismissed *fuehrers* and to continue to keep the people in bondage, in other words, the so-called Party of the Intelligenzia was trying to rule. What the latter was capable of doing we had seen on June 13, 1849, the events surrounding the abolition of the general vote in France. These people are o.k. for copy, but they are incapable of unity and, furthermore, they hamper each and any activity as soon as they assume a position of leadership within the Association. The French workers have understood this and they have done away with the threatening servitude both here in London as well as in France in eliminating the merely writing elements from their ranks.

Quite similar to France, the conditions arranged themselves in the German Communist Party, journalists and demi-savants have put themselves at the head of the organization, even worse, they have pretended that it was they alone who founded the organization themselves. In their view, the workers were mere zeros who would gain value alone by the fact that the aforementioned would stand ahead of them. As long as the workers would indulge this kind of comportment, they were amply praised, but the moment they refused this kind of blind obedience, they were called lowbrow, asses, scum and pack. Since Marx and Engels have arrived in London the formerly tightly-organized workers' association and the Labor district of London have been completely disorganized, as personalities were put above factual matters and each and every one was persecuted who did not have sufficient non-autonomy not to blow the horn for these people. The first personal attacks were directed against Willich, whose popularity - that he had attained among the workers with his actions in Germany, Besançon and in the last German revolution - was meant to be annihilated at all costs. The so-called intelligent and writing people could not brook a man of action at their side. In this case, it was a matter of nothing less than the principle - and here Willich and all the workers were completely in accord with Marx and Engels - it was just a conflict about personalities. Marx himself declared himself in this manner more than once, although, of course, he would blame Willich for it. The plots that were harbored against Willich in the Workers' Union as well as in the Association - and that were reinforced by people like (Ferdinand) Wolff, Liebknecht, Haupt, etc., and whose task it seems to have been, to disinform and to split the Party and who for this purpose had instituted a complete spying network - we may not possibly fully account for here. Nevertheless we will, hopefully, be able soon to give you oral communication in the matter. May that suffice, in the Association as well as in the Workers' Union the most drastic scenes occurred, which even threatened to turn into a general roughhouse. That under such circumstances neither the Association nor the workers' union would increase is self-evident. Quite on the contrary, a number of valiant old members got disgusted and left. When Schapper came to London he found the occasion to remark, the first night of his arrival, with what hatred front was made against Willich and when he argued against such comportment, the aforementioned group would take him on equally with unrequited meanness.

Finally, with the incident to be related in the following, a complete breach occurred when the local workers and exiles declared a majority that bordered on unanimity that they could not continue to be and work with the aforementioned. The incident in question happened as follows: Willich was injured in the émigré committee whose member he was in a manner, that he felt he needed to declare his immediate resignation. He explained himself in like manner to the members of the committee then in session and when he declared himself further the following day the members of the workers' union began to tear him apart with indescribable fury. His words were twisted, each and every one who did not speak out for Marx and Engels directly was treated in like manner, so that it came close to having these people be physically chastised from the part of the workers. Thus, the assembly parted in the greatest possible state of agitation. As Marx and Engels took flight they shook their fists against the face of Schapper and shouted in great fury: "We shall never forget you this!" These threats were countered by all workers with general laughter and merriment. The following day, Willich met a certain Hain, whom you are well enough acquainted with and who embraced the former with tears in his eyes when he first had come to London and had greeted him like a true friend. The conversation naturally turned towards the events of the night previous and Willich, who thought to be speaking with a friend, protested strongly about the twisting of his words and called this depiction of events a lie. As soon Willich had left, Hain had nothing better to do than to see Marx and recount the conversation with variations. At that point it was decided to eliminate Willich at all costs and by all means possible. How this was to be brought about was revealed two days later when the central committee was in session. There the conversation between Willich and Hain was again brought up and Marx, Engels, Schramm, etc., demanded that Willich would have to renege on his accusing Hain of lying. When Willich agreed to this only under the condition that they, in turn, would have to own up to the possibility of having erred, Schramm jumped up, called him a low-brow fiend and threatened to spit him in the face, if he were not ready to draw pistols with him. In short, Willich was provoked to accept a duel! Thus, Willich declared: "If you insist, I will draw pistols with you!" and he demanded the immediate removal of Schramm from the meeting because of scandalous comportment. Schramm, thus, removed himself. In the company of some French friends and the citizen Techow, Willich went to Ostende to meet the terms of the duel. Here the authorities and the police had been alerted by a private correspondent in the magazine *Précurseur* in which the German exiles were mentioned, as well, that Ledru-Rollin meant to hold a convention these days in Ostende with French refugees and democrats; there were present in town, as well, a Prussian prince and several Prussian officers. Willich and his enemies escaped capture only through a rapid voyage to Antwerp. There, finally, the duel took place. Schramm received a bullet in his head, after he had first shot at Willich and missed him. When the former came to, he extended his hand and declared that he harbored no personal animosity, he had only dueled himself with Willich out of Party considerations. When he further acknowledged Willich's standing and position in the Party and only added that he had erred, the latter shook hands with him. This handshake, however, did not hinder Schramm or his entourage to spreading the most vicious rumors later in London regarding the actual process of the duel. The whole affair then showed that Schramm had been held to eliminate Willich either by duel or by capture through the police.

We are now returning to the matter of the Association. In the same session in which Schramm had challenged Willich it had been decided to bring the whole matter before the General Assembly of the District of London, to which Marx commented: "You can do what you want, we will have the majority." The convening of the General Assembly then was postponed with all manners of excuses, probably in the hope that Willich would not return from Belgium. When the latter finally did return and the majority of the Central Authority made no moves to call for a reconvening of the General Assembly, although it was peremptorily demanded by the majority of the federated members, finally to be able to escape this limbo, which, after all, threatened to imperil the entire organization, the date was set by the District Authority. The majority of the Central Authority which could now easily see that it had lost any and all trust of the workers decided at this point to relay the matter through a diplomatic move to an area which deemed more advantageous to it. This majority consists of Marx, Engels, Schramm and three other local, married workers, Heinrich Bauer (shoemaker), Eccarius (tailor), Pfaender (painter). At that time the latter three were held to vote with Marx, Engels and Schramm – although Bauer had recently, repeatedly and in public declared Marx and Engels to be scoundrels - we will communicate to you orally, otherwise several further sheaves of paper would have to be filled.

When Schapper arrived in London and he saw that instead of principles, personalities had been used, that no more Association letters were exchanged between members but only personal letters, that through all these personal intrigues nothing further was done for the organization of the Association and the latter was, thus, endangered to come to nought completely, he mounted the proposal in the Central Authority to hand over supervision of the Association to the District of Cologne and to have it convene a.s.a.p. a federal assembly. This proposal was dismissed with the remark that there were no forces in Cologne to lead the Association and that at the present moment the devolution of power would have to be avoided at all costs. Only in one of the following sessions a repeated minority proposal for a federal assembly on the 20th of October of the year was granted; further proposals, however, to bring as many forces as possible from Germany were dismissed summarily. It is clear for that reason that the present decision of the majority of the Central Authority to hand over management of the Association to the District of Cologne must have its own reasons apart - as you have been told previously. Those reasons are to remove the London workers from the Association through the Central Authority in Cologne, as they are believed to have sufficient influence there, to make their personalities count alone. In consideration, now, that drastic measures are necessary under the given present circumstances, in further consideration of the fact that a firm organization of the Association has to be established a.s.a.p., so that for the next proletarian revolutions in France and in Germany not only the oppositional pose will be struck and newspapers will be published, but the German proletarians will take their fate into their own hands and may come to power; and if that would not happen it would be our own fault; in consideration of the further fact that Marx and Engels are taking up a number of young half-literates and turning them into their personal minions whom they are fascinating through dreams of future political power by which they are trying to rule the Association; in consideration, furthermore, of the fact that Marx and Engels are trying to turn the Association into an instrument of personal power and on the other hand they completely neglect it in places they do not deem of direct personal usefulness, the year 1848 in Cologne proves, when they sacrificed their position as members of the Central Authority for the position as editors-in-chief of the *Neue Rheinische Zeitung*; in consideration, finally, that the so-called coterie of literati may be of use for us outside of the Association, that within it, on the other hand, they would hinder any kind of organization, any kind of unifying process, any kind of action, the District of London, composed of 40 members, has unanimously drawn the following conclusions:

1. The previous members of the Central Authority are stripped of their functions

2. The citizens, Marx, Engels, Schramm, Wolff, Seiler, Liebknecht (student), Pieper (teacher with Rothschild), Pfaender, H. Bauer and Eccarius are excluded from the Association

3. 'Til the ordering of the federal concern at the convention of October 20th the following people are being commissioned with the management of the Association: Schaerttner from Hanau, Oswald, Dietz from Wiesbaden, Gebert (former leader of the leading district in Switzerland), Willich, Schapper, Fraenkel and Lehmann. (The last mentioned made up the minority in the former Central Authority.)

As we are communicating these decisions to you, we are asking you to make them known in the congregations under your direction and to give us report in turn a.s.a.p. of the state of affairs in your districts.

We expect further that you will do everything possible, that the federal convention of October 20th be attended by large numbers.

Fraternal kiss and handshake."[80]

Leaders would be – August Bebel wrote later in his study on Fourier – in revolutionary times "only tools, never movers and shakers and they will be cast aside, as soon as they overstep this function and try to assume the movement for their own egotistic interests and arbitrary affairs instead of managing it in the interest of the have-nots." So much that can be said for Bebel. Furthermore, as we can see, Stalin's procedures against the Central Authority had a prior example. With Marx it ended with a bullet to the head. With Stalin the bullet stuck in the head after torture had coerced all desired confessions.

Marx, in essence, confirmed the core of the information quoted above, when he wrote about it ten years later: "To complete the history of the Association I shall remark: On September 15th in 1850, a schism occurred in the bosom of the Central Authority. Its majority with Engels and myself transferred its seat to Cologne, where the leading circle for Middle and South Germany had been residing for a long time and where the greatest concentration of intellectual forces outside of London could be found."[81] In plain English that meant Marx handed over - against the bylaws and positioning himself against the workers and underlining it in leaving the labor union - his group in Cologne, the former seat of his *Neue Rheinische Zeitung,* the function of the Central Authority. Breach of bylaws up to the present is in all Communist Parties the most serious reason for exclusion. In the Stalinist system that meant, furthermore, often the death sentence.

The bylaws of the Association of Communists, ratified at the second Congress on the 8th of December in 1847, had stipulated in paragraph 22 that the members of the Central Authority be elected "from the District Authority of the location to which the Congress has transferred its seat." They were subject to the democratic control of the members according to paragraph 25 and "they were removable by their electors at any time." Putschist Marx had failed in the German middle-class revolution! Against the bylaws of the German workers he led the putsch initially with better success, but simultaneously he smashed the first German Communist Party into two feuding Associations. The bylaws could not be altered by the Central Authority, but only - according to paragraph 30 - by the Congress. The latter was meant to convene annually and it was meant further to publish next to the circular letters "a manifesto in the name of the Party."

Thus, the *Communist Manifesto* of 1848, according to the view of the democratic Labor Communists, was not the birth certificate of Marxism, nor the foundation of a "theory in outlines," to repeat Engels, but it was a declaration of will and intention of the Secret Association.

The Central Authority was further subject to firm democratic rules of engagement, but in no way was it subject to "Marxism." To avoid abuse of power and cult of personality paragraph 35 of the bylaws stipulated expressly: "The Central Authority has its seat in the Convention, but it does not have a decisive vote therein." The bosses were at this point, in contrast to today, only equal among equals. And the Communist ideology after all, it may be remembered, lives by its commitment to equality.

A year later, at the end of 1848, there was, as previously mentioned, a new Central Authority in London, upon which Marx and Engels had no influence. This Central Authority renewed its bylaws and the Party constitution, as well. And now we are confronted with a fact that is historically highly charged: These bylaws are not made out, like the previous ones of Marx and Engels, Marxist-Communist, but Labor-Communist, viz. they are made out in Social Democratic fashion. They are not geared towards Communist world revolution; they are tailor-made for the needs of the general national Labor Party. Following a statement of Roeser, one of the responsible and leading members of the Association, these bylaws came about shortly after the foundation convention of the Communist Association, because Marx had dissolved the Association in Cologne in 1848 unilaterally.

Marx was bitterly opposed to those bylaws and he demanded new ones peremptorily. Why? That will become immediately apparent when the texts are compared. Bylaws of the Association of Communists of December 12, 1847, article 1: "The goal of the Association is the striking down of the bourgeoisie, the rule of the proletariat, the abolition of the old society based on the class contradictions of the middle-class and the foundation of a new society without class distinctions and without private property."

Federal bylaws of the revolutionary Party of November-December 1848, article 1: "The goal of the Association is the institution of a unified, indivisible social-democratic republic." Here's the proof. Likely under the influence of their French comrades the German workers had understood that Social Democracy is a higher level of the international Labor movement in theory and in practice than Marx-Communism!

On this later basis the new non-Marxist Central Authority managed to acquire new members in Germany, among them Martens in Hamburg, one of the key figures of the German Labor movement that did not serve Marx!

The bylaws of 1848 reinforced the fact that the members of the Central Authority can be dismissed at any time just like any other functionary, as well as the fact that the Central Authority has a seat in the convention but it does not have a decisive vote; in short, the workers insisted, against Marx and Engels, upon the right to remain within democratic rules of engagement. And now something even more interesting happened: When Marx-Engels, in breach of the bylaws, did not appear in front of the General Assembly in London and did hand over the management of the Association to their compeers in Cologne - which proves that Marx deemed the workers simply incompetent to rule the Party, the intellectuals alone had the right thereof, they directed their Cologne stooges to draw up new bylaws. And that was by no means coincidental!

These new bylaws were sent out in December 1850 by the Cologne adherents of Marx to the lower Party members, i.e., a few months after the dismissal of Marx-Engels from the Communist Party. Marx had grandiloquently declared the "theoretical weaknesses" of the present bylaws, i.e., Social-Democracy, would need to be eliminated. Marx confirmed the new Cologne bylaws. Small wonder, they had been fabricated according to his directives and he brought back verbatim "the striking down of the bourgeoisie" from the previous version of 1847.[82]

However, the Cologne version contained even in its first article a strong and unmistakable jibe against Marx, as here it was declared for the first time that the Association be "secret and indissoluble," in all other respects, however, it was tailor-made for the dictatorial desires of Marx. It established the cancerous growth of the Communist Parties, the possibility of the cult of personality and of power abuse, not as an exception to the rule, but as a systemic rule in itself! All and every organizational principle of the German Labor Communists had been excluded. Even today this kind of framework is ruling the essence of the Socialist Unity Party of Germany, i.e., commands or directives are given only from the Central Authority. The Party is fully militarized. Who engages in intellectual or spiritual mutiny, who dares to criticize in a genuine manner, will be shot down on the practical-political plane. Independent and free discussion within the Party itself is impossible. What is to be discussed is being commanded prior to the act. The lower echelons solely have to report about the execution of the directives.

The prerogatives of the Central Committee, pardon me, of the Central Authority, are described as follows in the bylaws of Cologne – there we go again, all the noxious crap obviously comes from the West. Their members now according to article 9 – not as up to that point and as it is the usage with all functionaries everywhere – now cannot be dismissed at any time, but only during the convention! The Central Authority from that point on, according to article 11, did not report to the workers in the given district, but only "to the convention". In this manner Marx-Engels safeguarded themselves against a future dismissal.

Article 17 was completely new and unheard of and it was definitely tailor-made to Marx's advantage in his power struggles with the workers: "Conflicts among particular individuals of the same congregation will be decided conclusively by said congregation, in the same district the congregation of the district, of different districts the Central Authority; personal pleas and complaints are to be brought before the convention." Right, smart and wise! The heavenly Party Secretary can be accused only by the heavenly Party convention. Who draws up the heavenly agenda? The heavenly Party Secretary! Oh, Nikita, if you only knew!

Why do I have to think at this point about that ancient fable according to which in the animal kingdom one day the plant eaters and the meat eaters concluded a great peace and a fraternal association? None should be persecuted or devoured; all should be free and equal. That's at least how things stood on Sunday, the day the treaty was concluded. From that day on everyone was equal. Only on Monday the meat eaters had already become a little bit more equal. Except, as vicious rumors had it, the pig! Now the Cologne bylaws never acquired any practical importance. There would be no further convention that would be able to ratify and corroborate them. As a historical document, however, to unmask Marx they were of inestimable value.

The roots of the cult of personality, thus, clearly lie in Marxism itself. Its excesses and egregious consequences for the Communist world movement of our days - see the XX Party Congress of the Communist Party of the Soviet Union, see the Maoist cultural revolution, see the family economy of Romania and Korea, etc., see reform Communism - have been ideologically prefabricated in Marx. Except that for Marx we are dealing with nothing more than the schism of a secret society of some hundred members and sympathizers, about whose political fate half a dozen people had to decide. Today Communism has been split officially and worldwide into Marxists-Leninists, Maoists and reform Communists. The reformation period of Communism has begun. Will there be an ideological peace of religion? It could be concluded in other places than Augsburg or in Westphalia, after all. But as we have seen, this was not even made possible at the earth-shaking Karl-Marx conference of the Communist Party of the German Democratic Republic. Sometimes villainies are not revenged until some hundred years later; they are revenged, nevertheless, and all the same. Wiley tacticians may achieve a temporary advantage with dishonorable practices, as a general principle in the long run they are always the losers of world history. The end does not at all justify the means. Vicious means defame and defeat even the holiest ends. So much is to be said for the sad history about the very unscientific birth certificate of our almost scientific, crappy Communism.

Let us now turn to Marx's main work, the first volume of *Capital*. It was published twenty years after these stories about and around the *Communist Manifesto*.

Part II:

The Economic System of Marxism:

Economic Ideology and Practice

1. The First Volume of *Capital* from 1867

At this point Marx fans don't have to shrink back and lay aside the text in protest and discontinue reading. I would be happy to have the contrary be proven to me, as who would be glad, after all, to lose a faith in something that makes life so nice and easy? Now, we are going to the roots! We are now tackling the presumptive capital achievement of Karl Marx that has been praised abundantly by so many and read by so comparatively precious few: *Das Capital.*

We have seen in the first part of this study what is the matter with the philosophic-historic "first scientific achievement" of Marx, namely, the materialist conception of History, with which Capitalism had its direct demise prophesied ultra-promptly: in plain English, nothing whatsoever! We are now turning to what was supposed to have been the "second scientific achievement," namely, the economic theory, to see what that was, in turn: Not only nothing but even less than that.

In contrast to the professional Marx cheerleaders,[83] Engels in his old age stated dryly on February 21, 1888, in the preliminary remarks to his pamphlet *Ludwig Feuerbach and the Decline of the Classical German Philosophy*, that he himself and Marx had only laid down their material conception of History in 1845 in the *German Ideology* as an exercise in self-clarification, but they hadn't bothered to publish it. "The section on Feuerbach remained unfinished. The finished part consists of an exposition of the materialist conception of History, which only proves how incomplete our insights of economic History still were at the time."

In October 23, 1884, Engels had commented in his preface to the first German edition of Marx's *Misery of Philosophy – Answer to Proudhon's Philosophy of Misery*, that this work had come about in the winter of 1846/1847 at a time when Marx was trying to reach clarity about the basic framework and foundation of his new historical and economic approach. This proves that it was only in 1847 that Marxism had been laid down in its rough outlines, in other words, it was at that time unfinished. Marx had reached clarity subjectively within himself, not as yet objectively in science. He never reached that later stage as he remained an agitator and ideologue, but never crossed the threshold to become a scientist. He never discovered or understood fundamental principles, but on the contrary misunderstood them wholeheartedly.

Let us listen again one more time to the Elder Engels as to what he had to say regarding the economical positions of Marx in the introduction to the German edition of his *Wage Labor and Capital* on April 30, 1891: "In the 1840s Marx had not as yet reached a well-rounded conception of his Critique of Political Economy. That did not happen until the end of the 1850s. His writings which where published prior to the *Critique of Political Economy* [1859] consequently, would deviate in particular items from those conceived after 1859, they contain expressions and, indeed, entire sentences, which appear distorted or incorrect from the standpoint of the later works." Engels, who now published the above-quoted writing in an altered version, continues:

"My changes regard above all one particular point. Following the original, the worker sells to the capitalist his *labor* for his labor wages, in the current version he is selling his *labor power*. And about this alteration I have to justify myself. It is a justification to the workers so they can see that this regards no mere splitting of hairs, but one of the most vital points of Political Economy."

Engels continues to explain that in Classical Economy the value of a commodity is determined by the labor necessary for its production, i.e., its production costs, and the value of labor, i.e., the costs of the reproduction of the worker, is equally determined by that.

"What the economists considered as the production costs of 'labor' were not those but the costs to maintain the living worker … Classical Economy had come to a dead end. The very man who found the way out of this dead end was Karl Marx. And what the worker was selling," Engels continues, "was not his labor, it was 'his labor power.' This labor, however, is ingrained in the man and cannot be separated from him … what the economists called the production costs of labor are those for the worker and in that respect the costs to maintain his labor power."

Really, so the classical economists did not know what they were talking about? They did not have a clue that the costs of production of the worker really are those to maintain his labor power? In other words, they were supposing that the physical and mental powers of men existed clearly outside his body? In this discombobulated, contrarian manner only a Hegelian mind can think. But let's take a closer look at that!

We would like to help our con man, Engels, out with regard to the English pedigree of the discoverers of exploitation, of surplus value, of labor power, which is being purchased and sold. A mere 350 years prior to Marx, Thomas More was writing in his *Utopia* which appeared in 1516 in Loewen and was available in 1524 in German and it was published again in East Germany. in 1976 by Reclam publishers and from this later bootlegged version I am quoting, that there had been a surplus of goods - and from this surplus springs in Marx's utopian manner Communism, life according to one's needs, - if the rich scapegrace, who "uses twice as much of goods that are being provided by the *labor power* of others"   would only be put to work himself.

Now at this point Engels cannot say Marx had not read Rodbertus - pardon More - because Marx is quoting said stellar lawyer, Lord Chancellor and saint of the Roman Catholic Church, who knew precisely what was going on in the business of Political Economy, as he was making up to 100,000 gold marks annually and he cites him as the King's witness of the birth of capital "soaked in blood and muck" when discussing the original accumulation of Capital in the first volume of his *Capital* so soaked in spirit.   More, apparently, taught Marx another thing or two when he alerts the latter of the statist regulation of the price of the commodity Labor with the following words: "Indeed, in some places prisoners don't perform public works, but when a private person is in need of wage laborers, so he rents the *labor power* of them arbitrarily for the given day in the market and pays for that the stipulated wage, just a little bit less than he would have to pay for free wage labor."   So here More provides on top of the Capitalist private person who exploits the wage laborer in addition the completely un-Marxist theory of the wage laborer who is free in a double sense of the word ...

More complains bitterly that the common order gives everything to the "person of leisure and the cadgers," while not granting care for age and illness to "peasant, collier, day laborer, teamster and blacksmith," that is the class of the peasants and workers, "without whom no State could exist," a negligence that is truly shabby, as: "it [the common order] abuses the *labor power* of the best years of their lives ..."   And More gives the remedy in addition which Marx appropriates for himself, as well: Money has to be abolished in order to deprive the rich of their greed and fun "to acquire property unrightfully,"   and in order to prevent them from purchasing "the strenuous work of the poor as cheaply as possible".

And that is how according to More Communism would look like after, with the abolition of money, the greed for money would have disappeared: "What great burden of untowardnesses would thus be discharged with, what rich seed of crime would thus be extirpated at the root. Who would not know that embezzlement, theft, larceny, strife, unrest, altercation, revolt, murder, betrayal and poison mixing, which now through punishment are more pursued than limited, would wither away through the abolition of money and that furthermore fear, disquiet, sorrow, exertion and wakeful nights would disappear the same moment money would? Indeed poverty itself, the sole state as it appears, in which money is really needed, would instantaneously wane, if money were abolished everywhere completely."

Common acquisition of livelihood under omission of any kind of monetary circulation is the summary formula of Thomas More and Charlie Crap. More summarizes in no uncertain terms that "private property and money" put justice and equality into question.

There is surplus and labor power galore according to More in his polit-comic view, when it is said that exploiters and drones live off the labor of others, who they suck dry down to their very last drop of blood and that the rich with legal means of the State betray the poor of their earnings.

The abolition of money and the introduction of the duty to work as a constitutional principle anchored in the Constitution of the G.D.R. could still be taken from More by Marx. For the six-hour day and the praised ideological tolerance Marx may not have had the ink to copy that, as well. His inkwell must have been dry at this point. Not a problem. For that we are deep in it today!

But let's proceed with the English lineage of Communist utopias:

In the first volume of *Capital* Marx is quoting Thomas Hobbes in the chapter *Purchase and Sale of Labor Power:* "The value of a man is as in all other things equal to his price, that is to say, as much as is being paid for the use of his *power.*" This was written two centuries before Marx, banned by the latter as all things revealing into the endnotes. The equation of labor and labor power that Marx had been used to from the Classical Economy had become second nature for him, that he even uses it uncritically in chapter X of the *Anti-Duehring.*[84] This later work was first published in 1878! Engels explains here within a few pages just ahead of chapter X which was written by Marx, how important the distinction was between labor and labor power, as it engendered the theory of surplus value, which were the "most epochal merit of Marx's work."[85] This epochal blind alley is mentioned by Engels again and again and he continues to defend his friend — "Marx, who was the first to develop that and why labor could have no value!"[86]

Developed first, his own achievement, scientific novelty — here again the integrity and character of Marx are at issue. Did he get the concept of labor power from Moses Hess? The latter used it long before Marx. Did he get it from Hobbes - see above - as he must have read him, since he was quoting him? Did he get it from the English economists, the Socialists and Communists, who had drawn revolutionary consequences from Ricardo's theory of value with regard to exploitation, surplus, labor power? Who wants to may seek and he or she may find! I will confine myself here to the work of the German, Lorenz von Stein, as Marx had maintained, Stein had plagiarized him, Rodbertus had plagiarized him, etc., etc. All of them had plundered our poor Charlie, if we are to believe him, except that all the above writers had published before Marx!

Stein not only represented the materialist conception of History, which Marx had copied from him and from Wilhelm Schulz in a more shallow manner, but he had also laid out the insights which were, according to Engels, leading directly to said blind alley in such an epochal manner. Marx had plagiarized Stein thoroughly; we have just learned from Engels that Marx did not arrive at a well-rounded perspective on the economy until the late 1850s, but, nevertheless:

From 1849 to mid-May 1850 a three-volume work of Stein was published in Kiel which dealt with the social movements in France.[87] As we have seen Stein had already created a sensation with his bestseller about Socialism and Communism in 1842 among the German intellectuals. The rest of Marxism, after what is left from the achievement of the Social Democrat, W. Schulz, in the economic sense, is Steinism alone.

Stein had predicted the revolution of 1848 correctly in 1842. He had made that prediction based on his recognition of objective social movements and he now, in 1849, continues to call "the law of social movement more important than the facts of Socialism and of the social revolution." He does not, like others, think "that he has found a way through the labyrinth by thinking" he equally "would hold the key to the great riddles in his hands," but, so he continues modestly after his truly impressive performance that he had tried to find "that *social law* and give it name and content."[88] Here again Marx is much more awkward and clumsy, still with a general delay of exactly 18 years, when he postulates in the preface of the first edition of the first volume of *Capital:* "It is the final goal of this work to unveil the *law of economic movement* of modern society." Never mind that the goal should, in general, be final, the terminology used is, indeed, revealing: see the book titles of Stein and Schulz, never mind everything else!

That the economic movement would be the primary one had been settled by Stein and Schulz in reciprocal feedback with the political class struggles at a time when Marx was still writing anti-proletarian articles. "True progress of human understanding never rests upon individual insights; it comes about solely through the discovery of the *great general laws* and through the consciousness of entire peoples who absorb them."

Class struggle, as Stein continues, will bring "the working, unpropertied class of society that is dependent on the class owning property" the power or participation in power and it will be used, "to turn the condition of this class that is by the nature of its mere labor dependent into one independent and free in material respects." This should be the issue of the social revolution and the content of the much strained "social question," which will "never be solved by a single individual or a book." Stein, however, believes in a solution, he believes "this time with its beautiful harmony of all the most noble of human powers."[89]

Stein makes it clear that political revolutions always strive for power and property and he says this of Capitalism: "Next to the productive Capital there remains the mere personal capacity to produce. The latter is labor power which inheres in every person, per se ... Productive Capital, on the other hand, inasmuch as it reaches beyond the individual capacity to produce (that was a perfectly valid view in the 19th century as every entrepreneur was also his own engineer, manager and businessman at once) is in need of the labor power of those who do not by themselves possess Capital. In this manner, a natural and organic context is created."[90] (With Marx this simply reads as "an organic context" between Capital and Labor.) We may assume that Marx did not overlook the labor power which was highlighted and italicized in the text, his epochal, blind alley discovery after all?

And what about the surplus value?

As he is defining the coercion to accumulate, Stein expands: "The getting bigger of every Capital nevertheless rests, just as its genesis, upon Labor; and that is, of course, in that manner that the overflow [Ueberschuss] of the value and price of the product above and beyond the usage [Verwendungen] and costs will be added on to Capital. The main subject of the costs is inevitably wages. The higher the wages, the lower the gain; the lower the wages, in turn, the higher the gain of Capital and its growth, as well. This strife of the different Capitals amongst each other, in which each strives to become greater, which we call *competition* or *co-emulation,* necessarily leads to the adjustment of the wages at the *lowest* possible point. It is completely incomprehensible and unwarranted to reproach the acquiring Capital for that; it lies in its nature to act in such a manner and no other.

This lowest possible wage finds its limits in the needs of the worker; it devours, nevertheless, the gain that he could make and puts it with the gain of the Capital of the entrepreneur, instead of leaving it to the worker. The gain that is made in each and every connection of one Capital and Labor for a specific acquisition or for the enterprise fuses solely with Capital. If that gain were to go to the worker it would not go to the capitalist. In this manner, Capital and Labor step outside of their harmony and the contradiction ensues between the two great classes of society geared towards acquisition.

This contradiction has its specific character. Gain lies in the *interest* of Capital and it also inversely determines of the worker who does not have it. *The interest of Capital, hence, is set against the determination of the worker.*"[91] And Stein continues: "*Who does not have Capital, may not arrive at getting it.* In this manner the propertied and the non-propertied classes become propertied and non-propertied *states;* property and non-property is fixed in the tribes and races [den Geschlechtern] and the order of society becomes a fixed and closed one." Stein now puts the freedom of the individual into focus for the reader as a measure of his analysis and he declares the Capitalist economic order to be "as a contradiction with the idea of freedom inasmuch as the development of human communality is fixed and frozen at a certain point and so this society which is free in its nature becomes *factually unfree*. In this manner society does not only exclude non-proprietors from the acquisition of Capital, but moreover, it makes Labor without Capital *dependent* upon working Capital, that is, the non-possessor becomes subject to the possessor. This dependence as a permanent state is a dependence *of the working state upon the proprietorial one*."[92]

Stein calls surplus value the "overflow of value" above and beyond the costs of wages. According to Marx, surplus value is that kind of value which is worth more than the value of labor power. The value of labor power finds the monetary expression of its worth in the price, that is, in the wages of Labor. Where is there any new value or originality in the surplus value of Marx? It is Steinian value; nothing goes beyond the understanding of Steinian surplus value. In his way Stein never made any self-important ado about this factual statement, he says merely that he is repeating here well-known principles of Political Economy!

Non-Comrade Professor Dr. Stein defines in a crystal-clear language intelligible for every worker and, therefore, in a definitely populist manner the organic composition of Capital and he proves, furthermore, that it is the labor power of the worker that creates both surplus value and Capital. He applies the principle of value of the Classical Political Economy fully and entirely, value and price are divergent parameters!

As we can see, even with regard to the second earth-shaking discovery of Marx we can discern the same old familiar circumstances; the tired semantic reformulations as the utmost scientific ultra-value of Marx-Crap. On the side, Stein is delivering here for Marxism the entire theory of Capital and wages. Moreover, he makes it unmistakably clear that the propertied class has full control of the powers of State and that the remedy for the proletariat can mean only one thing: Social reform or social revolution.

Even prior to Marx picking up his maxim of the dictatorship of the proletariat in his *Class struggles* from the French theories of revolution in 1848, Stein had written: "For that reason it is inevitable that with the advent of the rule of the proletariat a rule of terror will ensue ... The well-accomplished social revolution always leads to dictatorship. ... It declares itself to be the autonomous power of the State and invests itself with the Law, the task and the sanctity of the same ... And as this dictatorship stands above society, it soon takes on the character of that might which is by its nature elevated above society."[93] Not alone the devastating criticism of Rosa Luxemburg of Lenin's and Trotsky's dictatorship confirms Stein's prognoses.

The escape from the misery of the proletariat Stein sees neither in Socialism nor in Communism, but in *social* Democracy.

In the table of contents of his second volume, Stein treats the economic base before the political superstructure. Before he goes on to describe Socialism, Communism and Social Democracy as intellectual and political tendencies, he sets out to examine their material base. Even the organization of his topics in the table of contents provides a telling testimony against Marx and he treats there among other things: The industrial society, its reign and its contrary; the genesis of the reign of Capital and of the Capital possessors; the proletariat; the genesis of the industrial strata of workers; the wages relation; pauperism, its inmost essence and consequences.

Let us look at those passages that may elucidate the solutions of the issues at hand.

First and foremost, Stein does give an introduction into Political Economy that is comprehensible for the layman. This defines the production of commodities and explains further the dependence of the proletariat upon Capital. Herein, on one page alone, in the first two paragraphs, he mentions this enormous discovery of Marx, labor power, five times in a row![94] Furthermore, Stein defines capacity, be it physical or mental, as a commodity, i.e., as the "commodity of labor power" of Marx. "As soon as industry is established the *value* of things takes on another character. Industry satisfies needs and desires, but it awakens and stimulates them at the same time. In order to be able to buy the desires that have become industrial commodities, those selfsame materials have to become commodities that one sells. To the extent to which I am able to turn a material or a capacity into a commodity, it makes up the *measure* of its value. This measure finds its expression in *money*. By way of industry and the trade connected with it, everyone has to recalculate his possessions according to its *monetary value*. Money becomes the medium of the entire traffic of goods."[95] Clearly, Stein recognizes the role of money: "Money is, therefore, the element, that, nevertheless, always exists prior to industry and that has a steady influence, but that *becomes the determining factor for the entire industrial life of goods* only through industry. This statement of the utmost importance is not sufficiently recognized in Political Economy. The study of money up to now is only one of coins and at most of monetary circulation. What money is in its actuality can be recognized properly only through the concept of *industry*."[96] Stein then deals with monetary capital and of the connection of bank and industrial capital, describes State, current account and credit banks, to sum up as follows that "monetary capital in its narrower sense" would become the ruling power in the "economic society."[97] "Where, on the other hand, Capital has been created, there without any Labor a safe existence and a reputable societal position can be had; this is comparable to the feudal landed estates of the past and it is as in the latter the source of *laborless income.* For that reason, Capital is the main factor, the prior condition of all earthly enjoyments and of all personal developments; this alone provides security of existence, of enterprise, of prospects for the future."[98]

Stein discusses the division of Labor, and its "alienation," he indicates the role of the average price and he indicates further, that possessors of Capital rule over the entire life of goods and he calls industrial society a "Capital society." His summary reveals him as a genuinely precocious "Marxist": "In this manner, every exertion becomes, by and by, saleable and the human being itself becomes a sales item."[99] From this passage Marx derives his verdict: "In Capitalism everything becomes a commodity," i.e., everything becomes venal.

Stein's passage about the "dependent class in industrial society" is teeming with later "Marxisms" often verbatim or nearly so: Of the juridical liberty and economic slavery of the worker, of dual competition, about "slavery in the name of freedom," etc. We should highlight for our area of interest Stein's assessment that "labor power is the sole property of the worker and it is, furthermore, his only protection against impoverishment. His labor power nourishes him and his family, the average wages are the average quantity of his consumption. *As long as* this labor power remains unbroken and factually active, the worker remains well even without the savings of Capital. As soon as this labor power either stops or his employment stops, *immediate impoverishment* sets in for the worker, which will not be mitigated by the drawing from what better times should have brought on the side. As these "better times" consist only of the daily satisfaction of needs through daily work.

If there are reasons, therefore, which are independent of the nature of the social strata of workingmen or of the conditions of industry, which would destroy the labor power of the worker either entirely or leave him temporarily unemployed, it follows that the impoverishment and poverty *"will be an unavoidable companion* of industrial society and a *perennial evil within the social strata of the industrial worker."[100]*

This shows in what kind of a differentiated manner a social scientist proceeds. In the following Stein deals with the category "immiseration" or "miseration" upon which Marx, in dogmatizing, it puts all the "revolutionary" hopes of his "theory of miseration." In this manner, Stein once turns directly against Engels: "There have been some, like Engels, who would describe the situation of the workers in general as pauperism and they would in such a way elicit both pity, as well as gain further converts for their opinions."[101] But this is not so: who has labor power and labor is not a pauper.

On the other hand, Stein, in all his capacity of differentiation of his value judgments, leaves no doubt about his own undiluted perspective when he writes about the factory districts: "Labor, the source of all force, of all grace, reverts her divine nature in the industrial sector – she becomes the enemy of her own mother, of labor power! ... Recent times have brought egregious discoveries ... that ... an abuse of human beings and more precisely an abuse of workingmen is taking place on behalf of Capital."[102] - "The new sources of wealth turn into sources of need through a strange magic ... To the extent to which humanity manages to dominate and coerce nature, humanity appears to be coerced through other humans or through their own meanness ..." So Marx in a speech in London on April 14, 1856, six years after the publication of Stein!

At the end of his expositions of Political Economy, Lorenz von Stein honors the social and political views of Adam Smith, who had declared, "Labor is the principle producing element and it has, thus, to be the ruling element, as well," and who had declared further that "middle-class government ..." has only been installed "to defend the rich against the poor."[103] Stein further underlines and analyses the contradictory, antagonistic base of Capitalism in its development, as "in every society the propertied social strata stands against the non-propertied strata." He continues that the future European, as well as, consequently, the German expectations would be determined by the "fact that Capital and Labor stand against each other as capitalists and proletariat."[104]

With regard to this future expectation Stein gives neither the utopias of Socialism nor Communism a chance, as both, according to him, were in contradiction to the objective laws of social development. Stein's hopes are directed toward a free social state, towards the equality of Capital and Labor and towards the economic-material foundation of political and personal freedom.

It becomes apparent why Engels denigrates the ideas of this eminent scholar and man of noble character as "mere twaddling," and by now we understand a little more closely where Marx, in turn, got his own twaddlings from. However, this is not sufficient to put aside the "epochal" work of Capital. Context and content need to be further elucidated.

An adherent of Marx writes to the latter mid-September of 1850 from Cologne: "... for a long time we have been excited about the publication of your Political Economy. May I ask you to send us the manuscript with your conditions; we would then have it printed immediately with Becker and assure its distribution. It would be of great value for the propaganda."[105]

What Marx sent in response were a few old articles from his time at the *Rheinische Zeitung!* This and the letter refutes unmistakably the falsification in the biography of the Russians quoted in Part I, according to which censorship had impeded that Marx's *Political Economy* would have been printed even before the revolution of 1848.   Never in the 1840s nor in the 1850s did Marx possess a manuscript about economic issues ready for publication.   The only things he had from that period were some disorderly, unsystematic pieces of scrap paper and the theoretical quality was accordingly low.

His few friends, in turn, had to wait another 17 years. Then in the middle of September of 1867, 1,000 copies of the first volume of *Capital* appeared. In 1885, Engels published the second volume and in 1894, the third volume. From 1844 to 1894, the two *ersatz*-experts had taken a quarter century for the first volume and half a century for the complete work of the full exposition of their Political Economy! Let us remember the timeframe of the real classical economists: the theorist, Adam Smith, took ten years; the man of practice, David Ricardo, took two years to found the Classical Economy of England, not to plagiarize it. The content of Marx's work *The Critique of Political Economy* which had been published in 1859 was summarized again in the first chapter of the first volume of *Capital.*

Marx came to Socialism and to the materialist conception of History as the last of the Young Hegelians. As the last of the Socialists and Communists of England he came, after Stein and with the help of the school of Ricardo to the exploitation of Labor by way of Capital, that is, to the conception of surplus value: Marx, as always a Johnny-come-lately!

He was aware of that, at least in 1852, when he wrote: "With regards to myself, I can't claim the merit to have discovered either the classes of modern society or their struggle amongst themselves. *Bourgeois historical writers long before me had described the historical development of this struggle of the classes and bourgeois economists and had given an exposition of the economic anatomy of the latter.*"[106] He could have saved himself the 'either' and the 'or' could have been replaced by an 'and,' but it will be exceedingly clear all the same how to judge and categorize the *Manifesto* and the *Capital:* Excerpts and compilation materials, an ill-understood, incompletely described state of research of Political Economy and of Historiography, no original insights, no new value, no independent scientific achievement, only agitation, propaganda, ideology! "What I did in a new way," Marx continues in his letter, "was to prove the following:

       1.   That the existence of particular classes is tied only to a particular state of development." Yes, absolutely, that is correct, except only approximately so. For that reason, even the first sentence of the *Manifesto* is already copied wrongly;

       2.   "That class struggle leads by necessity to the dictatorship of the proletariat." For that reason, evidently, he

writes in the series about the class struggles in France that he took this maxim from Blanqui and I quoted that, furthermore, in the first part of the global society [Weltgesellschaft] and the London Labor Association;

        3.   "That this dictatorship only marks the transition towards the abolition of all classes and towards a classless society." Here all the Communists come into play, among the Germans especially Hess and Weitling, who all made exactly the same statement – including the period of transition. In part I, I have quoted how Marx attributed these merits about this "world-historic mission" humbly not to himself but to the "socialist writers." His own "merits" were exaggerated to the same degree to which he lost touch with real events.

With regard to Communism now: These views - at best of a futurological quality last copied from Blanqui - were quoted by Marx in his series *Class Struggles in France 1848 to 1850* in the *Neue Rheinische Zeitung – Politisch-Oekonomische Revue [New Rhenish Times – Political-Economic Review]* in 1850. If a "proof" is brought on for a non-existing fact, then that is decidedly more than science!

With regards to the law of motion of society: A discussion of Lavergne, Schulz, List, Stein; and the English economists will follow below. Marx was in awe of their classical, Socialist and Communist economics. At no time was he in awe of the economic policies of the English royal house which had given these theorists a well-grounded empirical science. As early as from the 12th century onward the economic development of the country was directed according to these principles in a decisive manner: Prudent, circumspect and anticipating England was brought to bear to lead the nations with a successful policy of a completely un-Marxist synthesis of royalty, nobility and middle class. They should be well ashamed, these English, - not because they are today dumping all their trash into the North sea - but because they violated the only genuine science of Marxism-Crapism and its unalterable, objective laws, which our dear Charlie had just now fully come to understand in their midst!

The Scotsman, Adam Smith, on the other hand, began to work 100 years after the bourgeois revolution. Apparently, the political leadership of our "real" Socialism has to make blatant economic mistakes for another hundred years, before a new Adam Smith is presented to them, as Marx even turned our Adam into crap. The unscientific halo that hovers about *Capital* and elevates it falsely into being the "bible of the working class" and prevents the leadership, ideologically and theoretically, to perceive a light dawning upon them - in this case an economic-political one. The more they approach the Marxist-Communist goal, the more it recedes into the background: see, for instance, the intended redrafting of the program of the

Communist Party of the Soviet Union. The conflict between means and ends, because of the Marxist ideology, becomes bigger and bigger in any real-existing Socialism over time. It can be solved only, when Marx is not seen anymore as a scientist, but as the last rehash of the utopian system-makers. His goal is not economically feasible or viable, because his means violate and defy all economic principles and laws, especially the law of value! Nevertheless, what will prevail will not be the political means of dictatorship, but the objective parameters of the economic needs of the industrial production of commodities even within our unreal Socialism. These demonstrate on a daily basis that a ruling group of bureaucrats - who are more incapable than the Capitalist management structure thanks to Marxian manuals - are specifically incapable of developing science and high technology, productivity and efficacy, conduct and performance, production and exchange with simultaneous environmental protection in a sufficiently swift and qualitative manner.

"Moribund imperialism" carries our "real" Socialism by means of fantastic credits and refinancings of debts, by means of State-sponsored and private victual assistance through global economic crises and famines. The Federal Republic is doing this through the Inner-German Trade [I.D.H.] and through its third billion mark credit which given at increased interest rates breaks down the entire propaganda of the 9th Assembly of the Central Committee end of 1984, mentioned in the news with one sentence: Really, the G.D.R. is so incredibly successful that it doesn't know anymore what to do with all this West money, let's bring on more of these unwonted high interest rates! The crude oil deliveries of West Germany to East Germany for the refinement in the G.D.R. and return bring another billion - held against West currency this transaction could not be made anymore, we ran out of it some years ago. Furthermore, there is the 'swing,' unilaterally claimed by the G.D.R., the fixed positions from the Federal budget, etc. A third of the small COMECON States is incapable of repayment, like one-third of the developing nations, to the industrial Capitalist countries – what happened then to the sovereignty of the New Order?

The Communists are now celebrating the entire *Capital* as the theoretical source of their policies in general and their economic policies in particular! The population of the G.D.R. seems, nevertheless, to believe that the *ersatz*-Russians had been mistaken and, instead, grabbed the *Misery of Philosophy*, as Marx bequeathed his Capital to the Visigoths; after all, he was born in the West German township of Trier/Trèves on the French border.

Marx never quite managed to master Political Economy, given his alienation from reality and his Ivory Tower existence. From the middle of the 1840s onward he had given addresses on the topic to workers' associations. One may regard his *Economic-Philosophic Manuscripts* and hold them against what, e.g., Moses Hess was taking from the economic sources and was publishing at the same time!

Money, there, is for Marx the "general whore," apparently, a completely new economic category, or moreover, "the general procurer of men and peoples." He is here without rhyme or reason translating passages from Goethe's *Faust* and Shakespeare's *Timon of Athens*. Money is "the general discombobulation and confusion of all things, therefore, a world upside down," consequently, and this is Marx's logical inference in synchronicity with all his predecessors, the Capitalist world upside down has to be turned into the Communist world straight up in which there exists no more money. Here Marx must have discombobulated more than just money!

The issue of the law of value which deals with commodity, value, price, money, in turn, is not a specifically Capitalist one, but it is an ancient occurrence as ancient as the History of humanity itself and, what is more important, this issue will remain, as the division of labor will remain and will become more widespread beyond the given systems. Consequently, the functions of money will increase in significance on the national and international levels.

The mystical "explanation of money" has disappeared in the *Capital*. Well, Marx had ample opportunity to read up on the subject in Stein, and not alone there, and like Stein - as if by accident - he lets the industrial cycle from productive Capital be derived from money, to guard an individual nuance, obviously, a few years later than Stein. Nevertheless, Marx remained a mystic with respect to the deduction of monetary functions for Communism. He fetishized, demonized, dogmatized and set money as absolute as an incarnation of Capital, instead of comprehending what irreplaceable instrument content-wise and in technical respects humanity had created for itself for the regulation of economic relations. As a learned dogmatist, he set all social relations as absolute in connecting them in their origin with money. He should have at least known, as one philosophically trained, that it is methodically wrong to set anything as absolute and make it dogmatic. But then again, what were the workers saying when they threw him out of the Communist Party? "Half-educated element!" Alexander the Great of yore had engaged in wiser monetary policies in his global empire than the fervent Marx or his acolytes in their real-existing socialist system. The COMECON countries don't even have convertibility within their own borders, not to mention the rest of the world, although the Russians contributed to the Treaty of Bretton Woods, but without endorsing and underwriting it afterwards. Among Communists, who have been misled to such a degree by Marx, there exists to this day no comprehensive theoretical perspective, not to talk about a coherent foreign economic policy. Marx's "theory of monetary value" - given the circumstances of Special Drawing Rights [S.D.R.] of the I.M.F., the changed function of gold, the steering processes of the World Bank and the G.A.T.T. - has remained as invalid as it ever was. And the Soviets don't know any more today what they want, 40 years after Bretton Woods, and instead of buying and selling in world trade they turn back the clock to Stone Age practices: Will barter marinated herring for microchip!

The ideology bars the view of empirical facts and prevents rational solutions, but solutions are at least sought after: see Hungary, Poland, China, etc. Said countries all engage in a different foreign policy than the Soviet Union and that not only in their position towards the I.M.F., only Crapland East Germany stands loyally by the Holy Empire of Russia! But that not withstanding, long live the indestructible unity and cohesion of all Communist countries and the leadership of the Soviet Union!

Who deems these remarks sarcastic may look at the fifty-six lines on 'world money' in the first volume of *Capital* and ask himself or herself what that was meant to be good for in the 19th century? This passage contains general-concrete yada - yada - yada such as: "The exchange rates rise and fall every week, at certain times of the year they stand high against a certain nation, at other times they stand just as high for her." So that's how it goes?!? Spring, summer, fall and winter are God's children at certain times! One could get seriously furious considering the precious study time that is wasted on this crap from *Capital!* No analysis whatsoever, no answer to the why, wherefore, for what reason, what cause, from what context and, in addition, the above quote is just an explanatory(!) footnote for the mere mentioning of exchange rates in the main text. That passage alone should be enough for the thinking Marxist economist to change course!

In general, Marx is using quotes liberally but he does not have an expert opinion. He always ends up with an ideological deduction and this deduction is always the same: Capitalism is dying. That is the "almighty Marxism, because it is true," as Lenin was used to say in this context and for the same reason he added: It is a "manual for action." Now we could see from the example of Bretton Woods, how the Holy Land of Russia has been guiding all Fraternal Countries!

But then again, Marx really intended to elaborate upon all these open issues. He meant to break ground in at least as many topics as his classical forebears! His first sketch of 1857, that is after about 13 years of studies, envisioned for his *Capital* project at least six volumes: Capital, landed property, wage labor, State, foreign trade, world market and crises. These six projected volumes he reduced after five years to one that is "Capital in general" as he wrote Kugelmann in 1862. Another five years later the projection consisted of four volumes: The processes of production, circulation and the economic process in general and a history of economic theory. Marx managed to write just about the first one of those, Engels completed the other two, but the fourth even he did not manage. There we have it, this monumental scientific heritage, monumentally fragmented, verily a manual to fragmentary action!

It is indicative that Marx even from his conception saw economics as a theoretical matter, i.e., in his case that meant to reduce it to an abstract-non-signifying, ideological formula entirely devoid of content. For that reason there is nothing about application of the theory in the deleted volumes of State, foreign trade, world market! For that reason, the theory remained ineffective, degenerated into ideology, aloof, unusable for the practice; no manual for action, solely a bounced letter of credit drawn upon the prophesied Communist future! These prophecies have by now become verifiable through historical and economic facts. These facts refute Marx completely within the Communist world movement, within Socialism and within Capitalism! He "proved" economically what many had proven before him and what no reasonable human being would deny: That everything in the history of humanity is in motion, change and development – what a terribly dangerous prognosis for the status quo in Germany - and that this is true as well for the property conditions and the changing political conditions of class and power. Such decisive conditions of production shaping the future like the stock market or the corporation he barely even noticed. He did not have even the foggiest notion of monopolies, state monopolies, of multinational and international monopolies, of national, supranational and global mechanisms of economic regulation and direction in today's Capitalistic-pluralistic world of the democratic West.

So, what did Marx achieve in concrete terms? Let us listen to his loyal stooge, Engels, of what the latter has to say about the state and quality of the principal life's work of Karl Marx, he is writing the following in the preface to *Capital*, vol. II: "To get the second volume ready for printing was not an easy task. The great number of the mostly fragmentary elaborations at hand increased the difficulty. Only one script [IV] was at much as possible edited ready for printing. ... The large majority of the material was not fully worked out linguistically; drafted in a language in which Marx was used to do his excerpts: negligent style, often coarse, humoristic expressions ... it is the writing down of the thoughts in the manner in which they develop in the mind of the author. Next to passages that were nearly fully elaborated there were others which were barely sketched; the material of illustrating facts had been collected, but not ordered, not to mention worked out; at the end of the chapter under pressure to come to a conclusion there were often only a few fragmented phrases as cornerstones of a development here left unfinished; furthermore, the hand-writing often illegible even to the author himself."

And in the preface to the third volume Engels declares: "When publishing the second volume in 1885, I assumed that the third volume would pose only some technical difficulties, with the exception, nevertheless, of certain very important passages. And this was, indeed, the case; but of the difficulties which just these important passages would pose for me I had no idea at the time ... For the third tome existed only a very fragmentary first sketch. As a rule, the beginnings of each passage were rather well worked out, even stylistically rounded. But then again, the farther one got the sketchier and more incomplete became the elaboration, the more frequent would become the digressions on minor additional points grazed upon during the examination, so the original point was left for later resuming, the longer and more convoluted grew the sentence structures, wherein only nascent thought notions were expressed ... But now regarding the details: For the first section the main manuscript was only useful very partially and with great limitations. For chapter 3 there were whole series of uncompleted mathematical analyses. ... Chapter 4 contained only its title. As the item treated herein was, however, of decisive importance, i.e., effect of the transferal upon the rate of profit, I worked it out myself. For that reason, the entire text has been put in brackets. In that context it became apparent that, indeed, the formula of the rate of profit in chapter 3 needed a modification in order to achieve general validity. From chapter 5 onward the main manuscript is the sole source for the rest of the section, although here, as well, many transpositions and additions became necessary. The greatest difficulties were posed by section V ... Here we are faced not with a finished sketch, not even skeleton that could be fleshed out in rough outlines, but only with an incipience of elaborations which more than once would end in a disorderly pile of notes, remarks, materials in the form of excerpts. ... Here I had no other choice but to hew through the whole convoluted mess, to confine myself to the possible ordering of what was at hand and make only the scarcest of amendments. And so I finished the main work on this section in the spring of 1893. ... From chapter 30 onward the real difficulties started. From here onward it was necessary not only to put order into the material of the footnotes and the process of thoughts that was being interrupted continuously by ancillary phrases, digressions, etc., to be picked up rather casually in other places altogether. ... Chapter 31 then was more elaborated in context. Then the manuscript had a long section entitled: *The Confusion* made up entirely of excerpts ... namely, about money and Capital, gold outflow, hyper-speculation ... Herein, practically all current views on the relationship between money and Capital are represented and the "confusion," thus, made apparent about what in the money market would be money and what would be Capital, Marx intended to treat critically and satirically. I have after many attempts reached the conclusion that it is impossible to constitute this chapter; the material, especially, that endowed with marginal notes by Marx has been incorporated where a context for it could be found.

Finally section VII was available as having been completely written out, but only in its first draft; the endlessly convoluted phrases had to be dissected and disencumbered to become printable. Of the last chapter only the beginning was to be had. Here the three great forms of revenue, land rent, profit, labor wages, were meant to be represented according to the three main classes of the developed Capitalist society – landlord, capitalist, wage laborer – as well as the class struggle given by necessity through their existence as factually existing result."

Do we need another witness after this king's witness, Engels?

I do not think that this is necessary. *Das Capital* is the *Confusion*. The good, old faithful second with childish-naïve credulity was hanging onto the great perennial student, who had been allowed to enjoy what Engels, who had not made it through High School, had been barred to enjoy. For years Marx, as a perennial student, had beleaguered the universities and had finally achieved his Ph.D., while Engels, after a commercial apprenticeship had been tied down to that "dogged commerce." For Engels a human being did not start below Ph.D. status, for most other Prussians it did not start below the rank of lieutenant. Vehemently did Engels defend Marx against the reproach in the preface to the second volume that Marx had plagiarized Rodbertus as the latter had already described in 1842 – now this is a really bad year for Marx, first Stein and now Rodbertus, as well – in a more sovereign manner than Marx, the state of affairs in "political economics," that is the macroeconomic conditions at hand including surplus value. Engels returns to this issue in the preface of the third volume, but it did not leave him in peace as he polemicized against Rodbertus as early as 1884 in the preface of Marx's first German edition of *The Misery of Philosophy*. I have demonstrated above in the case of Lavergne how much a defense of this kind is worth.

Now, Rodbertus is not alone in his reproach that Marx had used him "quite well without quoting" him.[107] Meyers, in his *Liberation Struggle of the Fourth State*, states that Marx had taken "demonstrably … the greatest part of his critique" from the publications of Rodbertus.[108] One need only read Stein in order to understand that Marx was merely repeating the state of research of the German Political Economy to which Rodbertus had contributed his part, as well!

It is positively astounding that Marx, who was so pathologically eager to fight and, although he knew of the reproach, that Rodbertus had dealt with the origin of surplus value more clearly and succinctly before him, never publicly repudiated that criticism! Why wouldn't he have done so? Why did he attack the parliamentarian and Minister in his *Neue Rheinische Zeitung*, but never the economist in the scholastic literature? No, it is not necessary to take too hard or strenuous a guess!

Engels's defense of Marx with regard to surplus value is structured like in the case of Historical Materialism: Our Marx didn't know anything, didn't read anything, didn't know Rodbertus, didn't look at the relevant literature, and didn't look at the academic journals of Tuebingen University. He only knew the direct reproach and commented on it in private, not in public; as Engels tells us, if Rodbertus "maintains nothing else, then Marx would not care; and if Rodbertus held his own representation to be the shorter and clearer one, he could let him have that pleasure."[109]

Considering that this is supposed to be Marx's "main achievement," what Lenin called the cornerstone of Marxism, this indifference is absolutely mind-boggling. Why was he so indifferent? Because he knew what he had copied where, reformulated the content with linguistic sleights of hand and had then presented it as his own achievement! He left it to Engels to save what there was to be saved and Engels did Marx that favor for better or worse. I shall now juxtapose the various irreconcilable statements of Engels with regard to Rodbertus. The respective first statement refers to his preface of the *Misery of Philosophy*, the second to his preface of the second volume of *Capital*. The former was written in 1884, the latter in 1885.

The "progress" in the process of falsification should be noted:

1.   "It – this refers to the Socialist-Communist interpretation of Ricardo's theory of value, as the foundation of the theory of surplus value of Marx – led in *many cases to insights into the origin and nature of surplus value, which far exceeded Ricardo*, so for example in Rodbertus."

2.   Rodbertus "only rediscovered a truism with his surplus value".

1.   "At the time when Rodbertus *Understanding*, etc., appeared, *it was absolutely an important book.*" It has to be seen "on a level with the achievements of his better English predecessors". Well, the better ones would be on a higher level, wouldn't they? But there may even be a 'deeper level'":

2.   "What Rodbertus had achieved furthermore in economics rests – with regard to the 'truism' of surplus value – on the same level." It is really bad, Frederick, when one grows not only old, but senile on top of it!

It is well to remember that Engels communicated to Mehring that Marx had "not the foggiest idea" of Political Economy! The science in the meantime had not stood still. In the preface to *Capital* Engels maintained that Marx had treated monetary theory and labor wages for the first time scientifically, which proves nothing more and nothing less than that Engels neither read economic journals nor treatises, in short, that he was as remiss in understanding the discipline as Marx himself and he simmered by himself dimly in unsplendid isolation.

But even assuming the case that Marx had deduced the principles expounded in his *Capital* directly from Ricardo without Rodbertus, Stein, Schulz, Lavergne, etc., as Engels maintains, what does that prove? That he was in comparison to others again a Johnny-come-lately, who cannot reclaim groundbreaking research for himself at all!

By the way, it is frankly not credible that Engels in his old age was proud that it was not Marx, but he himself who had to cut open the books after the former's death which treated of the subject that Marx had dealt with all his life! A strange methodology for an academic, indeed, and one can only concur with Bakunin when the latter reproached Marx that he had "compromised the cause of the proletariat ... through his incredible vanity, his mean and unfriendly character and his tendency towards dictatorship within the Party of revolutionary Socialists."[110]

For completeness sake let's go through the traditional line of political economists with regard to surplus value. Rodbertus, long before Marx, had correctly defined surplus value as "unpaid labor" and Marx quotes Rodbertus, who he - according to Engels - did not know at all, as Engels himself another passage of the latter, where Rodbertus elaborates that surplus value would be engendered, "as wages from labor only make up a part of the value of the labor product."[111] And how does Engels himself define surplus value? *Marx would say solely*, writes Engels, "*that surplus value consists of unpaid labor, which is a simple fact.*"[112] If Marx, indeed, took his excerpt of Rodbertus in an "ironic manner," why does Engels then take this selfsame "ironic" statement as ironic in Rodbertus, but in Marx serious as science? Poor Marxism-Crapism!

But to take the cake entirely, in the already quoted *Capital* preface Engels writes: "That Marx knew then very well, even without the help of Rodbertus, not only whence but how 'the surplus of the Capitalist be engendered,' his *Misery of Philosophy* proves in 1847 and the presentations given in Brussels in 1847 and published in 1849 in the *Neue Rheinische Zeitung* about wage labor and capital".[113] One may well turn to what I quoted at the beginning of part II from this "wage labor and capital" from Engels! And, furthermore, we learn from him at the end of his preface to the *Misery of Philosophy*: "It is hardly necessary to draw attention to the fact that the mode of expression used in this writing does not concur entirely with that of *Capital.* So here there is talk of *labor* as commodity and of purchase and sale of labor instead of labor power."

That is not only outrageous, it is outright scandalous!

Marx was well acquainted with everything that needed to be known about surplus value on the basis of the findings of macroeconomics which were generally known and this before he even started to articulate his epochal dead-end economic theory! He even knew that "exceedingly well" even before he knew "the commodity of labor power"! Engels, Engels, if you were still a member, you would now have to be excluded again from the Workers' Association because of your unwitting complete unmasking of Charlie Crap! Because Marx at that time rejected not only the theory of surplus value of Ricardo, but also his theory of value, as well! But, whence did Rodbertus know about surplus value? He knew it, in essence, from Adam Smith and the latter's followers and they were, in turn, drawing on Thomas More from the 16th century, that is three and a half centuries prior to Marx! They had deduced profit, rent and interest from unpaid labor performance, i.e., from the "surplus labor," that kind of labor, that is, which exceeds that labor performance above and beyond the "production costs" of the worker, so-called by Engels. More-work or surplus labor creates more-product or surplus commodity and it, hence, creates more-worth or surplus value. These are rather high levels of abstraction within the theoretical model to explain the industrial mode of production which was well known to all economists prior to Marx. From these abstractions Marx derives the super-abstraction "surplus value" by means of "labor power." Where he got these concepts from, we have already seen: from Stein, highlighted five times, just to be sure they could not be missed. One would have to be a veritable Hegelian hair-splitter or an ideological fanatic in order to believe that this now would be a new science, because nothing can be done, anyway, with surplus value and value in a concrete way. It only becomes concrete at the point when I ask how the industrial, the agricultural and the financial capital actually make their real profit or gain. And that question the economists prior to Marx were well able to answer! Consequently, for the scientific practice everything was clear. Our Mr. Crap was again too late at this point. To add something at all he hegelized profit to make it average profit, but even that was nothing new. This was a well-established scientific recognition prior to Marx that roughly-equal capitals would bring roughly-equal profits. Here Marx falsely explained this process in a reductionist manner - see Engels critique of this issue quoted above. So even at that point were the men of practical experience agreed with the theorists, Marx did not see matters in a clear manner.

Marx is looking only at the competition between and within the different segments of the economy. He does not see the competition on the world market, the competition through quality, through service, through credit conditions; he does not mention the monopoly profit, about which others had already published, etc. In other words, even here he has not reached the height of the general scientific understanding of his day. Perhaps he should have read the academic journals from Tuebingen University, as well as their academic literature?

But he did read English academic literature! When Marx was just out of his diapers an anonymous author was writing therein in 1821 that the surplus product is to be paid "from the work of others" and Marx is quoting this in *Capital*. And as we have seen how good Engels may be at the art of exposure, we are going to listen to him one more time, as he says about this passage: "Our pamphlet is *only the extreme outpost of a whole literature*, that *turned the theory of value and of surplus value from Ricardo* in the twenties in the interest of the proletariat *against the Capitalist mode of production*."[114]

Many thanks, Mr. Communist of the Bourgeoisie, as Weitling would say!

I think the phenomenon that Marx and Engels, wherever they were resident, never gained influence of the labor movement, never were taken for real, has to do with the fact that in England the history of economic theory was well known and, therefore, it was never possible to sell Marx as this great theoretical beacon of light. Marx was bitterly disappointed that his first volume of *Capital* was never even reviewed, much less printed in England during his lifetime. Marx, after the revolution of 1848, held a fleeting influence over the left wing of the Chartist movement. The latter then wrote a kind of Marxist program with the result that Chartism, formerly the mightiest, erstwhile proletarian mass movement, hit rock bottom at the end of the 1850s.

Engels now holds that the surplus theory of value of Marx "struck like lightning out of a blue sky and that in all civilized countries,"[115] while the surplus theory of value of Rodbertus – no kidding, the latter has one, as well? – fizzled out without any effect whatsoever. Perhaps it was a lightning ball that was rolling around for quite a while? It took, after all, the entirety of four years for the first thousand copies of the first volume of *Capital* to be sold in all civilized countries. The scholars must have virtually fought over these copies on a global scale!

Of the friends and party comrades or former comrades Engels, Dietzgen, Schweitzer, Feuerbach, Ruge and Freiligrath, of the scholars Duehring, of the publishers Lange were the ones who made comments. That's how it struck in 1867! Freiligrath literally hit Marx with a hammer, when he wrote him in a letter: "I know that on the

Rhine many merchants and factory owners have gotten very enthusiastic about the book. In those circles it will serve its true purpose – and for the scholar it will become moreover indispensable as a work of source materials."[116]

As the sole German scholar, namely, the non-tenured lecturer, Duehring, had reacted to this flash of lightning; from the circle of experts came otherwise the verdict, Marx as an autodidact had overslept a full generation of economic science! Nobody deemed it even necessary to engage theoretically at that level. A Russian friend of Marx, Lopatin, member of the general council of the First International, published the volume in 1872 in Russia, as the censorship office did not deem it fit to have any effect on the workers. Even up 'til now, where is the worker, who would read this work, his so-called "bible"? The workers didn't read the work then! At best they were reading Lassalle or Duehring's *Capital and Labor*, which had appeared prior to Marx's *Capital*, as even Bebel did call Duehring an excellent socialist theorist and the father of Karl Liebknecht thought likewise.

Duehring then had engaged in a devastating critique of volume I of *Capital* of Marx. There was talk about a fragmentary-doctrinaire attempt, of scholasticism of sects, Mandarin punditism and polyhistorics in footnotes, of elitist, arcane and representational flourishes. Duehring attacked Marx massively for his notorious drive to dogmatize and for his fatal overvaluation of the economic factor: "What is missing is the guiding idea that the political formations, in turn, determine the economic ones," he wrote and accused Marx, therefore, of a "misapprehending ideology." Bernstein reports in his book about the Berlin Labor movement how Duehring attacked Marx "from the left."

Duehring proved that Marx stood clueless in front of the demands of the workers at least to be able to make specific statements about the future of their movement, that his positions exhaust themselves completely in coarse catchwords and slogans - and not even original ones if one thinks of Blanquism - precisely because he did not possess the creative imagination to find out, how a future economic and social system was meant to be shaped. Does one still wonder at this point why Bebel began to discover Fourier for the German Social Democrats? The latter's utopia brims with incentives for the formation of the socialist daily life, it incites creativity, while Marx's ornery slogans smirk down from banners and walls, crude and enervating to "enlighten" the citizens of our real-existing Socialism on a daily basis.

Duehring was wielding a sharp blade in Prussian Berlin against the "lectern Socialists and nepotistic professors," by the way. His first attack was directed against Wagner, tenured professor at Humboldt

University, in which Prof. Dingbat holds tenure today and he did so via litigation. Wagner had taken a work of Duehring and published it under his own name – a real scandal ensued. Be consoled, there is nothing new under the sun!

Duehring attacked the Prussian State in a decisive manner, as well; he even defended the Parisian *communards* publicly in Berlin!

He was not only held in respect but outright admiration among the workers and the young intelligentsia. Thus, it came about that no one among the theorists or men of practical experience did deem Marx's capital achievement to really have been one, unless it were to be a capital misapprehension. At that point now, Engels literally flipped out! After a decade had thus passed, he wrote on May 24, 1876, soon the "Lassalleans would be the clearest minds" and not the men from Eisenach. Engels now struck and wrote his polemic *Anti-Duehring* the following year in the German Social Democratic party magazine *Vorwaerts* [Forward] in installments. Here we have the first comprehensive representation of Marxian eclecticism wherein one may distinguish the elitist interpretations of Plato, the bureaucratic-centralist tone of Campanella, the oversimplified theory of dictatorships of Blanqui as well as the democratic-humanistic "reform-Communist" tunes of a Thomas More, depending on what sides and in what contexts one is willing to put one's stake.

Engels encountered little that was conducive with his series of articles. At the Party Congress of 1877, again in Gotha, it was demanded peremptorily that the printing of these attacks against Duehring be shelved. August Bebel opted for a compromise solution, when he proposed to publish Engels' work as a pamphlet and enable Duehring to give a counterview on an equal number of pages. But to analyze this in detail would demand a chapter in itself which would take us away from our declared mainly economic aim. Thus, we leave Engels' polemic with said German scholar aside. His other polemic which he wielded mainly against an Italian savant is equally exhilarating. He undertakes the latter in his preface to the third volume of *Capital* in 1894 and therein he returns to the theme of Historical Materialism about which a scholar from Padua factually remarked a plethora of experts had developed it long before Marx. Engels here appeals to the Italian Socialists, to "tear out the stolen peacock feathers" from their professor as Marx was supposed to have discovered that "everywhere and always the political conditions and events would find their explanation in the corresponding economic conditions."[117] For real, here we have a genuine discovery, not a fragmentary one, as in the other prefaces and this is 1845, not 1847. We could like to skip the procedure of having to re-invoke all the fine and foremost German minds, which would have to be unleashed at this point to "tear these stolen peacock feathers" out of Marx.

Engels is aghast in his preface that "the Italian" had taken Marx to be a deliberate "sophist, paralogician, blowhard and hustler," all these quite fitting epithets, because Marx would console his readers "every time he is stuck, with the conclusion of his theory in a forth-following volume, which he knows only all too well, *he is incapable and unwilling to deliver.*" Here the question imposes itself, whether Marx at this point in recognition of the real scientific problem, still had the intention to publish volume II and volume III? Whence did Professor Loria take this assumption? Or was there more than an assumption, i.e., a written or oral communication to this effect? I don't know, but that would explain, why Marx never finished the following volumes and why he did not even fight with Rodbertus with regard to the core question of his plagiarized critique of Capitalism. That is, Marx, where he became definitively positive, had given from his *Capital* a completely erroneous deduction of the construction of Communism. Here we have, actually, the second crucial issue, but we will come to that presently.

Here Engels makes a statement about Loria that, in fact, rather characterizes Marx and himself in a striking manner: "Unlimited gall, combined with a slick bypassing of unsolvable issues, heroic neglect of received kicks and blows, quick reappropriation of the achievements of others, impertinent hustling for PR, systematic organization of fame via nepotism amongst comrades – who could herein be his equal?"[118]

And the Italian continues to enrage Engels to the point that he wrote an extra "addition and postscript to the III volume of *Capital*" in 1895. Furiously, he calls Loria a "midget" and a "donkey," etc. It becomes evident that the vocabulary the German Labor Communists used when excluding Marx/Engels from the Party has remained the same, but how does the old German proverb go: Who curses is always right!

What is it then that enrages Engels to that extent? Loria had simply asked, what Marx had stated differently "then to repeat the axiom of the orthodox economists in a reversed manner that the value at which commodities are sold does not have the right relation to the work that has produced them." And Engels quotes Loria, furthermore, who states that Marx at the beginning of his work said "the exchange could only equalize two commodities through an equivalent equal-sized element that inheres in both, namely, the equivalent quantity of labor contained in them." At the end of his work, after Engels had published the third volume of *Capital*, Marx on the other hand maintains that "commodities exchange in a relation very different from the quantity of Labor contained in them."[119]

Loria now asks, whenever there had been "a greater theoretical bankruptcy," and "when had there been committed a scientific suicide with greater pomp and circumstance?"[120]

Now as Engels is running out of steam, he becomes especially courteous and he calls Loria a "Southern Cagliostro," who had shown up the "clumsy Northerner Marx." At the beginning of his postscript to the third volume Engels writes, on the other hand, that it would be necessary, "to bring up to date to the state of science in 1895 important individual additions of the text written in 1865."[121] The big question, now, becomes what did Marx work on from 1865 onward in his capital work until his death in 1883? Why had he not corrected the mistakes and made the addition himself? He didn't want to or he couldn't do it? However that may be: Engels is contradicting himself and Marx, once more, in one and the same breath. But who would want to complain?

It is entirely understandable that Engels lost his cool, when he had to read in Loria's text: "Is it really true that Marx wrote with the intent of publication, this mass of unconnected notes, which Engels compiled in loyal friendship? ... Is it, indeed, certain that Marx would have published those chapters on the median profit rate, wherein the solution that had been promised for so many years has been reduced to this hapless mystification, to this vulgar play of empty phrases? It will be at least permitted to doubt this strongly?"[122]

If we compare Engels own representation -which I have quoted in detail above - about the state of the so-called "third volume," then it becomes consummately evident how right Loria was. But Engels was insulted in a twofold manner, as Loria answers his ironic remarks about the origin of the materialist theory of History, that "if Aristotle had not outlined it, Harrington had proclaimed it without doubt in 1656 and it was then elaborated by a bevy of historiographers, politicians, lawyers and economists long before Marx."[123]

There we have it!

The "Southern" professor as a professional at least knew his subject matter, just as did his German, English and French colleagues. Engels labels Loria, whom he also calls "the illustrious," as a vulgar economist. All European scholars and scientists, experts in theory and practice, were vulgar economists in his eyes, who did evaluate the not-quite-vulgar Marx correctly[124] or ignored him with full justification. Engels could not convince the Association of Communists of the theoretical halo of Marx, but he managed to do just that in the later Social Democratic movement for some party functionaries from Germany and Russia, who in their naked struggle for survival had no time or leisure left to go through wads of academic literature. Engels failed again in doing so with the intellectuals of Western Europe who thought independently and researched critically. The critical academic professionals from the departments of History, Philosophy and Political Economy had unmasked Marx completely in his own time. Consequently they ignored him completely, because they considered him beneath all criticism of what Engels erroneously considered to be scientific. Russian illiterates, on the other hand, had to take credulously and believe what they were hoodwinked into by the authorities. As far as the Russian intelligentsia is able to lay hands on the factual material, which is difficult given the extent of the censorship, which even the party press has to submit to, they all become dissidents! Whatever facts deemed to be detrimental for the soul's prosperity of the Communists in the East Bloc countries are being withheld from thinking minds by the Secret Police in the most caring manner and where a thinking mind may not be converted; mind and man are disbarred from liberty. Consider this progress of Humanism! Our Bloody Uncle Joe, for his anniversary depicted in *Neues Deutschland* with the pure white uniform of the generalissimo, as is well known, took off the heads with the brains of any prospective dissident to preclude any possible further disturbance to his affairs of State.

Brothers and sisters of the Golden West: You have to hammer by all ways and means possible facts, facts and again facts into the brains of the East! The war of minds is being furthered and asked for by the East, don't wield it slovenly and insufficiently, please, take the ideological class warfare seriously as the obverse side of peaceful coexistence! After all there are always enthusiasts, who will fall for the visions and dream-fares of Charlie Crap and his political exploitation through merciless, cynical power-brokers!

But why not give Marx himself the word for his "economic" defense! He wrote on February 22, 1858, about his Outline or *Grundrisse of the Critique of Political Economy*, which would become ten years later the first chapter of his *Capital*, to Ferdinand Lassalle: "If I had the time, peace and the means to work out the whole thing, before handing it over to the public, I would condense it immensely, as I have always preferred the method of condensation." Professional Marxists have always only identified the materialistic-dialectical method, how negligent! The condensation method of Mr. Crap would solve all scientific milk problems! Much becomes apparent here about the economic qualities of Marx-economics! Here the question arises, as well, how this man spent all his precious time - as a day job he preferred unemployment benefits from Engels - that he never found the time to work correctly? Even more distinctly Marx describes the product of his intensive quality work a quarter of a year later in a letter to Engels, dated May 31, 1858: "It is the deuce that, namely, in this manuscript (which would make a thick volume in print) everything goes topsy-turvy like turnips and coleslaw." What a pity that Loria did not know this letter! So then, it was the deuce, or devil incarnate, responsible for everything going topsy-turvy like coleslaw and turnips in Marx's mind, because language is the material reality of thought, or isn't it? Now, at least, we know!

So that was the state of understanding of Marx after fourteen years of study of Political Economy, an insufficient self-clarification! In the same timeframe Ricardo would have finished and printed his main work seven times! Marx began to rework it, but then was not satisfied with it, he simply could not even master the main issues, as here there was no question of agitational-political yada - yada - yada, but serious problems of the general Political Economy were at issue. And so he wrote as an intimidated, poor shrimp of a man, to the brilliant stylist, Lassalle, again on November 12 of 1858 in a miserable letter: "I do not strive for an elegant representation, but I only strive to write in my average manner ..." With that we shall be satisfied, as for the great mass of our students in the subject of Marxism-Leninism, why should we exert ourselves with this crap, the C is the A of the average Communist Joe! The lament about the "mediocrity" of the grades in Marxism-Leninism is only matched by the lament of all leading cadres in the State and Party apparatus of East Germany. This mediocrity is ingrained in the subject itself, not in its communication!

At this point, Marx waxes triumphant and here he causes great embarrassment for Engels, Brother Engels, who did not know all letters, gets mighty scared; as Marx here maintains in this letter to Lassalle, that this study of his would promulgate "for the first time a correct notion of the social conditions in a scientific manner." Now to Engels and all following sycophants: Correct your historic image of Marxism! Nothing doing scientifically with 1845/'46, 1847, 1848, nothing doing with the *German Ideology*, nothing doing with the *Misery of Philosophy*, with the *Manifesto*! Here the Master is stating it clearly and unmistakably: he invented Social Science in 1858! Should in the future Engels' various prefaces that state facts otherwise not be put under censorship? Moreover, we should really forget with increasing speed that in this great, earthshaking, original, erstwhile Social Science from the outset "by the deuce everything got discombobulated like coleslaw and turnips"!

As we now need to live with these discombobulations and Marx is here even contradicting Engels, it is no wonder that the Russians have this slovenliness in their propaganda. In the preface of the *Grundrisse*, which appeared 1953 in East Germany, the Institute of Marxism/Leninism builds upon Engels' hypothesis that Marx had articulated "his" theory of surplus value before 1848 and that he had used it against Proudhon. In the authorized Marx biography, which appeared thirty years later, from which we have already quoted not a few lies, something truthful after all shall be brought up. Here the Soviets deem the interpretation of Marx to be correct: "The second discovery, i.e., the foundation of the theory of surplus value, he would only make at the end of the 1850s."[125] Pray, why is this story of our "Classics" not called *Twothousandandhalf a Night*?

Of course, Marx had an excuse for Lassalle in the letter last quoted for his overwrought mediocrity. Marx let the latter know that his "dumb, wooden manner of writing ... derives from a sick liver." Some write with their head, their heart, mind and hand, but it is also possible to use a typewriter. Marxism after all is omnipotent.

What does Marx have to say with regard to the economy? How is Capitalist production of commodities directed? Let us summarize the content of all three volumes of *Capital:*

Productive Labor creates value and surplus value. The latter is split into the gain of the industrial, the agricultural, the commercial and the financial Capitalist. They are making profits, which derive from unpaid Labor exertion. Competition now hinders the Capitalists from making individual profits, as on the market prices fluctuate around the value, because there are differing price bids. Prices are influenced by supply and demand. Thus, median prices and median profits ensue. Extra profits and profits from monopolies because of scientific, technological or other advantages will be leveled sooner or later by the competition that follows. Investment capital always flows into those areas of the economy which promise high profits. From the resulting glut of the market the pendulum of profit strikes back, the production is throttled and looks for new spheres of capital investment. In this manner the anarchistic, unplanned macroeconomy keeps itself in a state of equilibrium. The market-mechanism safeguards the micro-economic, interproductional and macroeconomic necessary proportionality for the individual and productive consumption. Resurging disproportionality on the market is being equilibrated by crises. Crises reduce the oversupply through price decay, on the labor market through the decline of wages and the cycle of money, labor power and capital begins anew.

That is all that is written in the three volumes and that is absolutely nothing new, measured by the state of research and development of Political Economy in the middle of the 19th century. All this had been known to experts at the latest in 1776 when Adam Smith's *Wealth of Nations* had appeared, Marx, on the other hand, came to terms with his own ignorance and Engels blew it out of all proportion to make it appear "epochal."

It was Adam Smith who had already stated clearly that Labor and Land are the sources of all wealth. He recognizes economic conditions as conditions of social classes, although he is not one of those historians whom Marx mistakenly credits with this discovery. The French historians also based themselves upon the findings of the English Political Economists. Smith had grasped value/surplus value/profit/average profit as well as he had grasped the functions of money. In his definition, profit derives from unpaid labor and he determined the level of the necessary labor wages according to the fluctuating costs for the means of subsistence of the workers' families. Clearly, Smith condemned the social weaknesses of the early, still underdeveloped industrial society – even given all his positive valuation of the productive development - when he wrote[126] that "a society cannot be booming and happy, when its largest part should be poor and miserable."

Parts of the working class suffered during the times of Smith and Marx, as well as in the developing countries today, more from the underdevelopment of Capitalism than from the system in itself.

It has been remarked that even Smith had had precursors, whom he esteemed highly, like Petty and McCulloch. Both already had developed the Law of value – which Engels attributed to Marx and which the latter had never understood – and the labor theory of value, as well. Thus, Prof. Dr. Smith as the theorist and Ricardo as practitioner had jointly founded the theoretical structure of Classical Political Economy.

David Ricardo did his main work between 1814 and 1817, before Marx was born. He put the class difference between Capital and Labor into more precise relief. He called workers in invoking slavery "living tools" and he donated money out of his own pocket to their most prominent representative, the democratic Labor Communist, Robert Owen, whose ideas were later adapted by Weitling, including the one that money should be replaced by the introduction of time-units, in order to help mitigate the material misery of the English worker through their unionized/syndicalist self-help. Marx, as well, gave Belgian workers money out of his wife's funds, not for union projects but for political putsch attempts.

Ricardo demanded with great emphasis freedom of speech, press and freedom of congregation for the workers. He also developed the labor theory of value further and applied it to monetary theory. The categories labor wages, profit and land rent he developed further, as well. In foreign trade he created the theory of comparative costs for the international division of Labor, which still carries weight today etc., etc. In all that Ricardo underlined strongly the objective character of the economic laws and we shall not forget at this point that the English Classical Political Economy propelled the materialist conception of History significantly, especially in Germany. Smith and Ricardo as opposed to Marx were not denizens in an ivory tower, aloof from the real world. They were, from the horse's mouth, well informed through their professional life and their excellent circle of friends which included the greatest minds of the country in politics, economics and science, much in contrast to the two-man incest team, Marx-Engels. The genuinely classical writers in practice had abundant material for their research and analysis. They were able to generalize theoretically and they did not need to become ideological lunatics, instead, as Marx had mixed the ideology of Blanquism with the theories of Classical Political Economy, again coleslaw and turnips discombobulated together, highly-charged ideological French teachings grafted arbitrarily upon the economic substratum of Germany. Neither theory nor ideology - let's stay with agricultural metaphors - had been homegrown on Marx's own pile of manure. Nothing original grew there. While the classic writers rightly postulated the validity of the law of value for all eternity, or at least for as long as there was industrial production, Marx wrongly prophesied the abolition of the commodity production, of the law of value, of prices and of money. As opposed to and in contrast to the classic writers, Marx deduces "his communist demands" from the "necessary breakdown of the Capitalist mode of production that unfolds in front of our eyes more and more on a daily basis,"[127] as Engels put it. What broke down, instead, or better, apart, meanwhile, was the ideology of Marxism and the Marxist national economies lag behind the Capitalist mode of production in all decisive political and economic parameters. With the social ones it is different. Smith and Ricardo - long before Marx - had proven their empathy with the suffering of the nascent proletariat. Their successors elaborated in the first half of the 19th century, i.e., fifty years prior to Marx, the social components of their teachings that were critical of society, as well.

I have to add at this point that Party propaganda always held that the sources of Marxism – the classic German philosophy, the classic English Political Economy, the French teachings of Communism – were bourgeois theory, but their elements were, instead, proletarian ideology. This statement is outright false! From Classical Political Economy no Communist social teachings can be deduced. It is true, in turn, and that is being camouflaged, that the English, French and German Socialists and Communists did "produce" Marxism. Marx can, thus, not even show any original value of thought in his ideological deductions of Historical Philosophy or Political Economy, not even to mention in his theory!

Where English Classical Political Economy had mainly investigated the role of production and circulation in the genesis of national wealth, the Socialist-Communist successors of Ricardo turned mainly to the question of how the distribution of wealth could be managed with greater social justice. They came to speak of the theory of surplus value in an exceedingly perspicacious manner. As precursors of the Labor movement here, Bray, Gray, Hodskin and Tompkins should be particularly mentioned. These men defend in a manner intelligible to all workers the economic interests of the working class against the abuse of power of Capital. Even a Soviet colleague maintained that they had "brought to their logical conclusion the main consequence of this theory,"[128] which can only mean that Marx had not been able to do so anymore! Now, now, here we have these Russian cloak-and-dagger dissidents again! What a mess is brewing around our Master Charlie Crap.

Now even Marx himself owns, for example, that Hodskin had "understood the nature of Capital correctly,"[129] and I shall add, published it and made it known long before Marx! Marx, in the same breath and in the same passage, mentions the Communist, Bray, as well: "The workers, up to now, had given the Capitalists the Labor of an entire year in exchange for the value of half a year of Labor – and whence derived the inequality of power and wealth which now exists everywhere around." Are there still further questions regarding the alleged theory of surplus value of Marx? There you have it!

Hodskin, who held more brilliant, more differentiated and more realist views on original accumulation, on the accumulation of Capital, i.e., on societal Labor as a whole, etc., than Marx, which, had they been heeded in our real-existing Socialism instead of the phraseology of the latter, it would have saved society much trouble and the people much suffering. Thus, Hodskin virtually puts Marx's "second discovery" into his mouth: "Labor, the creatrix of all wealth, is not a commodity."[130] This can be garnered, nota bene, in Hodkin excerpts of Marx! And Marx has copied more from the anonymous source quoted above: *"If you call Labor a commodity, so it yet is not one..."* and then he adds: "what is brought to the market is, indeed, not Labor, but the Laborer. What he sells the Capitalist is not his Labor, but the temporary use of himself as a working power."[131] Indeed, not only Stein and Rodbertus, but the English Communists, as well, spoke of Labor power, hence derives this epochal discovery - as our second Johnny-come-lately Engels would have us believe - not from Marx; that alone is certain!

As to those for whom all this does not suffice, he or she may read Ricardo as he cites Destutt de Tracy: "As it is certain that our physical and spiritual capacities are our original wealth, the use of these capacities is a kind of Labor."[132] At this point, we have reached a position which lets the author of the anonymous writing say that the hairsplitting fight in Political Economy derives from the fact that words are used by different persons in a different sense.

Furthermore, Marx corroborates in his excerpts about the theory of surplus value, J.B. Say, as well, in that the latter "had made a giant discovery" when he wrote, that "commodities can only be bought by commodities," that, therefore, consequently not Labor, but Labor power be a commodity. Next to Stein, Rodbertus and others "labor power" is here spelled out in full, even in bold print, and Marx continues to "discover" it in the writings of Hodkin, Say and our anonymous writer: Thus, Marx was a terrific discoverer, let us here, for once, wholeheartedly agree with Engels.

For his own self-clarification not for publication - didn't we find that somewhere before? - Marx, thus, continues to write about this anonymous writing: "This barely-known pamphlet contains a drastic step above and beyond Ricardo. He designates the surplus value or profit directly, as Ricardo calls it (often also as surplus produce) or interest, as the author of the pamphlet calls it surplus labor..."[133] Marx makes a note to himself to the extent that this was already said by Smith and Ricardo, although not with the same clarity and absoluteness. Surplus value is, thus, defined unmistakably as unpaid surplus labor; its various forms are mentioned. Engels in his preface to *Capital* falsifies this into a discovery of Marx. As if the classical economists did not understand that surplus value can be produced either extensively or intensively! Only a cranky intellectual completely off his rocker and out of touch with the world can raise to the rank of a theory such absolutely rudimentary and self-evident truths! Marx contradicts his hairsplitting thoughts on absolute and relative surplus value again in the 14th chapter of *Capital* vol. I completely in the sense of these dialectic - it would be better to say sophistic - smoke screen and mirror sleights-of-hand, of which Ruge accuses Marx, with which, as it is well known, everything and nothing can be proven.

What is, thus, left of the "cornerstone" of Marxist theory?

The old story from part I: Hast thou not stolen the goose, or Gans, i.e., from the German classical theorists - then thou hast stolen from the Classical English economists! Marx acknowledges in his notes again written only for self-clarification that the author of the anonymous pamphlet had already traced back all surplus value to surplus labor and that he called the general form of surplus value, in spite of its concrete forms of profit, land rent and monetary interest, "interest of Capital." But that is unscientific in Marx-Engels view! Scientific, on the other hand, is "their" concept of surplus value! The reason is that he creates surplus value from surplus labor and surplus product. The English are speaking "slang," Marx with his hyper-Hegelian mumbo-jumbo, on the other hand, creates pure science! Really?!? And that, the English author writes, in essence, these discombobulations should be discontinued in linguistically separating neatly between the content of the different concepts, which he did, indeed, and which Marx could have learned in kindergarten, had he only attended it.

To summarize:

Surplus value equals unpaid labor, that according to Classical Political Economy, according to Socialist and Communist economics, according to German Political Science, and it is being produced by exploited Labor. As usual, Marx as perennial Johnny-come-lately, seizes this fact last, but then raises the claim to be the exclusive discoverer. In the reverse - in a backhanded way - this statement is correct, but never mind that! We of the "real" Socialism are always ahead and if being ahead means behind, then we are behind ahead with Comrade Crap!

Plagued by a bad conscience Marx, in the first volume of his *Capital*, does not breathe a word of from where he derived all his wisdom. Engels is trying to camouflage the plagiarism in the second volume of his do-it-yourself-work, in waxing eloquent about Marx having quoted Hodskin in the first volume. That he did, indeed: The quotes there are so discombobulated that truth is turned into its contrary. Just now we saw the extremely positive valuation that Marx gave Say in his notes used for self-clarification. Who feels like it may open *Capital*, volume I, and check in the index under Say and then read the published text. Say is mentioned in about a dozen footnotes, never in the text, and how? Lo and behold: "This Jeremiah who dissolves the half-truths, truisms and fallacies of Adam Smith in resounding general phrases of no significance, He who has otherwise brought forth nothing but "trivialities." "Say, who gets lost in phraseology," "the nullities of Say," etc. This makes up for a fine self-portrait of the snotty arrogance and mean insincerity of Marx. Have Bakunin and Loria exaggerated their case? By no means, if anything, they have understated it!

But that is still not enough. The professional plagiarizer, Marx, is accusing Say, of all people, of plagiarism. He is crying wolf and in the old time-honored tradition of, thus, trying to detract attention from the real culprit, he is showering with invectives the very people from whom he has copied "his" main tenets.

"The manner in which he exploited the Physiocrats at the time lost writings for the furthering of his own 'value' demonstrates the following example: The famous phrase of Monsieur Say 'products can only be bought with products' (on his sheets for self-clarification he wrote: commodities) appears in the original as 'produce can only be paid with produce'."[134] Thus, produce, product, commodity against commodity - the commodity science be praised as the only genuine science, the scientist Comrade Crap as the only genuine scientist, the genuine commodity Marxism-Crapism. All genuine commodity is compromised and can be bought; everything genuine is, therefore, genuinely venal!

Just to recapitulate: Marx started his analysis in his *Capital* with the subject commodity and its form of value and he maintains with a straight face in two thousand years of scientific history nobody within the human species had managed to solve the riddle of commodity and its value – HE alone has managed to do so. This is awesome: How could humanity have gotten along for two thousand years without genuine production of commodities, without sales and purchases, without Marx?

Following the exposition of the economic "achievement and performance" of Marx, it is as yet necessary to give an exposition of his political and social deductions. "The greater social wealth, functional Capital, scope and energy of its growth and, therefore, the absolute quantity of the proletariat and the productive power of its Labor, the greater would be the industrial reserve army. The labor power at disposition is being developed by the same causes as the expansive power of Capital. The relative quantity of the industrial reserve army, thus, grows with the potencies of wealth. But the greater the industrial reserve army in relation to the active labor army, the greater the consolidated overpopulation, whose misery stands in inverse proportion to their labor pangs. The greater, finally, the Lazarus strata of the working class and the industrial reserve army, the greater would be pauperism. *This is the absolute general law of capitalist accumulation* ... that in the measure in which Capital is accumulated, the conditions of the workers, however high or low their payment, have to become worse. The very law finally that keeps the relative overpopulation and industrial reserve army constantly in equilibrium with the scope and energy of the accumulation, is forging the worker tighter to Capital than Prometheus was tied to the rock by Hephaestus. An accumulation of misery analogous to the accumulation of Capital is engendered. The accumulation of wealth on the one pole is also an accumulation of misery, labor pangs, slavery, ignorance, brutalizing and moral degradation at the counter-pole."[135] ...

A commentary of this "theory of misery or miseration" from which Marx was seriously expecting social revolution is superfluous. This kind of thing disqualifies itself. Where does an "absolute law" reign here, where Marx had generally "proven" that social laws are only effective tendentially? Or, one may ask any Labor union member what he or she, for example, thinks of this ridiculous "theory of wages"? The political conclusion that Marx draws reads as follows: "The centralizing of the means of production and the socializing of Labor do reach a point, where they become unbearable with their capitalist shell. The shell is, thus, exploded. The bell is tolling for the private property of the Capitalist. The expropriator is getting expropriated."[136]

To assure that the genuine Marxists in our country will not get irritated I shall quote what is the party line:

"As long as there are capitalists and workers in the world, no book has ever appeared that would have an equal importance for the worker,"[137] as Engels decreed with regard to *Capital*.

"In *Capital*, Marx founded the central category of Historical Materialism, the economic formation of society,"[138] was the proclamation of the Central Committee of the Socialist Unity Party and First Party Secretary Ulbricht highlighted, furthermore, that the materialist conception of History, as Lenin stressed, had progressed from a hypothesis to a scientific theory. Good Lord, Walter! Now the science that was decidedly to have been founded according to Marx in 1858 has been relegated again nine years further down? Had Vladimir been aware of that at all?

What Marx did think about the expropriation of the expropriators we shall have a look at now. Here we have his sole concrete manual for action. And those priceless pearls of wisdom can be found in his Critique of the Gotha Program of the German Social Democracy.

2.The *Ignored Marginal Notes of the Gotha Convention of the German Social Democratic Party* of 1875

The *Marginal Notes* together with the *Manifesto* and *Capital I* make up the most important documents of Marxism. In my analysis I am not concerned here with the political aspects, which are merely the repetition of the known thesis of the dictatorship of the proletariat, but with the predictions that Marx made about the establishing of Communism. According to the official Party jargon it is here that he "first uttered the thought of the two phases of Communist society."[139]

Now, whatever he is quoting there - the transitional period, first the Socialist and then Communist phase, the abolition of private property and money, the temporal issuing of 'labor notes' instead of money - all that can be found in Owen and Weitling, in Fourier and the St. Simonists. Marx is calling all these utopians, as he does Reybaud as early as 1841. He, nevertheless, took over from them everything that he deemed usable, including the concept of the formation of society, and hence he himself remained a utopian. Today's Marxists still hold the utopians were unscientific, because they had been unable to say how the new Communist formation of society was to be established. Marx, on the other hand, was supposed to have shown the way, the way of the dictatorship of the proletariat that is. Without any kind of dictatorship whatsoever the Labor movement had been able to create a social-democratic model, as for instance in Sweden, with a degree of personal freedom and a standard of living, for which they can only be envied by workers who are living in a dictatorship. But let's stick to History. Why did Marx criticize the German Social Democrats?

In the year 1875, Germany saw the unification of the Socialist German Labor Party and the General German Workers' Association, a.k.a. the "Eisenachians" [from the homonymous East German town] and the Lassalleans. The men from Eisenach, under the leadership of Bebel, Liebknecht, Auer, Geib and Bracke, tended ideologically more towards Marx than Lassalle, who, at the stage, when the debates about the unification of the two parties entered their decisive phase, had been dead for a decade. Marx now saw his chance to exclude the dead Lassalle from the programs of the German Labor movement. Lassalle had been the great antagonist, whom Marx feared during the former's lifetime as he had supported him financially and as he had been his spiritual and mental superior. The low-brow, even anti-Semitic spite, which Marx and Engels had poured over Lassalle in their letters, now became public disguised merely in theoretical form. Marx could never overcome the envy when hearing Germany's workers sing: The trail which had blazed Lassalle daringly we follow!

Lassalle had dared everything in Germany, while Marx shot off smart-alecky commentaries from the safe shelter of English democracy, the same deal as when he acted as the editor-in-chief of the legally safe Rhineland, when others drew fire in Berlin.

Now when Marx was writing the *Marginal Notes* of the *Gotha Party Program*, something remarkable happened: Although the Eisenach Party leadership, among them Marx's friend Wilhelm Liebknecht, were in disagreement with only a few passages of the outline, they insulted Marx completely. They filed away the accompanying letter from Bracke that came with the *Marginal Notes* without even losing a word about it. That shows how even "Marxist" leaders thought about the "classic" writer Marx. Again and again, just like during his exclusion from the Communist Party, Marx, the self-proclaimed erstwhile sectarian chief of sectarian chieftains, was not heeded by the movement of the proletariat!

Marx's criticism of the program was only published in 1891, at the occasion of the preparation of the Party Convention in Erfurt in the *Neue Zeit* [New Times], the Social Democrat weekly. Engels, not the Party leadership, made it public after Marx had died and the theoretical heads of the Party had become bound to Engels through personal contact and financial support. In this manner, Marxism became theoretically preponderant within the program of German Social Democracy. Practically, thank God, it never became a force.

When Engels published the marginal notes, he deleted the most offensive expressions of Marx, as he had always corrected the autodidactic economist. Marx, by the way, had announced in his letter to Wilhelm Bracke from May 5, 1875, that he and Engels would distance themselves from the program at the convention. As the leadership of the Social Democrats proved to be completely unimpressed by this announcement, Marx refrained from following it up. He had been severely humiliated. Nobody in Germany accepted our self-proclaimed leader of all working men! How could someone outside of the Party, outside of the country, outside of the people, have the gall to dictate to the German workers their program? The German working class in the 19th century was as suspicious of the remote control from the West as it was of the remote control from the East in the 20th. For the German Communist Party in 1946, the Marxist principles and tactics from 1875 were valid, when it came to unifying with the Soviet Zone Social Democrats under Otto Grotewohl. The criticism of this unification by Marx is still highly regarded by today's Socialist Unity Party, as they believe, in view of the many small potential Grotewohls of today's Social Democratic Party which the West section of the Central Committee imagines to identify, that

History could repeat itself. Marx felt in 1875, as did the German Communist Party in 1945, that the Social-democratic system of thought of Ferdinand Lassalle needed to be completely erased for the Communistic views of Marx. This is expressed in his criticism of the Gotha Program as follows:[140]

He is writing in the first section, "that the human being that has no other property than his labor power has to be the slave of the other human beings in all societal and cultural states," who have made themselves proprietors of the material conditions of Labor. The former can work only by permission of the latter, thus, he can *live* only by their permission. That is, indeed, correct. This is especially true for our unreal Socialism, as there we have only one and sole, omnipotent employer without competition and that is the One-Party State. The Party controls everything without being controlled in turn. Those who like to emigrate will get fired. Thus, they become by Party definition antisocial and, therefore, risk imprisonment. Catch 22! If they are lucky they regain their freedom through West German marks.[141] Was it that freedom Marx was thinking of when he felt in his youth that everything should revolve around the freedom of man?

The most important part of the criticism of the program consists of the fact that Marx is here talking for the first and last time in concrete terms about the Communist organization of the distribution of the popular revenue created by Labor and of the construction of a new social order. His instructions are as follows: "Within the society that is founded upon the unionized society based on holding the means of production in common, producers do not exchange their products; in like manner, the Labor used for the creation of these products does not appear as value of these products, as a material quality possessed by them, as now, as opposed to Capitalist society, the individual works do not exist in a roundabout way, but directly as elements of the general labor."

In plain terms this reads: Marx is speaking of products, not of commodities, i.e., use values are not sold, but they are directly distributed without money, the market is a detour. So much is clear. What is not clear is whether he is speaking of cooperative or syndicalist production, i.e., a kind of workers' self-government or of a central State planning. These outpourings of Marx are simultaneously and correctly quoted by the Communist Party of the Soviet Union, as well as the Communist Party of Yugoslavia for their widely diverging economic models! Here the general prognosis from *Capital* about the annihilation of the Capitalist production of commodities and the abolition of money is reiterated in more detail and in this manner Lenin and his Supreme Economic Council have used it successfully to the complete ruin of the Russian economy, because, as Marx continues: "What we are dealing with is a Communist society, not as it developed upon its own base, but on the contrary, as it emerges now out of the Capitalist society, that is, emerges in every respect, economically, ethically, mentally, still tainted by the features of the old society, out of whose womb it came. Consequently, the individual producer - after deductions - receives exactly what he gives. What he has given is his individual labor quantity. Let's say the social working day consists of the sum of the individual working hours. The individual working time of the individual producer is his delivered part of the social working day, i.e., his share thereof. He receives a certificate from society, that he has delivered so much Labor (after deductions of his work for the communal fund), and he is drawing, by virtue of this certificate, from the societal stock of consumption goods as much as an equal amount of Labor costs. The same quantity of Labor that he has given to society in one form he receives back in another. Apparently, the same principle here rules that regulates the exchange of commodities, as far as it concerns an equivalent exchange. Content and form are changed, as under the changed circumstances nobody can give anything else but his or her Labor and as on the other hand, nothing can become individual property except individual means of consumption. Although with regard to the distribution of the latter the same principle rules as with regard to the exchange of commodity equivalents, there is always the same quantity of Labor in one form exchanged against the same quantity of Labor in another form."[142]

Let's translate that again: The worker does not receive money, but a certificate, see many writers, last Owen and Weitling, who say the same thing and see Lenin, who practiced it! On the certificate a time unit is registered. Here we may regard the consummate incapacity of Marx, which prompted the German economists to say that he had overslept an entire century of economic science. We might as well make that two hundred years, because simply time does not equal time. Time as a measure of value is something else than a mere time unit. Marx never comprehended the first thing about the law of value.

On a pluralistic basis, given the competition, time is contracted and condensed. Thus, the time spent and, accordingly, the value per each use value is tendentially lowered. In full use of the working time, with careful preparation of production, with the continuity of production (and so on) a higher efficacy is attained than if there is sloth and lack of motivation of the labor force.

Nevertheless, the real performance can be only determined in the market and only by way of the price mechanism. The highest-performing producer can supply most cheaply, bring down the prices and either eliminate the competition or limit it. But precisely this mechanism Marx would want to have annihilated by his unified economic property structure. In lieu of objectively effective economic laws now you have the planning bureaucracy which regularly fails according to plan. Marxism produces within the system of "real" Socialism against the laws of motion of industrial production, which Marx has plagiarized without comprehending them. The working day of society does not consist, as Marx writes, of the sum of the individual working hours, but it consists of the highly differing and varied performance(s) achieved in that time! Even St. Simon had come up with the postulate for Socialism that Marx made the leitmotif of it: "Everyone according to his or her capacities, everyone according to his or her performance." But: Performance can no longer be measured after the abolition of money and price! Nobody in the Socialist Bloc today still thinks about following Marx and abolish money, as this was done at first in the Soviet Union and later attempted in other Socialist countries. Even from that standpoint Marx is as dead as a doorknob; the more they are trying to resuscitate him ideologically. The worker, in fact, does not draw from the common stock of goods by way of a "certificate." The whole of Communism actually is nothing but a "certified" appearance! Apparently there is an entirely different principle at work than the one that Marx is teaching, as one hour is one hour equivalent in minutes and seconds, but not in work performance and value!

But since value has to be determined, how else would it be possible to plan on all levels; arbitrary subjectivity in our "real" Socialism takes the place of real macroeconomic parameters. Here lies the crucial issue that explains why our victorious Socialism, in matters of high technology and economic performance, is falling permanently behind the moribund and dying imperialism, whose death many ardently wish for in this, our country and does not get anywhere near the levels of labor productivity of the Capitalist industrial countries! The conflict of end and means in the economic ideology of Marx is clearly and painfully apparent. Our "real" Socialism is economically speaking nothing more than State Capitalism half-castrated. Formally there exist against the teachings of Marx money and the production of commodities, but de facto the monetary functions and the law of value are stifled: The prices are derived administratively. The whole dilemma of all attempts and approaches to liberalize, improve and all other economic reform waves rests on just that untenable principle of Marx. The story will continue in the same old - same old manner and we will always run increasingly behind the State Capitalism of the West as we have done since 1917 and 1945. Our "real" Socialism will not instigate an economic reform unless an ideological reform is instigated previously!

That "content and form" of the economic laws are going to be changed in Socialism, Marx was aware of; what he didn't see was that they would be distorted beyond recognition. His way of thinking developed in ideological not in theoretical terms. And even here he is falling back into the antiquated theory and he speaks of "Labor," not of his epochal "labor power." Perhaps Marx himself was not, after all, a full-bodied, genuine Marxist?

In the second part we find those passages in Marx, which had been wrong in his *Capital* and now that they have become superannuated and antiquated, did not get any better in the process, "that the system of labor wages be a system of slavery ..., which will become harder to that extent as the societal productive forces of Labor become developed, regardless of whether the worker gets more or less pay." Close the Unions, Comrades, and don't mind the low wages! It is the same old, broken record since the days of the articles of Metvissen in the *Rheinische Zeitung.* From 1842 to 1875, Marx had not learned one new thing; he sticks by his theory of miseration - an absolute misery, indeed!

Now there was one item among all the items of the program which was meant to fight the possibly worst form of misery: namely the misery of child labor. The workers were peremptorily demanding its prohibition. What did Marx have to say about it? He based himself on the foundation of Prusso-German law: "Here it becomes absolutely necessary to give the age limit. A general prohibition of child labor is incommensurable with the existence of heavy industry ..." It may be well to read this egregious phrase of this genuine friend of all great and small human beings again and again! Should the Party leadership have insisted upon bringing this to the attention of the delegates? Perhaps, then the publication of those shameful sentences 15 years later, written for the event of the Party convention in Erfurt and its programmatic debates, would then have become moot. Perhaps the deputies of the unification convention would have welcomed it if Marx had told them that in furtherance of this brainstorm, he had sent his daughters to the factory of his friend Engels for the purpose of their exploitation from their tender age bracket on upward? Or were these Marxian ruminations about child labor meant only for proletarian children and not the children of the Baroness of Westphalia, as Mrs. Marx was wont to print on her calling cards? The workers, Marx continued to lecture, uttered all those noble, pious thoughts. The prohibition of child labor would be "reactionary," in Marx's view, because the regulation of working time and workers' protection, i.e., the "early conjunction of productive Labor with instruction would be one of the most powerful means of transformation in today's society." Long live the cultural revolutionary Marx with his shock troops of minors and underage!

We still have to look at the "corrections" of the Marxian hobbyhorse as he is speaking here in his programmatic criticism not merely of dictatorship, but of the "revolutionary" dictatorship of the proletariat in the transitional period of Capitalism to Socialism, which is meant to let the statist suppression of the population wither away.

Yes, today's Marxists-Crapists take this very seriously, as they did with his proposals as to money and the other recipes. They explain how the role of the State becomes more important and elaborate and how the Party would grow and grow; thus, they have applied Marx creatively and turned the practice into the opposite of the ideology.

In his *Critique*, Marx, by the way is rendering homage to the humanistic tradition of freedom of conscience in his inimitable way: "Anyone may have to execute his or her religious as well as physical execration without the Party putting its nose into the matter." This maxim is really practiced in our real-existing Socialism. The Party stays away. Only the Secret Service, completely unaffiliated with any one party in our One-Party State, puts its nose into the matter, as we may see with reference to the murder of the Polish priest Popieluszko.

After these passages Marx is repeating the theses that caused the French Socialists and Communists in the *French-German Annuals* not to cooperate, as in his eyes the "toleration of the bourgeois 'freedom of conscience' would be nothing but the toleration of all manner of religious freedoms of conscience." As we can see, even here he has not learned anything new! Oversimplification and dogmatization writ large, in youth as in old age! Religious thought, an inalienable human right, he demands to abolish. His ideas of freedom of conscience are scandalous and barbaric.

At this point, Rosa Luxemburg's criticism of Lenin becomes valid, who thought in this matter just as Marx did: Freedom is always the freedom of those who think differently! And Karl Liebknecht, Wilhelm Liebknecht's son, simply and wholeheartedly rejected the Marxian theory of History in its entirety. At the cradle of the German Communist Party in the 20th century we find the same basic attitude of Marx's critics as that of the Association of Communists in the middle of the 19th century. In the 19th century the cardinal criticism was directed against the personal-dictatorial claim of power of Marx himself; in the 20th century it was directed against the practice of the Marxist dictatorship of Lenin. How the leading minds of the German Labor movement felt between those two periods can be gathered from the fact that they rejected Marx's criticism of their *Gotha Program* and further, most essential here likely was the position of August Bebel with regard to the Party principles of Marx, which were formulated in the last statutes of the Marxist splinter group, Association of Communists, which brought about the institution of the leader's personality cult.

The Central Party archives of the Central Committee of the Socialist Unity Party contain[143] the literary estate of the longstanding functionary of the Hamburg Labor movement, Joachim Friedrich Martens, with the explicit injunction: No right of publication! This estate contains a hitherto unpublished letter to Martens from October 20, 1867. Bebel herein explains his positions towards the democratic principle of organization and he adds in a passage marked "confidential" that he had instituted an "outpost" [Vorort] instead of a "committee" that would be in the position to *control the leadership.* This "outpost" principle goes back to the democratic structure of organization of the General German Workers' Fraternization lead by Stefan Born, whose Central Committee was effective and in session during the year 1850 in Leipzig, as well.

This now is crucial: Bebel early on took issue with the organizational principles of Marx, when the continuous committee of the convention managed the affairs of the later Social Democratic Labor Party, a.k.a. the "Eisenachians," although he had joined the First International one year prior to his letter to Martens. Bebel anchored the democratic principle of organization deeply in the bylaws of the Eisenach Party. He let a control commission be convened to exclude any flights of despotism of the leading functionaries. Again the local members were supposed to vote for the control commission and the latter had the right to dismiss management, just like in the bylaws of the democratic Labor Communists prior to Marx!

There are other interesting, unpublished documents in the literary estate of Martens. One John Philip Becker, who was leader of the popular militia in 1849 in Southwest Germany, and as of 1860 Marxist partisan, and publisher of the organ *Vorboten* [Vanguard] of the International Labor Association, wrote to Martens on January 31, 1873, from Geneva: "Future generations are, of course, going to establish new ideals well above our current concepts and the spiritual and ethical warfare will intensify as it continues to last. The realm of heaven lies in the way to the realm of heaven!"

One is inclined to believe that one is listening to the Wilhelm Weitling of 1849 or to the Edward Bernstein of the end of the 19th century - these men were all more realist in their political ideals than the utopian Marx. Today they are all - except Bernstein - co-opted by the Communist Party propaganda like Bebel, Liebknecht and Luxemburg, to reconstruct a line of continuity that fits the latest ideological matrix.

In the G.D.R. the forgery and falsification hit rock bottom in the cases of Luxemburg and Liebknecht. The Socialist Unity Party under Ulbricht ran a smear campaign against "Luxemburgism" as a perverted variant of the Social Democratic ideology. Did she not underestimate the role of the Party and was, thus, an adherent of the theory of spontaneity? Had she not criticized Marx and Lenin's theory of accumulation because of its arbitrary rule? The traditional line of the

Socialist Unity Party was still upheld in portraits of Marx, Engels, Bebel and Liebknecht as late as 1968. Now this is different, not only with the Communist reconceived concept of Prussia and its Fredericks, but also with the Janus-faced Luther, the enemy of the peasants, as well as with Rosa Luxemburg. We now celebrate an organized annual pilgrimage to their graves headed by the Polit Bureau of the Central Committee as far as they can walk.

We know how deeply democratic was the thought of Rosa Luxemburg. What was the thought of Karl Liebknecht, her wayfarer, fighting comrade and founder of the Party? Here are the following summary valuations of Marxism, which refer to the materialist and economic conception of History. Liebknecht wrote "Studies of the Laws of Motion in Social Development," the same laws of motion to which was already made reference above:

> "*The Materialist Conception of History – A Critical Summary*
>
> It is not 'materialist,' has not a shred of materialism in it, at least not in its genuine, philosophic sense; only, perhaps, with regard to a materialism in its vulgar-moralizing sense. But then not even that!! As the ideologues of all spheres and the surplus sphere, as well, have their 'economic conditions', their 'economic base', their 'social structure' and their 'feudum.'[144]
>
> Even the materialist conception of History is in its main lines a psychic-intellectual one, i.e., the factors that it regards as essential, are mainly psychic-intellectual ones.
>
> They are not in the least 'economic.'
>
> It proceeds from food and reproduction at the base, but leaves the shelter and surplus sphere out of consideration.
>
> It makes the equation food = Labor, although the spheres of shelter, sexuality and surplus need Labor, as well.
>
> The entire economic sphere is conceived in too narrow and distorted a manner.
>
> The 'ideological superstructure' is insufficient and even wrongly defined. The relationship between ideology and 'economic conditions' is misunderstood.
>
> The ideologies are falsely limited as they regard even all that which has become 'economic conditions,' economic base, social structure and even that which has become feudum and the reproductive and nutritional sphere as ideology, although the psychic-spiritual element defined in such a manner, that goes together with the merely physical one, be it dualistically, be it monistically, as 'body' and 'soul,' make up the spiritual-psychic content, the spiritual-psychic essence of the socially regulating factor. What is there 'materialistic' about even these socially

regulatory factors, about the economic conditions? They have next to the material a spiritual-psychic essence throughout, through which they alone are related to human society, which alone makes them social appearances.

Within the essence of the Social the non-material element is already contained.

In their last modifications (by Engels) the theory has again become so indistinct, so isolated that it loses its entire characteristic formation – just like in the definition of my father [Wilhelm Liebknecht]."[145]

In such a critical manner the much esteemed and experienced German Labor leader, Karl Liebknecht, regarded the heritage of Marx. Had he and Luxemburg not been murdered they would never have allowed the following Stalinization and the complete Encrampment of the Communist Party of Germany. We are back with Marx, said Rosa Luxemburg during the founding party convention of the Communist Party of Germany at the end of 1918, under his banner, but what kind of a banner that was in the positive sense she knew as little as Liebknecht. Marx stood alone for the programmatic postulate familiar and clear since the Chartists' movement: The working class was meant to take over the political power. Rosa Luxemburg had an entirely unbiased approach to Marx; she even spoke of the "garbage chamber" of Marxism.[146] In contrast to Lenin who clung to Marx with a dogged dogmatism, she looked at the things the way they were.

In spite of all the alleged "science" of Marx, the leading minds of the German Communist Party of the 20th century were badly endowed. And that was true, as well, for their co-fighters. They "had only rather hazy notions of how to achieve Marxism. That had to put a damper on the development of the revolution just like the policies of the opportunistic forces,"[147] Neues Deutschland wrote on the occasion of the 66th anniversary of the October Revolution. At times you can find truth even in the most unexpected places, i.e., in the central organ of the Central Committee of the Socialist Unity Party! It is unfortunately, not yet, possible to forge everything. N.D. should only have added that these extreme obscure and impossible notions came directly from our ever so revered classical writers of Marxism.

Let us now turn to the question how Lenin in practice dealt with instructions of Marx and how today's practice of our real-existing Socialism deals with the rather contrarian and clumsy economic ideology of his,

3. Lenin's Application of the Marxist Ideology for the Construction of Socialism and its Refutation in Practice

"The classic writers of Marxism-Leninism regarded the machine-driven mass production with an organic separation of Labor and a respective interconnected technology as the adequate base for Socialism. That was the perspective mapped out in theory. In practice, however, the Socialist revolutions have not found those conditions in one single national economy of one single country."[148]

This is another way of explaining the entire disregard of the "theory" of Marx by Lenin and the Stalinists in practice in a rather cavalier manner. In the official lingo of the Party, not of one member, but of the entire Central Committee of the Communist Party of the Soviet Union, the same insight today reads as follows: "In his reflections on the peculiarities of our revolution Lenin, in his last work, came to the following conclusions: 'that the general laws of development of the entire world history, single stages of development which constitute a particularity either in form or in sequence of development, but in no way exclude that, are, on the contrary, to be accepted' – 'Modifications of the accustomed historical sequence.' 'Accustomed sequence' for him meant the attainment of such a level of development of the productive forces and of culture, as is necessary for the construction of Socialism. As Lenin clearly states, such a level has not been reached by the Old Russia. The victory of the Great Socialist October Revolution has made of it immediately the most progressive country in respect to politics. The modification of the historical sequence following the thought of Lenin consisted in the workers and peasants getting power, at first to overcome on that basis the material-technical retrogression of the country and bring the productive forces up to a world level. Some of our present problems and difficulties are historically linked directly to the tasks engendered by the modifications of the 'accustomed sequence' and to the fact that they have not been solved to a thorough degree. Their full solution will bring the broadest range to the unfolding of the advantages of Socialism in all areas of social life up to the gradual transition to the stage of Communism."[149]

To resume: In no country has the practice of "real" Socialism corresponded to the Marxist theory. If we are being told the contrary by the Communist Party of the Soviet Union, then even the most pious neo-Stalinists in the Socialist Unity Party of Germany will believe it. They will, nevertheless, believe in Marx, because that in their eyes is dialectical thinking. I myself have lived long enough in this intellectual prison, so I understand that mindset well enough.

In the context of the discussions of the new Party Program of the Communist Party of the Soviet Union, the debates are astoundingly open and taboos are, if not broken, at least discussed in a critical manner. "To these topics belongs the issue of socio-political crisis in the development of the Socialist countries."[150]

The political crisis in Soviet Russia is generally considered as the summit of these crises, which reached its climax with the Kronstadt uprising. It was an inner conflict. The "dictatorship of the proletariat" had to suppress the sons of workers and peasants militarily, put them before a military court and then before the firing squads, just as the czar had done before it - four years after the so-called Great Socialist October Revolution!

How could it have come to that? The Kronstadt uprising was no isolated incident; strikes, demonstrations, peasant revolts were the order of the day. Why?

Not because Lenin had ignored the instructions of Marx from his *Critique of the Gotha Program*, but precisely because he had heeded it, the bloody conflict between the popular masses and the party had come about! But just that patent fact is denied even today. The responsibility, according to the official version, was not that of the impossible ideology of Marxism, the responsibility was not that of the party, but the responsibility was that of the ignorant and lethargic masses! Let us listen to a Soviet author in whose article the whole discussion of that program culminates: "A role is played here by the concept of 'war-time Communism' with regard to the development of the revolution and the attainment of its goals. Lenin has this to say about it: 'We, who are being carried by the wave of enthusiasm, we, who have awakened the enthusiasm of the people - at least the general political one and then the military one, as well - we counted upon solving the great immediate economic tasks directly (as well as the general political and military ones) upon the basis of this enthusiasm.' In other words, it was believed to be possible to 'achieve the immediate transition to Communist production and distribution.' This transition was connected to the following measures: the nationalization of all possible forms of economic activity; the centralization of the economic and political management; the expropriation of the bourgeoisie, including the country bourgeoisie; forced labor of all working men, including the mobilization of the work force for the key areas (militarization of Labor); general duty to work and other unpaid Labor; concentration of the entire surplus product in the hands of the State; leveling of the material conditions and transition to the leveling victuals exchange system of the distribution by the State; reduction of the role of economic stimuli to a minimum. That was - if you wish - the socio-economic model of 'war-time Communism'. This model geared towards the transition to Communism was by no means a voluntarist invention of the Bolsheviks, but the expression of the aspirations of the revolutionary masses of the country, the urban proletariats and the poverty of the villages. The 'communization' was effected and even forced above all from below, while Lenin in this period repeatedly called for the slowing down of the pace of nationalization, the building of the communes, etc."[151]

Once I am going to quote other sources we will see how mendacious this depiction really is. 'War-time Communism', of course, instituted military leadership methods everywhere, as long as there was war and civil war, but this was by no means the most typical feature of this policy, but the direct transition to Communism was to be implemented! Marx had wanted the proletarian revolution in Germany seventy years ahead of Lenin. Why would Lenin not have wanted to have it? And in the following our Soviet author cannot deny the questionable character of this wanna-be-communist experiment: "Contained in this model is a certain utopianism. Even Fidel Castro, who nourished similar views in the 1960s, had to admit as much, self-critically. The aim - the direct transition to Communism without intermediary stages - apparently, had been set at too high a level; it did not correspond to the realistic and particularly the economic possibilities of the country, its cultural level, as well as the socio-psychological readiness of the majority of the population. Even in Vietnam the keeping of the methods of 'war-time Communism' objectively hindered the economic development, a conclusion the Vietnamese Comrades had reached themselves. Like contradictions exist today in other economically-underdeveloped countries, as well, who have chosen the Socialist path of development.

By the way, Lenin ... remarked, 'that there apparently exists a law that demands of the revolution to go beyond that which it can cope with.'

This utopianism derived mainly from a revolutionary 'romanticism' of the masses ..."[152]

In plain English this reads as follows: As within the cadres of the Communist Party of the Soviet Union the truth about the New Economic Policy [N.E.P.], which should actually be called the Old Economic Policy, had never been published. Some of Lenin's successors stumbled into the same trap, which would lead them to the brink of self-destruction! Today this is being corrected as the Russians are no longer capable of safeguarding economically the overzealous Socialist experiment of certain developing countries.

Suddenly, the inner crises of our "real" Socialism may be publicly identified as a warning to those putschistic adventurers from certain countries, who are not paying heed to any objective or subjective preconditions. Nevertheless, the Cubans, Vietnamese, etc., followed faithfully the sole concrete, immediate directives of Marx and Engels, as both regarded the transitional period as very short and they advocated introducing labor money, that is, time-certificates and direct product distribution early on in the Socialist phase. It appears strange that the illiterate masses of Russia would know all that so precisely. Or did that have to be attributed to the "leading role" of the Party? Or was the Party, on the contrary, defenselessly exposed to the onslaught of the Communist uprising masses and could they not lead them? Riddles are here piled upon riddles! Let's proceed methodically and sequentially to solve them and we shall find that this "certain utopianism" really will reveal itself as the accomplished utopia of Marx himself!

It was none other than Lenin himself, and not some subordinate flunkey, who stipulated the "abolition of the commodity-oriented organization of the economy and their substitution by a communal, Communist organization, in which the market would no longer be the regulator of production, but the producers themselves, the community of the workers."[153] That, to a T, is the position of Marx. The law of value as the regulator of anarchic production is meant to yield to planned production itself and that presupposes communal instead of private conditions of property. Commodity production, so teaches Lenin, is Capitalist production under all circumstances - note the method, here we have the same over-extreme and over-dogmatic position as the one of Marx! - or it will transition into it.[154] Therefore, Lenin demanded right after his putsch, which stood in complete contrast to the Marxist "theory of revolution," to institute the exchange of products, i.e., to abolish purchase and sales, trade and money, especially to exchange industrial against agricultural products. For that reason also, he ordered, as early as at the end of October 1917, to capture the population by force in so-called consumer syndicates.[155]

Lenin, like Marx, was expecting to achieve a drastic increase of the productive forces from the abolition of commodity production and, therefore, an immediate material supremacy of the New Order above Capitalism. What happened, instead, was an economic catastrophe! After three years it had become too embarrassingly big to hide. Our anti-Capitalist revolutionary, Lenin, who had just established the dictatorship against the proletariat and the peasantry of Russia, as Luxemburg had correctly written, discovered suddenly - and, thus, qualifying himself as the greatest counter-revolutionary - that the system of State Capitalism (as it had been developed particularly in Germany under the conditions of World War I, that is, the imperialist war and coercion economy) was actually the better model for Russia than the one of the German, Marx. "I'm saying that State Capitalism would actually be the remedy for us ... because State Capitalism is something centralized, well controlled, well calculated and socialized and it is that, precisely, what we are missing."[156] That is what he wrote after the Peace Treaty of Brest-Litovsk. These are the extreme liberties Lenin was now taking with Marx: The dictatorship of the proletariat has to be established in order to implement State Capitalism in Russia! Could we not have had this in an easier and cheaper way? The dictatorship of the proletariat now suddenly served to resuscitate and reinstitute the toppled, underdeveloped Russian Capitalism more perfectly upon a German base - is it possible to reach a more moronic conclusion? What had been Loria's question? When had there ever been a greater suicide in theory, and we may add in practice, than here? From here on the insurmountable contrast between ideology and practice of our unrealistically-existing Socialism is now fully apparent!

To add insult to injury, simultaneously with this "escape" Lenin praised the solid work ethics of the non-revolutionary workers of Western Europe and juxtaposed it after 1917 unfavorably - can that be believed? - with the miserable work ethics of the Russian worker.[157] This problem, as it is well known, does exist until today. The root of this problem lies not in the least in the laziness of the Russian worker or peasant, but a political system, which is lethal to the spirit, nerves, will power and performance of the people and which is regarded by them as an exploitative dictatorship, which is best fought by a permanent performance refusal in the sectors of industry, agriculture, transport and services. In former times revolutionary crises came about through the higher development of the productive forces. The real-existing disorder of Socialism today owes its crises not to an increase of performance, but to a performance refusal.

Furthermore, Lenin demanded categorically to learn from middle-class scholars. That sounds like the dialogue that was broadcast recently by the second West German Channel Z.D.F., between the Soviet Planning Commissioner and the former Federal Secretary of the Economy, in which the Russian expressed the desire in the face of the complete breakdown of Soviet agriculture that the Germans – meaning the real Germans from West Germany, not the Soviet Germans from the East – should send specialists, technical gear, seeds and cattle, so something would come after all of the manure and lands of Good Old Russia! Has the world ever seen a greater regress than this supposed greatest historical progress?

Lenin's admission that there was no concept - O Comrade Crap, how that just has to hurt! - and one would have to learn from the masses[158] "from below, on the basis of experience," is sufficiently clear. In contrast to contemporary writers, Lenin seems to be of the opinion utopianism had proceeded from above and now the masses would have to correct them, doesn't it, Comrade Ambarzumov?

One may read the articles of Paul Scheffer, the correspondent of the *Berliner Tageblatt*, who is being highly regarded by the Russians in the mediation of risky politico-economic transactions, how Lenin actually did learn; the Russian peasants took his tax collectors and commissars tied them to boards and sawed the latter apart slowly, castrating them in the process, the representatives of the new authorities. They cut off their testicles, labeled them "nuts" and sent them as the detested tax in kind and natural goods to Moscow. In the face of such conditions the most stupid and backward apparatchik would have to undergo some learning process!

In such a brutal and bestial manner the peasants proceeded with those who had just promised them peace and land! Why would they do that? Simply because the economic policy of the Bolsheviks was more dire than the czarist one! And not only the peasants, but the workers, as well, in unison with their workers' management, would turn against the central leadership, they would sabotage openly the latter's nonsensical directives in order to stop the insane course of the total abolition of commodity production. Above all, the resistance was directed against the ukases of the Supreme Economic Council. The latter proceeded mercilessly with complete nationalization. Marx had always pleaded for the total nationalization of peasantry, including all landed estates, not only in the demands during the revolution of 1848/'49, but later, as well. He was against any cooperative or syndicalist principle. Now this, the Bolsheviks would not dare, they ignored that item in Marx's program, but with regard to the sectors of artisans, trade and industry they proceeded as Marx had stipulated ... The Supreme Economic Council nationalized everything. It abolished taxes, the costs for services like power and housing rent, transport tickets didn't cost anything anymore and they, thus, produced a deficit of the State budget of incredible proportions and inflation beyond bounds, because: the State incurred costs and ever more costs, but it didn't have any revenues! Had Lenin possibly not read the "law of money circulation" of Marx, or did that also have no validity at all? The incredible budget deficit compelled Lenin in his actions to now abolish money completely! Of course: If I abolish money, there will be no further deficit. Of course: Death cures all illnesses!

Everything was captured by force, registered and distributed. Wages were thrown back to the barter system, i.e., the workers received their wages in kind instead of money, etc. In short: Lenin's directive to annihilate Capitalism in its economic form, the commodity-producing society, was entirely implemented. Organized chaos reigned supreme! Production broke down completely. Of the approximately four million workers of czarist Russia only one million remained. More than half of all industrial outlets had to be closed. Workers could not buy sausage, bread, schnapps and cigarettes anymore at any street corner, as Capitalist trade had been abolished as a matter of course and the Socialist version of it could not establish itself! There was distribution, allotment, but no trade at all.

The Party itself, like the economy and society, was in a state of complete and utter disarray and corruption. In an article about "the Crisis of the Party" Lenin remarked: "The Party is sick. The Party is being rattled by a high fever." It was a question of the corruption and enrichment of the Party members, the higher ones on account of the lower ones, the lower ones on account of the workers. For that very reason Lenin let all manners of victual rationing be shortened at the X Party Congress in February 1921 and that Congress passed the resolution "to fight decisively against the abuse of position and material advantages by Party members," as well as a "course for the equalizing of the Party members in all material respects."[159] Lenin let, depending on the case, 30% to 60% of the Comrades be excluded from the Party. God, what a weal and boon such a procedure would be today for the Socialist Unity Party of Germany! Only in this later case it would have to be 90% and 98% of them from State Insecurity.

To resume: The "scientific policies" of Socialism especially invented for the industrial proletariat, annihilate the proletariat instead, the Communist Party and the results of the Socialist upheavals and instituted State Capitalism instead, which to this very day shapes today's U.S.S.R. and the world system of our real-existing Socialism. Applied Marxism failed in the revolutions of the 19th as well as of the 20th century.

To resume: Not for the proletariat alone, but for their federated partner, the peasantry, as well, applied Marxism brought catastrophe. Even Lenin's general economic policy cut asunder all economic threads between village and town and that's were he failed most of all. The comptrolling departments to eliminate the black market trade between city and country had to be dissolved and victuals from the West had to be imported for 10 million gold rubles. This happened after the X Party Congress had accepted Lenin's proposal, which went as follows: "Let us revise our policy with regard to the peasants."[160] Lenin, however, had disregarded from the get-go the special "theory" of Marx with regard to the peasant issue and he had elaborated the agricultural policy, the decree on the land, on the basis of the voter directives collected and summarized by the social revolutionaries. Had he followed Marx on this issue, as well, he would not have survived his adventure.

To resume: Neither in the revolutionary policy nor in the policy of allies did Lenin adhere to the ideology of Marxism. As long as he kept Marx's instructions, he endangered his "revolution" and the alliance of class powers that held it together. *Practice shows: Marxism is an ideology alienated from life, detrimental to the interests of the people and inimical to them.* Only: The Russians are well off. Lenin, celebrated as the "continuator" of Marxism, has given them the possibility to break completely with Marx and to embark on their own path of a paradigm of Socialism that is pluralistic in both its economic, as well as its political aspects, a kind of socially-stabilizing State Capitalism, without unemployment, and with increasing wealth for laborers and peasants.

But who finally will liberate the one and only and greatest of all German Democratic Republics from Comrade Crap? How disastrous Marx was for the working classes of Russia is officially documented. It suffices to read, among other things, the calculation Lenin made in 1921 before the delegates of Soviets of All-Russia! It suffices to read the Bolshevist sources on the catastrophic famine, the egregious conditions in those cut-off regions isolated on command, to which the German settlements on the shores of the Volga also belonged. Thirty millions of a starving population there were according to the official statistics. And officially "only" five millions of those died – through war and civil war? No! On the contrary, it was because of the catastrophic economic policy à la Marx, as Lenin well admitted!

The proletariat had become five times as poor in the years of 1917 to 1920, the peasants twice as poor as under czarisms – and this according to the official figures! No peasant was interested in cultivating his fields, what for? He had to hand over everything and would not receive money. The more diligent he, thus, became the more he got punished and for the worker the situation was likewise. That was the inner, decisive, essential root cause of the catastrophe; the practical economic policy according to the instructions of Marx! German science had a high standing in Russia and was this Marx with his "science" not somebody who had made this nameless Lenin great and famous?

The decay of production was further caused by a rampant hyperinflation, as ambiguously two systems existed simultaneously: partly, one was still or again trying to bring order into the economy through money. On the black market one czarist gold ruble was traded against 200,000 Soviet rubles, when in 1922 the State bank was reinstituted. Krestinsky estimated at the already-quoted Soviet congress that the monetary circulation of Soviet Russia amounted to ten trillion paper rubles! This insane policy of monetary emission was underwritten by the State Secretary of Finance. Did not even Marx have considerable practical and theoretical difficulties with money? From 1922 onward, each newly-printed ruble would get an "appreciation of value" of ten thousand with regard to the old rubles. Only after the gold ruble was reinstituted following strictly czarist monetary experiences and practices, it was possible after years to recreate more bearable conditions. Inflation, according to certain Soviet books, was unknown in Russia. This phenomenon became known only through the German hyperinflation in the 1920s. Marxist economic policies wreaked greater havoc among the working population of Russia than war and civil war taken together! How did it look, now, this dictatorship against the proletariat? Who used Marx against whom?

The Supreme Economic Council, the cardinal instrument of this dictatorship, had approximately 900 members. Measured by the yardstick of today's State bureaucracies this is not a great number. Of those 8% were workers and 19% were organized Communists - holy dictatorship of the proletariat, if only Marx had lived to see that! In other words, four-fifth of all those specialists of the Supreme Economic Council were not Party members. What happened here to the leading role of the Party? What a devastating verdict of practice over theory! And this one-fifth of Party muftis had to be kept in good spirits by way of special apportionments of victuals! Whoever would like to read up on all this in greater detail may read a great specialist on the subject, only: one has to read against the grain![161]

Things were going wild within the Party itself: Communists of repute turned against Lenin's State Capitalism. They declared that in this manner exploitation would never become abolished and they were right in doing so. For that reason, the Party opposition demanded "self-organization" of the working class; today we would say this is roughly the Yugoslavian Socialism paradigm. So there was not just the battle against Marx, but also the battle against Lenin with democratic and reform-Communist variations of policies.

Lenin knew whom to blame: "Russian Man is a bad worker in comparison with the progressive nations."[162] If what Lenin is saying is correct, then the Russia of today is a non-progressive that is to say consequently a regressive nation and, therefore, it should be a great example for the G.D.R. nation. Even here the intellectual kinship between Marx and Lenin shows. Neither man thought highly of his own nation. Nevertheless both, had they only known the traditions of their respective country, should have been forewarned!

With regard to Lenin, a digression into the economic history of Russia may be allowed. The German Political Economist, Heinrich Friedrich von Storch, gave lectures after the abolition of the Continental Barrier, to the family of the czar in classical middle-class economics.

Storch motivated the czar, true to the theory, to begin a system of free trade in Russia, i.e., to relinquish the protection and sponsoring of Russian Capitalism which was still completely underdeveloped. Genuine teaching meant everything to the czar as it meant everything to Vladimir Illych, after all it was a German who was preaching it and they should know before everyone else, shouldn't they? This later assumption was a capital mistake for the white czar as well as for the red one. Cheap labor from English factories glutted the Russian market in the 19th century, ruined the local manufacturers and reduced drastically, just like Lenin's policies, the number of proletarians. Czarist economics or, rather, mis-economics hit Russia more devastatingly than the entire Napoleonic military campaign! Again, Lenin's policies destroyed Russia more effectively than the entire world war and civil war considered together.

"The proprietors of land have no market, the factories are facing terminal ruin, precious metals have all been exported, the most solid houses of trade are facing their break-down,"[163] thus, List is reciting to Count Nesselrode the results of the deplorable czarist economic policy of the 19th century. The reports about Lenin's Russia at the beginning of the 1920s sound suspiciously similar; these fabled Twenties which were anything but golden in Russia. They are just described and stressed a little differently, much like the popular mind in the G.D.R. described the situation of our unrealistically-existing Socialism with regard to the effects of the world economic crisis of recent years: Capitalism, as we know it, Comrades, is facing the abyss, we, however, have gone a decisive step further!

Where did the white czar see an escape, a solution? He wanted to have the German national economist, List, that special friend of Karl Marx, as a leading theorist and practitioner at his court. List, who was already Honorary Consul in the U.S. system, declined politely.

Where did the red czar see the solution? As his predecessor he saw the rescue with List and in Germany, not with that stork, Marx, with his red beak! Marx was chased by Lenin from the Russian court theoretically and practically just like Storch [German for stork] was chased by the earlier czar. Ideologically speaking, both czars remain schizophrenic: yes, absolutely, in theory – both Marx-storks are entirely right; except in practice, unfortunately, it just doesn't work! It is a decided irony of History that both completely agree in this respect.

After all is said and done, one has to admire this incredible courage in Lenin, this ruthlessness with regard to his own person, when higher matters were at stake. Incisively, he states with absolute baldness: "At the economical front we have suffered a setback *as we tried to implement Communism* - it may be noted: not implement war-time communism – *in the spring of 1921, a setback more serious than was ever imposed on us by Kolchak, Denikin, or Pilsudski, a setback, which was more serious and more dangerous and cut more to the bone and marrow.*"[164]

How shall the worker work, when management, never mind czarist or bolshevist, is working like that? Should Lenin's verdict not be reversed and should it not be said: Russia's leaders are worse leaders in comparison with those of the advanced nations? Only in this manner does it begin to make sense. Nevertheless, leaders are prisoners of their own ideology. From the toddling stage onward they had been inculcated with it. By the time they have overcome the ideology in their minds, they have gotten too old to change anything. They don't have the force anymore to bring out the creative potential of the people. The system of Marxist Communism is not capable of being reformed. It will implode, slowly and in torment for the people, of its own inner contradictions.

If I were pious and at home in Russia I would pray that God give Russia a new Peter the Great and that he should go to the West as a labor immigrant! He should take a good, deep and hard look at everything that is going on there and leave his ideological shamans at home. He should then look around not only in the area of technology and the economy, that is, at the base, but he should also look around in the areas of the superstructure, as well. There he could learn, say in the Socialist International, or in the parliaments of the E.U. and the European Council, how multinational and global problems are prospectively solved in such a manner that they take an efficacious economic effect. He could then copy all of that and still retain the social stability of his own system. At that point, Russia would become a paradigm for all who want a Social Democracy, as the utopia of Communism is economically unfeasible. A pluralistic social base, a pluralistic democratic superstructure and, thus, the imminent danger of the annihilation of humanity would be banished! Would that not be cheaper and more secure than our present hyper-armament?

"The History of all times and countries," List is telling us, "demonstrates exactly how the industry and wealth of the peoples is fundamentally determined by their political organization." And he continues:

"There have never been a people suppressed by despots that had had a developed industry and general wealth." However, he does not get dogmatic about his insights, "Certainly, even despotically-ruled nations managed to attain a certain level of wealth, if they had had the good fortune to get a series of benevolent rulers. But to abide by a word of Czar Alexander, that would only be a lucky coincidence." Then List quotes Montesquieu and his *Spirit of the Laws:* "In a nation that is kept in servitude, work serves more for sustenance and maintenance than for development; in a free nation work serves more for development than maintenance."[165] This would precisely explain the transfer of know-how from West to East.

Democracy and industry are synonymous, List maintains. "The nobility of Venice committed collective suicide, when it annihilated the democratic element. Industry demands a government mindful of the people, whose policies are directed towards one goal throughout the centuries."[166] This historical circumspection of this "vulgar economist" may be compared to the historical myopia of Marx! Now we can see, as well, why List preferred to stay in Germany instead of becoming a counselor at the czar's court.

Since these sentences have been written, History has corroborated through another century and a half of practice: Without political democracy there is no effectively functioning industrial system to be had. Or in other words, without a pluralistic base there is no democratic superstructure to be had. The economical system of Marxism annihilates freedom of personality, objectively as well as subjectively. It guarantees economic dependence and personal servitude. Juristically speaking, it throws the free worker back behind any middle-class constitution. And at this point we are reaching the historic question, whether the unscientific, but real-social-communist Bolshevists could not get a little smarter? Let's get back to them from our digression into History!

Lenin did not only demand the abolition of commodity production in a general or theoretical way; in his new Party Program, drafted after the victory of the Communist Party, as well as in the constitution of the Soviet Union, he let the abolition of money and the "attainment of the general equality of the citizens of the Republic in the area of commodity production and distribution" be emphatically proclaimed. For that purpose 37,000 industrial outlets, down to one-man-installations, and these were many thousands in themselves, would be put under the control of the supreme planning committee. They were managed from Moscow in a qualified way and I can't tell you how: Without telex or telephone that is! Here it becomes apparent how the classics change the classic age: A horse – a kingdom for a horse? No, not one, 37,000 horses for 37,000 equestrian messengers through night and wind and ice and snow for the Marxist non-vulgar economy! Why would great concerns in the Capitalist industrial nations keep 20,000 to 30,000 deliverers? Today's Russians are so in awe of the Japanese economy performing so well. Do they realize that there approximately 80% of all metal-processing companies are small or family-run businesses? And this today, in the age of the multinationals!

The Supreme Economic Council, which was presided over by Prince Obolensky, now Comrade Ossinsky, a "left-wing" Communist, later "democratic centralist" and adherent of Trotsky, was meant to abolish the dysfunctional economy, because after all, as Marx-Engels had written, planned Socialism had to get rid of Capitalist anarchy and, hence, get rid of the misery of the proletariat and not prolong it indefinitely. But even the left-wing Prince did not manage to find anything concrete in the general expositions of our yada -yada - yada classics. Even Lenin and Stalin did not find anything, either. The issues began to top and topple each other: What kind of planning? Total planning? Partial central planning according to general regions, according to local areas, a mixture of everything? Planning for industry, agriculture, infrastructure, budget? With money as had, or without money, with *ersatz*-money, with the time-certificates as directed by Marx? Value-oriented planning or planning according to use-value? Statisticians of all countries unite! How many onions and how much toilet paper does suffering humanity need? The Russians even then possessed excellent statistics. Every town was able to calculate exactly for Party control and Secret Service control that it had 30,000 inhabitants, when it needed 15,000 certificates for victuals. Today the same system goes in our real-existing Socialism; Soviet tradition has to be esteemed highly. Corruption is as high on the agenda today as it ever was, to bring up just one event: the State Secretary of Fisheries assassinated during the Andropov Administration, who had marked caviar as herring tails and put the difference in foreign currency into his own pocket. But that is an ancient, time-honored tradition; one need only read the literature, Gogol's *Revisor* is no exception. Does the legend not go around that Peter the Great had the pockets of his minister sewn closed? In the Council of Ministers of East Germany I have observed people, who have been delegated by their *ueber*-Russians to come here - strictly official may that be understood - "to organize" furniture non-existent in the U.S.S.R., under the radar, that is, which was being needed for Soviet dadshas. When our Visigoths then one day dared to ask in Moscow itself, whether they themselves, in turn, could not sleep in one of those apartments thus endowed, the categorical answer of the dear congregation of brethren was that this would not be possible, because the furniture was too good and new, made in the G.D.R. directly, sorry! What are we complaining about? Nothing changed since our happy feudal days with the princes and the dukes.

At first, Obolensky managed, grace of Marxist-Leninist instruction, to delete millennia of development both in their civilizational and in their economic aspect. Who says, this was not a breath-taking revolutionary velocity? Production was entirely centralized and completely messed up. The nationalized metal industry still had an output of 2 to 3%; the textile industry had an output of 6% of their pre-war capacity. The railways transported 10% for the same period. Coal production had been reduced from two billion puds to 520 million puds. In short, the Marxist planned economy brought exactly the opposite of Marxist prophesying. One may well remember Lenin: Not war or civil war was to be blamed for this catastrophe, but sheer and bland economic unreason! Trade, the white and legal market, had been annihilated; the country had been thrown back to the pre-industrial trading in kind. After the "first victorious proletarian revolution" one lived again like during the darkest times of feudal Absolutism. The proletariat went back to the village, to escape unemployment and starvation, the "fabled class in itself" dissolved and shrank back by 75%. The only thing that flourished was the black market! It was impossible to live a normal life, to govern at all. The solution out of this screaming contradiction was seen in the terror of the Cheka and this principle holds true to this very day. Criticism, for instance, is orally very much in demand, practically suppressed. Criticism again, even without political action ensuing thereof, can be branded at any time as ideological diversion inimical to the State. Thus, even scientific controversy becomes impossible. However, if there are no theoretical solutions geared towards long-term processes, then there will equally be no effective economic developments sustained by future-oriented technologies. This is one of the defining features of the continuous retrogression of the Marxist system.

That's what happened to the intelligentsia and to the industrial working men.

But what had happened with the largest and most pressing percentage of the population of about 140 million of which 75% were peasants? Lenin had turned them into mortal enemies through the abolition of the scanty trader's net. From where was the peasant supposed to receive what he needed for his scarce economies if not from the market? The peasantry was certainly not thrown into idle fits and starts of joy over the revolution. It had brought them only a 10% gain of additional farm land property, not counting those areas they had already cultivated under land lease. And the distribution proceeded just like in czarist times; taxes were levied according to the heads each family counted. The peasant received no forest, as he had been hoping for construction material and fuel, but even the forest commons were confiscated by the New State. We may remember of the impossible position of Marx on the peasant issue! Theoretically, peasants were the mainstay of the alliance; in practice, they were not only alienated, but actively turned into enemies – as in Germany 1848/'49. Here again the crass cap between theory and practice becomes apparent. Further, it was not at all the case that the peasants were clamoring to liquidate the landlords or to oust them. This was done, by and large, by the shock troops from the city and the peasants were mobilized by them more often than not against neighboring landlords instead of their own, as it was generally the case that the peasants refused to turn against their own lords. The new Soviet lords levied against the peasants thirteen different taxes to be paid in kind and on top of that they had to be available for unpaid horse-team transport and delivery services. Even here this was the epitome of proletarian Absolutism, the most sinister Dark Ages came alive through such "progressive policies" and more sinister than anything that man had ever known – see the Chernenko quote above.

How did the peasants react? They reduced their cattle quantities. There were districts in which there was 0.4% working cattle per farm. Thus, only 10% of the arable land was cultivated even in the famine areas! In addition to the reduction in cattle quantity, and in pastures and fields, the peasantry let go two-thirds of the prospering home industry in the village in order to escape the new, more brutal exploitation under the Soviets. Any older person in East Germany will vividly remember analogous conditions here, the first in the early sixties, when against all rhyme or reason large-scale collectivization was effected by the Socialist Unity Party shock troops in the countryside. There were long lists of meat and sausage distribution instead of victual certificates and the people could read from the shop windows: Meat and sausage – gone! They went as well. And the wall came, instead!

The peasants reacted then as now, especially since Stalin had driven the Marxist policy so inimical to the peasant to new heights of perfection. They are, in turn, punishing their authorities by way of underproduction, just as the EU peasants are punishing theirs through overproduction. A member of the Soviet government declared in 1922 that before World War I the workers received an average of 4,000 calories a day, during the war it was 3,750 and under the dictatorship of the proletariat it had been reduced to 2,700, too little for intensive labor. Were they, thus, lazy as Lenin believed? It was after all his policies that brought the country, the workers and peasants to the brink of ruin. Even the Communist food outlets, the poor relief and soup kitchens, did not help anymore at that point. The Russian people were paying the bill under the new dictatorship as they had always done, now through increased misery, with tears, hunger, bitter need, blood and death. Informers were rampant and so was imprisonment, forced labor and the firing squads reigned.

At that critical junction when the country threatened to suffocate in chaos completely, strikes, anti-government rallies, revolts and large-scale death through famine, Lenin finally changed course in the eleventh if not the thirteenth hour, decisively and thoroughly. He commanded the N.E.P., the New Economic Policy, which was nothing more according to Marx's favorite expression than the "same old crap." Lenin had, after the instructions from *Capital* and from the *Marginal Notes of the Gotha Program* had not worked, no other thought than to organize everything again in exactly the same manner as it had been organized under the czar. The new course meant taking recourse to commodity production, to the reintroduction of money, to the reinstitution of that exploitation that had not been abolished in the first place in more civil and slightly more bearable forms. Taxation and wages in kind disappeared. Market and trade were legalized. Services had to be paid again like taxes, stamps were again moistened and in foreign trade tariffs were again levied. The Communist ideology of revolution had been, by and large, buried. Not only the economic autodidact, Marx, but the ideology which he had copied without rhyme or reason had become an entire and wholesale failure. The integral State model of Communism failed globally in the 20th century as it had failed locally in the 19th. Then the workers had told Wilhelm Weitling: Your Communism is a "non-thing,"[167] i.e., a non-sense! It doesn't work. It doesn't work in business, it doesn't work in the family, and it doesn't work in bed. And the consequence became: Let us live like we did before, we are going to sign off on the Commune.

At this point, Vladimir Illych in person, actually, signed off on the practice of the Great Commune, however: Just like all other ideologues in our "real" Socialism, he avoided scrupulously saying, the Marxist ideology is the culprit. Why is that? No power can exist without ideological justification. But the members of the Soviet Polit Bureau, of course, all knew from long experience that Communism is a utopia, no doubt! They subscribe to *realpolitik*, not to ideology. Gromyko publicly cast spite and aspersions upon Reagan, the "ideologue." Their profession consists of fooling the people, and especially the younger generation, as thoroughly and perfectly as possible. This deceit is the precondition to sustain the dictatorship against the proletariat.

To resume again: Practice, even according to the Marxist philosophy, the touchstone and criterion of theory, has unmasked the so-called "scientific" Communism of Marx as utopian. Thence dates the spiritual decay of Marxism, which today has split into three tendencies and which is, thus, not only ideologically split, but split in its aspect of power politics. The superpowers, who are supposed to be Socialist China and the Soviet Union, let ferocious proxy wars be fought in Cambodia and Vietnam, after they had engaged in ceasefire directly at the Ussuri.

Proletarians of all countries unite, had been the battle cry at the foundation of the Communist Party. Communists of different countries annihilate each other, seems to be today's maxim. That's how the new social order works. It is, all things considered, nothing but the old order.

What other decisive proof does the N.E.P. put forth for the refutation of Marxism-Leninism? Well, no juridical form of property rights of any kind, be they syndicalist, unionist, private, societal or statist, can be made responsible and liable, that the commodity-money-value relationships exist and, therefore, the exploitation in the shape of the wages system; but on the contrary, the unsublatable material societal division of Labor between city and country, within and between the various macroeconomic branches of production, between industry and the crafts, between domestic and foreign markets, etc. No power on earth can stem or stall this division of Labor. No country can produce or manufacture the billion-aspect gamut of products alone. On the local, national and global levels the division of Labor will become ever more important in the future - disregarding the analogous ecological and demographic movements completely. Consequently, Marx's plagiarized thesis, the unification of all property relations to be the cure-all of all social issues, is an unworkable, scandalous nonsense and an enormous one at that! Unified property impedes the law of value to work and, hence, it impedes that kind of efficacy needed for the rapid increase of Labor productivity and, thus, it impedes the victory of our pseudo-socialist State Capitalism over Capitalism proper which would allow for mixed forms of property.

The end - means conflict in the ideological economy of Marxism is unsolvable. By way of economic means our real-existing Socialism can never overcome real Capitalism. The N.E.P. was forced upon the Party leadership by the conflict of the Party with the rural areas and the peasants. The latter wanted to make money, live better than they had lived under the czar and they wanted to be able to buy what they needed to live and to work. Instead, the Communist Party brought them Medieval structures of forced contributions and unpaid horse-team services. At this point, everything became a historic joke, because whence derived the division of Labor? From the peasant! As long as there was hunting, fishing, natural fruit gathering in common, neither purchasing nor the market was needed. When one peasant began to cultivate the soil, the next one raised cattle, the third one sheered sheep's wool as their cardinal and prime occupation, then exchange and trade became a necessity. The more commodity production developed the more trade, money, market gained in significance. Without the societal general worker in his national, regional and worldwide form, today's civilized humanity could not exist. And this holds true not just for the productive area, but also for the unproductive one. But even here the legendary verbal acrobatics of Marx are helpful: Private Capitalist planning and management of the production processes are being defined as unproductive and exploitative, the same activity in our unreal Socialism is held to be the exact opposite. Officers and functionaries under Capitalism are parasites inimical to the people; the bureaucrat of Party or State or Secret Service in this surreal Socialism of ours by definition and statistics is a 'laborer' so that their daughters and sons can get a place of choice in college or university. "Labor veterans" are being honored with high orders of merit all the time, which include material and financial advantages, as well, see *Neues Deutschland.* These are strange workers, indeed: They are admirals, generals, Stasi-authorities, popular police officers and army brass, Party honchos, etc.

Our students begin to ask even in their freshman year why they are given the percentages of workers and employees in only general and not in differentiated terms. Well, State secrets are not disclosed in our genuine Socialism and who talks with others about facts in the government guest house or in the government hospital, in the datshas, or in the restaurants, or at home, or in the tulip field will find himself or herself soon interned. Beware Comrade Snoop-dog, who is always present, even the imported bugs never sleep. Anything that can earn West currency needs to be kept on a high performance level. In this matter, and in this matter only, we have an excess of order whereas everything else may be consummately snafued and discombobulated.

By the way, since all Stasi-agents, policemen, all members of the armed forces are, by definition, workers, the Socialist Unity Party is clearly and without a shred of reasonable doubt a workers' party. Our homefront *ersatz*-Russians have clearly learned their lesson from Russian statistics! These "workers" are led by managements staffed 53% by graduates from colleges and universities under the leadership of Dr. *honoris causa* Erich Honecker - according to the speech of the General Secretary at the 10th plenary session of the Central Committee of the Socialist Unity Party held in June 1985 - in other words, they are intellectuals. In order to dissimulate this fact, no leading Party or State functionary in the G.D.R. officially bears academic credentials or titles. For years G.D.R. propaganda has tried to make it clear to the working class that they are being led by the working class themselves and not by intellectuals. Furthermore, the percentage of the employees within the party management is not disclosed, but with this lack of disclosure the ideology big shots get more disavowed than they are themselves aware, as the true workers are much more intelligent than many of the so-called *intelligenzia*.

Given all the pseudo-success of Socialism mainly based on verbal acrobatics, the governing class, nevertheless, proceeds from facts in their own internal analysis. As the international division of Labor is important for them, Socialist commodity production today is no longer rejected, but intensified. Even in that respect Lenin gave the prime example: Take credits from Western foreign nations to bolster Bolshevism in need, import new technologies in the same manner, allow mixed joint ventures with foreign companies, etc. Without the N.E.P. there would have been no development towards Rapallo. Today all this is repeated in the shadow of Helsinki. Rapallo and Helsinki are indicative of the policy of co-existence of Russia, i.e., that contemporary strategy here is treated at length in the first part to destroy the Western pluralist democracies by way of exported class warfare!

State, diplomacy, economy go for peaceful co-existence and good business. The Party goes for class warfare and world revolution.

As the head men of our unreal Socialism are always simultaneously functionaries of Party and State, the practice is as schizophrenic as the ideology of Charlie Crap. The foreign-policy and foreign-trade hermaphrodite N.E.P. revives again on a higher level. The polit-economic bastard N.E.P. - law of value simultaneously applied with State stipulation of prices, a consummate nonsense! - was being killed by Stalin as early as 1924. At this point, even Rapallo was not a matter of grave concern anymore; German development aid workers were put on trial as "sabogents," the hard-working, high-performing peasants were liquidated with their agricultural economies, which brought about new and worse famines than under Lenin. This Blanqui-Marxism in its most purist form practiced by the *fuehrer* and father of all working men against Lenin's N.E.P. experiences devoured more Soviet men than did World War II in its entirety. Just prior to it – according to today's official figures of the Political Main Administration of the Red Army for the occasion of the 40th anniversary of the victory of Hitler's fascism – Stalin had 82,000 officers, starting with Marshall Tuchashevsky down to the battalion commanders. The Russian people won that war all the same. They were not fighting for the Communists - they were fighting for Mother Russia.

The N.E.P. and its foreign-trade variation, economic co-existence, were and are mere tactical ancillaries within the larger Russian strategy to attain the goal of world revolution in stages, however, that strategy had not been successful in the "revolutionary post-war crisis" until the middle of the 1920s, in spite of all putsch attempts of the Stalinist COMINTERN that were staged in Germany and elsewhere. As it is well known even Thaelmann's putsch attempt in Hamburg was abortive – at this point that was it, for the moment. N.E.P., co-existence, promises and contracts would be broken domestically as well as internationally, constantly and continuously, for nothing but crude, stark and naked power politics.

Lenin at the beginning of the 1920s had to make concessions to the peasants, to the masses of the people. Once the country had recovered somewhat Stalin annihilated at the end of the 1920s all autonomous agricultural economies. Lenin had to make the treaties of Brest-Litovsk with the Germans. They were shredded, once the time had come for that, in the eyes of the Soviets. The Communist Party of the Soviet Union made the Hitler-Stalin Pact and shredded in this manner all promises it had made to the Communist sister parties, because they were counting on territorial expansion on account of Poland and the African colonies. They dissolved the Polish C.P. and had their leaders shot. In this way, as well, they were helping the anti-Marxist, Hitler.

The Communist Party of the S.U. signed international treaties in the Anti-Hitler coalition which would guarantee the Germans the unity of their State, but in practice they practiced the opposite of the professed. The Soviets signed the Helsinki Treaty in 1985, but they are still trampling human rights underfoot on a large scale. They are preaching peace and they are simultaneously waging a barbarous war against the Afghan people, where they are trying out their new weapons system on women and children. Will Afghanistan become the equivalent of the Spanish Civil War for World War III?

As much as they breached treaties, they did have a rather cavalier and elegant way to interpret and break their own self-developed ideological principles.   One of their most important postulates after 1950 was the announcement of the existence of the world peace camp and the imperialist war camp: two camps, two systems, two world markets.   Sure, nothing is possible without material-economic rationalization.   Let's stay with the world market: the ideology is Eastern, the effective prices are almost Western, and they continue to increase.   However, unlike in the Western markets they never fall again.   What has been driven up remains up for the benefit of Russian exploitation! The Russians ask for world market prices from their satellite states for energy and raw material deliveries, which are atrociously overpriced, measured by the costs of production and the average income and price levels within the COMECON countries.   Part of the performance has to be made in labor power directly. This investment sharing cultivates the more remote regions of the U.S.S.R. at the cost of the smaller COMECON countries. Well, since the days of the N.E.P. the Russians know about money and exploitation. The G.D.R., for instance, today has to deliver four times as many ships, train engines, excavators, derricks, travel and cooling wagons to the Russians than it did have to ten years ago. On the other hand, the latter reduced their oil deliveries by 10%. They are selling their oil, instead, against West currencies; they deem these ugly inflationary papers beautiful, what an aberration of taste!

The U.S. has to pay extremely high interest rates when they are trying to attract investment capital, the Russians don't even bother with such rates.   The conditions of exploitation in our real-existing Socialism are clearly echeloned according to Marx even in matters of foreign trade, after all, he did not copy *everything* wrongly and, for that reason, the stronger party sucks the weaker bloodless.   The one economically more potent accumulates Capital, wherein the military and political hegemony of Russia speed up that process mightily in the COMECON, that is, it depends on extra-economic parameters. As in this manner all COMECON countries have to bear the additional costs through increased investment sharing and the terms of trade get worse and worse. As the U.S.S.R. did not only reduce the delivery of oil to the G.D.R. but to all their other satellite states, they were able to sell those extra quantities to the West against convertible currencies. Ten years ago two-thirds of Western trade was done by the smaller COMECON countries; today this is done by the Russians. Poland and Romania have become insolvent. The most powerful Socialist community of States is unable to refinance them. So perhaps Marx was right after all with his plagiarized theory of immiseration?

Perhaps now, after this catastrophe, another change will come as it did under Lenin? Within the pale of dictatorships, of course, the most radical, surprising and incalculable alterations cannot be excluded. In 1920 Lenin shut off ideologically each and every one of his adversaries, who was speaking out against the abolition of commodity production and demanded regular market relations with the rationale: "But free trade is the return to Capitalist slavery!"[168] One year later that selfsame Lenin wrote as follows, and here we are reminded of Engels annual progress against Rodbertus; our "classic writers" seem to attract this kind of change: "We will be able to allow the circulation of free, local commodity traffic in rather great quantities. With this measure we do not destroy but fortify the power of the proletariat."[169] Let's be very clear on this; here Lenin was not as yet thinking about national or world trade. Those insights came to him only later, when he finally understood that without Western Capital aid, especially from Germany and Great Britain, Russia would not be brought back to its feet. By now we know, mainly through the historical series of articles in the West German *Spiegel* magazine, that the N.E.P. and its peaceful coexistence were neither just economic nor merely peaceful. In conjunction with economic relations a clandestine cooperation of the German *reichswehr* had developed with the Red Army, of which the Russian leaders were hoping it would bring Germany even militarily onto the side of Russia, as the latter was keen on revenge for Versailles and that it would lead to a joint war against the Western powers. In this respect, as well, they followed the editor-in-chief Marx, who had written in the *Neue Rheinische Zeitung* at the end of March, beginning of April 1849, in the series about *Wage labor and Capital*, that: "every revolutionary upheaval, may its aim be ever so removed from class struggle, has to fail, until the revolutionary working class be victorious, *that every social reform shall remain a utopia until the proletarian revolution and the feudalist counter-revolution shall measure themselves with arms in a world war.*"[170] World war and world revolution had always been synonymous in Marxism. Trotsky adhered to that; Lenin disapproved of it for a time, after the Poles had beaten his army, see the above-quoted memoirs of Clara Zetkin. From the Russians you can hear the familiar word, "peace." However, never was there a word pronounced that would have disavowed the Marxian ideology of world war and civil war! This Marx quote makes it abundantly clear how drastically Marx had misunderstood the "lawful succession" of social formations, which he was, according to Engels, supposed to have discovered himself. Directly after 1849 he wanted the proletarian revolution in Europe! Marx, because he was in a hurry to become somebody, intended to do away with Capitalism altogether and jump one revolution ahead. Why, for all nines, did world history not do him this favor? Maybe it doesn't think that highly about Marxism after all? Perhaps it deems his over-the-top adventurist, viewed in historical contexts, completely off the wall?

As is well known even the mummified Marx of the 20th century has egregiously miscalculated in this respect. It seems to be quite difficult, all this business of scientific prediction and the insight and understanding of historical laws, as much as all the Leninists seem to have a monopoly on that front.

The total, complete and entire failure of the Marxist ideology in theory, as well as in practice, is being camouflaged in the S.U. as well as in the G.D.R. with rather spectacular ado. In the same manner and simultaneously with it Lenin's so-called "theory of imperialism" has also failed, although it is quite incomprehensible in the first place what should be so theoretically gripping about this little pamphlet of political agitation. Lenin does not waste one line on the analysis of monopolistic categories of value. His meager, measly writing is an attenuated, trite rehashing of Hilferding's *Finance Capital*. The terminology and the analysis of imperialism as the last phase of Capitalism, Hilferding had pre-published in the *Neue Zeit* [New Times], the organ of the German Social Democratic Party. In this respect the classic writer, Lenin, is quite akin to the classic writer, Marx, in content as well as in method. Plagiarize, miss the main theoretical thing, make thin pamphlets out of carefully wrought volumes and be always too late with the right insights! Engels could also be mentioned here, one has just to read *The Peasant War* by Zimmermann, then compare the poor copy from Engels - with which we would have them back together again - the three equals without equal!

Lenin, moreover, took over uncritically the hypothesis that commodity production would be undermined by monopoly, all economic movement would work towards centralization by the monopolistic State, only the leadership strata would have to be replaced and everything would be fine. In this manner, he reached the "modernization" of the historical perspective of Marx. Just imagine he had stayed with the views of the elder, politically more mature Marx, according to which one formation would only be doomed, when it does not give any leeway anymore for the development of the productive forces. Imagine Lenin had accepted Marx's hypothesis according to which Socialist conditions of production could be achieved only in a country with a highly-developed standard of science and technology with a qualitatively and quantitatively highly-developed proletariat, in association with other highly-developed countries - where would Russia be today? The historian may well ask about alternative possibilities. Nothing in the History of Humanity has to happen just and absolutely as it did; no red-flag and no brown-shirted dictatorship, no Marxism and no Fascism as anti-Marxism. And nothing has to be repeating itself, either, what has happened in Russia and in the Russified part of Eastern Europe - to the detriment not only of the proletariat, but also to the detriment of the peoples and nations.

With these thoughts let's come to the here and now, to the present time: Neither for the domestic market of the COMECON countries nor for their foreign trade is there a unified theory or practice as we had come to realize earlier. For that reason, the Polit Bureau does cast aspersions upon the economic theorists for their incompetence; however, who in turn says why the system cannot be reformed, will be done in! But, nevertheless, the conditions, having become more and more unbearable, force reforms time and again, which are regularly praised as the mother of all solutions and then they fail with equal regularity! The end - means conflict and the objective laws of economics are always stronger than the subjective views of the leaders. One may look at the resonance of these experiments in the G.D.R., compare the debates about the introduction of an economic accounting of the 1950s with the new economic system of planning and management in the 1960s and these with the stipulations in the Party program in the 1970s. Each time it is about the same problems, and that goes for the 1980s today, as well. In intervals of about ten years the attempt is being made to find a solution for the latent crisis situation within the national economies of the COMECON. The time periods of the open outbreak of the crises characterize, as well, the crises cycles of the underdeveloped Western European Capitalism of the 19th century. Eastern European State Capitalism does orient itself upon Western standards, historically speaking, not just through special trade arrangement via Genex, Intershop and the particular currency Forum checks. Simultaneously, the strategic warfare within and between the parties about the evaluation of the economic events in theory and practice lead to the most doggone fits, leaps and starts and to a constant disproportionality within the comparative development. Roughly sketched, this could be diagrammed as follows: a straight line from top to bottom on a white sheet of paper, with a second line oscillating wildly to the left and to the right of the first. Who or what is represented by the straight line and by the second oscillating line? The oscillating line is the straight line of the Party and the other line represents the Comrade Party Secretary with his defiant, obstinate, dissident left-wing or right-wing deviation!

Erich Apel, former Secretary of the Central Committee of the Socialist Unity Party for Economic Affairs, shot himself in the mid-sixties just like his predecessor did in the same chair. Apel had refused to sign a new "friendship treaty" with the Russians; the plundering of East Germany by the Russians went too far for him. On the eve of the underwriting ceremony he set an unmistakable example of protest. Erich Apel, a capable and professionally-experienced engineer, had previously been lambasted systematically. If the apparatchiks do not understand anything, that, meaning "slaughtering" as it is called in the respective jargon, they do understand. Apel had been the man to speak for the New Economic Policy/Planning and Management [a G.D.R. attempt to implement Lenin's N.E.P. under the new circumstances]. As a man of practical experience he knew what he was talking about. He opened the introduction to the envisioned economic reform fearlessly with an attack upon the Russians, called Stalin by name and referred to the "collective management" of the Communist Party of the Soviet Union when he wrote the following:

"The law of value cannot be considered a 'residue' of Capitalism, which would be in the ultimate analysis alien, in essence, to Socialism and whose gradual extrication and exorcism from the Socialist economy would have to be a cardinal point of economic policy. As it is well known, Stalin developed this detrimental view in his work *Economic Problems of Socialism in the U.S.S.R.*

Because of that, in practice, an arbitrary limitation of the commodity - money relation was instituted and Socialist economics was oriented towards an insufficient application of the principle of material interestedness. That did not only lead to fallacies in other areas of economic theory, it also led to direct economic losses.

The law of value would not be an economic law if it could be violated with impunity. So, for example, the fact alone that the prices of a part of our products deviate considerably from the value parameter, i.e., from the socially necessary exertion of Labor, lead, in turn, to a misconduit of material interestedness, as well as to an increase of difficulties in the planning and management process."[171]

This attack did not remain without lethal effects. Apel here had generally taken positions which were revisionist in the eyes of the Russians and *ersatz*-Russians. For them he had gone too far in his interpretation of reforms; since Bernstein revisionism is a mortal enemy of Marxism.

Apel had demanded that to "bring the economic laws to bear with full force."[172] He demanded to abolish the bureaucratic, one-sided administration of the economy. The administration should "manage in economic ways with modern methods."[173] His criticism of the Russians shows how he assesses the current situation. He accuses them, justly, of complete incompetence and of macroeconomic waste. Of course, he affirmed planning as a principal instrument of socialist economic management, but he also wanted a sensible coordination of economic self-regulation with administrative steering, in other words, the best of both worlds while eliminating the disadvantages. But his is utopianism, an eclecticism that is not feasible.

Apel put gain from its subordinate position into the center of microeconomic and macroeconomic performance and he demanded a real cost-utility calculation and an effective formation of prices, which alone would make it possible to make gain and performance measurable. Consequently, he demanded also the re-evaluation, in other words, the correct evaluation of technical equipment, new percentages of amortization, new relations among costs, quality, price and gain, culminating in the keyword of industrial price reform.

He decidedly turned against the Russian theory of the inflexibility of prices, because these would lead to macroeconomic disturbances and waste – a very true insight, even then, directed against the hare-brained practice of subsidizing, which is typical for real Capitalism. Why should a State deemed Communist have to subsidize in the first place? Why doesn't it give the workers directly what they need in order to live decently and correctly? Is that not, after all, the clearest solution of "social problems" for which the workers movement had come about to begin with?

Apel's ideas were correct in theory, but in practice they could only be partially implemented. The problem was simply that: Who determines the prices for what product? Is the price fixed along objective or along subjective lines? Taken together with the general discombobulation of prices an objective stipulation of prices is just impossible. But why would that be so? Apel is giving the answer indirectly, when he quotes Marx in a manner of justification - even this is an inexcusable error, something like this belongs at the beginning: "Common production assumed, the temporal determination becomes imperative. The less time society needs to grow wheat, cattle, etc., the more time it gains for other productions, of a material or spiritual manner ... economy of time; in that concept all economy is ultimately epitomized. In the same way society has to economize its time with sufficient utility to achieve a production in accordance with their general needs. ... Economy of time, as well as *planned distribution of labor time upon the different branches of production remains the first economic law on the base of common production.*"[174]

Apel is here unwittingly revealing the unscientific character of Marx under the title *On the Elaboration of the Scientific Foundation of Planning*, whom he acknowledges in this citation from the *Grundrisse* only for the revelation of "main features ... of proportional and optimal development of the societal production and consumption." In a roundabout way he is calling the Marxist ideology an "abstract methodology," which produces "stenciled, schematic manners of thinking," as the textbook that he is criticizing in such a devastating manner, is teeming with Marx quotes. Such a man, according to the will of the Russians and *ersatz*-Russians, had no right to survive!

If one reads today Apel's appraisal of microelectronics written twenty years ago one would be prone to think one were leafing through the documents of the last plenary session of the Socialist Unity Party. With Apel's fall twenty years ago fell, as well, the concept of the introduction of microelectronics, to the greatest disadvantage and damage of the G.D.R. population. Instead of massive quantities of goods, energy, intensive in materials and wages, the G.D.R. today could export small matchboxes full of vital intelligence. This is one example of the extreme amplitudes of a conceptional and practical kind in the economic policies of the G.D.R. It would be enough to enumerate: Already developed and then completely aborted production of airplanes, completely neglected and now subsidized construction of apartments, completely destroyed infrastructure of crafts and so on and so forth. Here we have the wisdom and farsightedness of the scientific style of leadership of Marxism, to be always late with any and all innovations - as Marx always effortlessly managed to do. When will this pattern change? Never, as long as Comrade Crap is allowed to remain the figurehead at the helm!

Andropov, as the Secretary General of the Central Committee of the Communist Party of the Soviet Union, during a plenary session of the Party on ideology in the summer of 1983, lamented bitterly the lack of an economic science that would be capable of solving the problems of macroeconomics in a long-range, perspective manner. These laments can be heard with predictable regularity roughly every ten years again and again; even the ideological crisis has its cycles!

Marxism is not a theory, it is not a science, it is, instead, the greatest enemy of any living Social Science. Marxism is an ideology and an apologia, nothing else. It is a political system that lives off the forgeries and falsifications of empirical facts, that lives off the keeping secret of certain issues of its own press from scholars and students. One cannot expect from such a system that decisive analytical results will be brought to light that have scientific new value and would open long-term perspectives.

Perhaps in the future a man endowed with the gift of right action can be found within the leadership cadre of the Communist Party of the Soviet Union, who will muster Lenin's courage to make short shrift with that crappy Marxian scholasticism and who will introduce governing methods of the 21st century. Lenin clearly confessed to a false political course and he made the called-for corrections: "We assumed we had entered – after we initiated State production and State distribution and compared it to the previous one - another economic system of production and distribution."[175]

Even the classic Lenin did not know anything and he assumed erroneously that he had established a non-Capitalist system. Will a new Lenin ever be found, who will say the exact same thing for today's Russian system and who will draw from there really the sole sensible political and economic consequences of and for a Social Democracy? Lenin declared the Party had conducted an entirely false policy under his leadership from the "immediate transition towards Communist production and distribution."[176] When will a new Lenin say that the base for this false policy was and is nothing more than the false ideology of Karl Marx and that there is no such thing as scientific Socialism or Communism and that the exploitation of State Capitalism within our "real" Socialism cannot be abolished today or tomorrow and that there is no reason, therefore, to arm and arm and arm again for the annihilation of the system of private as well as State Capitalist exploitation?

When will a new Lenin say that money may not only not be abolished, but that the functions of the old gold ruble need to be re-established entirely, even on the global market? When will a new Lenin say that prices need to be determined objectively through the world market and, thereby, make performance measurable and stimulate it at the same time? When will a new Lenin say that only all this and then some would allow a genuine blossoming of a pluralist, social Democracy and that there can be no other alternative for the wage-earners in the U.S.S.R. because of objective laws of social movements?

When Lenin I was at the helm of the Russian State the people coerced him through strikes, political rallies and bloody uprisings to achieve the correction of the course of the Party and the people, thus, rescued Russia! Is it possible to have a revolution from above under Lenin II? Lenin I had announced: Learn, learn and then learn again! Lenin II would have to announce on the other hand: Unlearn, unlearn – and then learn everything again anew!

In the face of the slighting of economic science within the COMECON it would come in handy to be reminded of Varga, the leading theorist of the Soviets and the COMINTERN, who was one of the most glowing adherents of Lenin and one of the most capable political economists of his time. This very man wrote with regard to the failed experiment of Communism that it would lead nowhere at all and that it would, instead, produce the most atrocious dysfunctional economy and the most egregious waste. And Varga had at first been an adherent of the superannuated conception, revived by Marx that labor time should be set as a measure of value instead of money.

In 1920, the Supreme Economic Council set up a commission that was directed to make this fantastic law of time effective as Socialist law of value. A rather daring enterprise, indeed, once the value parameter is abolished, how shall the use values of a steam engine and of a sewing needle be made compatible? How many seconds may a sewing needle cost? How shall composite, sophisticated and simple, undifferentiated, highly-qualified and unskilled Labor be expressed in one and the selfsame time certificate?

How should a business calculate its production value, if it learns only in the aftermath, with hindsight, what the produced stuff was worth in hours? How shall the time exertion for production of each individual item and particle and sub-particle be measured statistically and organizationally?

If a high-performance business, high-quality staff with high efficacy delivers 500 final products a day and another, comparable business with bad management, slovenly staff, etc., delivers 250 items in the same time period - will these unequal performances be graced with the same time wages, i.e., the more lazy someone is the more he or she gets, in our case twice of what the diligent would get? The slower someone works, the more time he or she wastes and takes, the more use-value he or she is supposed to "buy" with their time certificates? Hurrah, that is the Communist paradise!

Performance is, thus, punished − that is how it is today in our real-existing Socialism - and the greatest scape-graces and do-no-goods receive the greatest wages. That is the crappy Marxian instruction for action; see *Grundrisse, Capital, Critique of the Gotha Program.* Marx crapped up the law of value, because he cannot differentiate between quality and quantity, economic summertime and wintertime! He is postulating a law of time for his "scientific Communism" that did not even hold true in the Communism of Yore! In May of 1921, the definite deadline to find a time measurement for the monetary system that Lenin had abolished, the Supreme Economic Council had found exactly nothing, in spite of its Commission ever so highly versed and educated in Marxism. Lenin, who had boasted in advance that Communism would reconstruct the urinals in gold for ideological reasons - otherwise he said not a word on the value function of that precious metal in this article on gold, which would indicate that he had not a clue about it, but of the "quality" of having-not-a-clue he did have a lot of - ruefully returned to the gold rubles of the czar. His successors are selling out that ever-so-cursed, precious metal to the gilded West. After South Africa they are the second largest exporter of said urinal material.

Once that intrinsically and essentially very un-Bolshevist ruble began to roll again, Lenin commandeered members of the Central Committee, who had studied Electro-Technology in Germany, to come up with a plan for the electrification of Russia. The creation of a source of energy was vital for the further development of the country. With regard to the further formation of Marxist ideology Lenin's new definition of Communism is quite interesting: "Communism means Soviet power plus electrification." Finally, a light had dawned on the Marxists! Soviet Communism, and that is the slogan of our students today, means a society of cavemen plus nuclear power plants!

When the gold ruble currency of the czarist empire and the technical-organizational conditions of German State Capitalism, including electrical energy, were applied to Russia's economy, the country managed to exit its misery little by little by way of Western help especially through German and English credits. At this point, the economic measures taken finally attained the expected results. Scientific Communism was dead; total State Capitalism was the command of the hour! In reality, Lenin and the Communist Party had foresworn the omnipotent instructions of Marx.

Critics chided Lenin that he hadn't heeded Marx's indication; commodity production could be abolished only once the productive forces had reached "the highest level" of their development. First, that is not true, see *Marginal Notes to the Gotha Program of the Social Democratic Party*, and second, and more importantly, here we are confronted with the totally false general view of Marx, his eschatological expectation! Productive forces will never reach "their highest level." Humanity evolves through historical becoming and unbecoming; there can only be a constant evolution, no final ideal, no ultimate system! The ideology and practice of Communism comes and goes, as does everything else in History. Perennial, eternal is nothing but constant change, which, however, will always proceed on the base of material, industrial and agricultural production. This production will always retain its division of Labor and its exploitation, as in the deeper sense of the economy those who are productive have to sustain those unproductive. The superstructure has to take care that the division of Labor will be conducted within bearable and tolerably just tracks.

For years East Germany prided itself with one of its agitational maxims, as countless as they were stupid - my God, how many dirty benches in parks or in stations could have been painted in clean red instead! - one that read as follows: "Long live the fundamental model of scientific Socialism, the U.S.S.R." Just a model wasn't enough; it had to be a fundamental model! That is probably one to teach us how not to do it. The dilettante treatment of the idea of development, the arbitrary eclecticism in the blending of German philosophy with English political economy and French Socialist-Communist ideology is, in practice, taking its revenge up until today. Marxism consists of an eclectic system of philosophic, historical and economical teachings that are intrinsically and fundamentally wrong.

The destruction of the economic bases and infrastructure of Russia through Lenin at the outset of his Marxist experiment, the chronic lagging of "real" Socialism behind the Capitalist industrialized nations measured in Labor productivity and efficacy, the inability to dominate and control disproportionalities, crises, unemployment, State bankruptcies and inflation within the world system of "real" Socialism, and worst of all, the mutual martial slaughtering of the fighting comrades amongst themselves, who all call themselves adherents of Marx and Lenin, Engels, Stalin and Mao, in short, the Marxist teachers, lead to the central philosophic problem of Marxist-Leninist ideology, i.e., to the liberation of Man, to his and her self-realization in freedom and peace, in social harmony and justice.

How can Man develop in this alleged New Order, how can he or she live, materially and ideatically? The practical results are only too well known, here as elsewhere, they provide a crushing indictment of the ideology. In the first part of my inquiry I epitomized them in the formula of proletarian Absolutism, certainly not a goal worth striving for. Marxist Communism cripples and destroys each and every thinking human being in the long run, just as every absolutist dictatorship has ever done. Marxist ideology is the enemy of humanity. Humanist needs cannot be planned by either the Central Committee or the Supreme Economic Council, to be satisfied in their wake.

It is high time to get rid of the irrational ideology of Marx, to throw the pamphlets of this propagandist of civil wars and world wars upon the heap of scrap paper, as his ideology is inimical to peace and that means in today's terms: It is destructive to humanity. Up to now there has been no like analysis of the alleged theoretical achievements of Marx in the form given here. We shall see what the informed discussion will bring, especially with regard to the tenets of Political Economy. On the one hand, Marx is being rejected as an over dogmatic adherent of technological productive force by the socially new ecological and environmental movements; on the other hand, he provides social concepts even for politicized parsons in the Federal Republic of Germany and elsewhere, who stand - oddly enough - upon the shoulders of Marx instead of the shoulders of Christ. So contradictory is the valuation of Marx in many other areas, as well.

It is not a question of overkill, of somehow making Marx even "deader" than he already is. What is at issue here is the deeper theoretical understanding of historical, social and economic laws that influence social development and their possible or impossible utility in their Marxist, reform-communist, or social-democratic respect. It has to be made clear in this context that Marx never was a scholar or scientist, but on the contrary, a stupid, but fanatical ideologue, a half-educated element, as the Democratic Labor Communists of his time appraised him, synonymous with dictatorship and inhumanity, the latter's very personification, indeed!

For the survival of humanity the humanist principle will have to be activated, not the principle of class struggle which consists of the over dogmatized isolation of just one faction within the working class.

Marx himself was an element hostile to workers; he called the tendency of the French *Atelier* in his *Critique of the Gotha Program* the tendency of "the reactionary workers," because they would not let themselves be dominated by an intellectual equally alienated from the world and their class. Compare the analysis in the first part of this work. This and this alone is the true and genuine Marx. There is no other. And that has to be made clear to all adherents! The history of human society is not historically and economically determined and dominated by an imaginary Marxist-Leninist law of development as the "classic writers" and the Central Committees of the Communist Parties have been preaching all this time. That is a stupid superstition! Every industrial society of today can dominate and master its common nature, just as every individual can master its own personal one. Nothing is subject to teleological processes, not the fate of a class, not the fate of our people, not the fate of our German nation. Man can master his or her own nature just as his or her social one and that's what makes him or her human; human in and by itself, not human in Capitalist or Socialist terms. Man shapes and orders in thinking and anticipating.

Why should a pluralist-democratic State of the West, which is endowed with higher scientific, social, economic and technical means and possibilities not be better able than Eastern State Capitalism to perfect its industry and agriculture, its infrastructure and service sector, but also, and that is the deciding factor, its social network in keeping all of its citizens' liberties? Who is leading and in charge of even the automatization of mental reproduction processes, the West or the East? Who has the perfect data banks, systems of communication, and computer brains of the fifth generation, the West or the East?

What does the ideology of Marxism have, to oppose all this applied science and know-how, an ideology that was retrograde, antiquated and adverse to progress even in the 19th century? The formula would be: Many tanks and then more tanks, but very little brains! Of course, the West may decline, as well, but then only of its own partial lack of brains in political respects which cannot be gauged from here; on the other hand, some things become clearer from the outside.

Western democracies can, given sufficient worldwide cooperation, develop their production conditions better and with greater alacrity whereby the Russians and *ersatz*-Russians will in peaceful competition completely run out of steam. The Capitalist countries were steeped in a catastrophic crisis in 1929, but Keynes taught them, how to do better in the future. For a quarter century, thus, the so-called economic miracle prospered worldwide. Everyone knows on what that was based, but meanwhile the conditions have changed. Why has the system of national and regional, supranational and global cybernetics not been adapted to the now again changed conditions? Then the social problems which accrue from the irresponsibly high unemployment could be improved and it could ultimately be banished entirely from a surplus society. Or would we want to opt for a real-socialist society of under consumption, of lack, of suppression of personality guaranteed by the State, in short: a Communist order?

Western macroeconomies are not only performing better; they are more pliable, faster in their reaction, more adaptable than the Eastern planned economies! On the Crapist-Marxist part of the planet the productive forces collided continuously with the conditions of production. How often have the Russians railroaded and stampeded workers' uprisings since 1945? Even then and there they had their N.E.P. experience! It began with the German workers: June 17, 1953. How often have the Russians disciplined, demoted and murdered the leading cadres of their sister parties? Always in following the recipe of Marx: Power alone is holy and sacrosanct, and who has that power, as our workers are used to say, will abuse it! On the other hand, in contrast to N.A.T.O., it is a peace-loving power. Entirely peacefully they have shot down the Hungarians in 1956, entirely peacefully their tanks have steam-rollered Prague in 1968. How often have they brought the world to the brink of that great social world war that Marx always so desired? Can these red imperialists be trusted at all?

If it is true, according to Marx's scheme, that productive forces and conditions of production have to collide permanently, then do these collisions, from 1945 onward - that is in the almost Marxist age - begin in the Capitalism of the West or the State Capitalism of the East? And with regard to us Germans: Who was it who commanded the marches against the Czechs and Slovaks, who mobilized against the Poles, the aggressive, revengist army of the Federal Republic of Germany, or the general staff of the East German army, so brimming with peace that one can hardly stand it?

When will the politicized parsons of the F.D.R. and the West German Communist Party actively advocate monuments to the victims of the Russian reign of terror, the slaughtered workers not only in Poland, but also in the G.D.R.? Would that not be more true to the spirit of the alleged liberator of the working class, Karl Marx, upon whom they are calling at the most inappropriate occasions? Or are they proceeding as the genuine German classic, Goethe, who ironically recommended: Be generous in interpreting and if you can't interpret then take the scrap paper used for something else!

For Marx that will not be necessary. It is necessary only to look at the historic fate, the practical application of his ideological hypotheses. It is merely necessary to regard impartially the catastrophic reality of the Eastern *demi-monde* in its historical and current aspects, to realize how Marxism has to be judged. As long as one remains caught piously in his abstract ideological teachings and as long as one mistakes them for a scientific theory, this may pass as rather workable. If one begins to test and investigate theory and practice, one loses all former illusions and those tend to end badly, by and large, anyway. Many will say: This is all well and good, but we know all this already. Certainly, who can live in a place where one can read, think, write and speak freely and clearly would, indeed, have to know what's what, because this is an issue of the fate of Germany in the controversy between pluralist plurality and Marxist simplicity.

But let us again remember Goethe: Error is constantly repeated in the deed. For that very reason truth has to be repeated incessantly in words.

Only in this manner can the necessary steps towards action be taken.

Concluding Remarks:

Pseudological Ideology and Politics

What did the Marxist-Leninist ideology and the political systems ensuing from it bring the working population in insights and positive change?

Has it abolished war, crises, unemployment, social misery, famine, exploitation, repression, terror and loss of liberty in our real-existing Socialism, or has it just reproduced all of the above on an ideologically more hypocritical level?

Has it realized the human rights guaranteed by the United Nations, but to this day not ratified by the Soviet Union, or are the international agreements regarding political, civil, economic, social and cultural rights only available from ponderous law tomes after they have gone through the shredder?

Has this ideology brought peace, autonomy and national independence to the suppressed peoples of the red colonial empire or has it treaded in the dust the fundamental values of human and societal coexistence, or railroaded them with tanks?

Has this ideology at least made this real-socialist State Capitalism and its "liberated labor" more joyful, more creative, more efficient and productive and has it, thus, enriched and improved the life of the working population materially more than that of the wage earners in the Western industrial countries, or is this ideology left by a large margin in all decisive areas of productivity, macroeconomic performance, high technologies and future technologies and environmental protection behind those of this dying Capitalism?

With these questions I am turning especially toward my Western colleagues of the faculties of the Economic and Historical Sciences: What I was able to do, I have done. Through the morass of lies and political misinformation of this ideology I have blazed a trail. No Soviet propaganda will be able to obliterate the facts that I have exposed here. But remember, much more remains to be done. Open the trail to a full forest clearing! Unmask Marx in a much more comprehensive manner; not alone as a mean, retrograde plagiarizer who cannot be taken seriously, who never even created new value in historical philosophy or economics, but as the peace-imperiling political agitator he is! Slap into his face the above-quoted maxim of Lucille Aurore Dupin, pseudoandronym Georges Sand, together with his world war propaganda and civil war agitation! There is more than enough reason for this: Inculcating entire peoples in hatred, having to zero in on their own as on an enemy image, agitating for doom, determined by an ideology which is directed by Germans against Germans, is more than life-threatening to humanity! For Soviet interests to mow down the German flowers of youth hither and yonder the frontier, that is the ideological drill in the G.D.R. Let the Russians fend for themselves for this alleged ideologically predestined world hegemony, but leave us out! No human life, no nickel or dime henceforth for this system!

Above all of Germany hovers the peril of nuclear annihilation, or annihilation through conventional weapons systems. This is an extremely irrational stage, historically unique, which can by accident be brought about at any moment. What would happen, for instance, if not the Russians flew their airborne weaponry into N.A.T.O. airspace, but, if, vice versa, N.A.T.O. inadvertently shot a missile into Soviet areas? We know only all to well how the Soviets are not even able to shoot straight. See the Korean civil aircraft accidentally downed recently or the coincidental crash of missiles, or Major Nicholson of the U.S. Military Mission. We know all too well how ersatz-Russians who pride themselves to be "Chekists" have others badly shoot for them, see the victims of the Berlin Wall. What would happen if the Soviets opted for a preventive strike in their pathological fear of the West, just because of disinformation or nerves? Or, what if they would deem themselves safe in their first-strike capacity within the framework of their Star Wars program. Germany and its children would get scorched like a torch just like one General Secretary of the U.S.S.R. threatened it would happen decades ago!

How could Germany evade the accidental, unintended martial catastrophe? Only if all atomic, biological and chemical weapons were to disappear from Germany including all military missions and all foreign troops. We would like to get rid of the Soviet military deployment in Germany including the SS 20s and worse.

How can that be achieved? Only if the Treaties of Yalta and Potsdam, i.e., the treaties between the U.S.S.R. and the G.D.R. and the Western Allied Powers and the Federal Republic of Germany, were honored that include the provision of a Peace Treaty for Germany in acknowledging its national sovereignty and boundaries. We will have to insist on the autonomy of nations and on the keeping of international treaties. *Let us follow the maxim: Peace, Liberty, Unity.*

Goethe, the most classic of our German classic poets, inculcates in us that it is not enough to know, but to realize, that it is not enough to will, but to do!

What needs to be done practically? Let us have a secret plebiscite in all of Germany with the following questions:

- Are you for the conclusion of a Peace Treaty with Germany for the 50th anniversary of the end of World War II in 1995, yes or no?

- Are you for a pluralist-democratic constitution of Germany, which will become effective with the ratification of the Peace Treaty, yes or no?
- Are you for an interim solution, beginning in January 1990, which has to be prepared immediately which shall include a union of customs, currency, passport and the economic and political sphere, between the two States of East and West Germany, between East and West Berlin, yes or no?
- Are you for the first election of the [new] German Reichstag in January of 1990, which will be given the task to work out a constitution for Germany, to represent the German Union toward the outside world and to prepare the Peace Treaty with the victorious Allied Powers, yes or no?
- Are you for the second election of the German Reichstag in January of 1995, which will ratify the Constitution, form a national government, which will sign the Peace Treaty with the Powers of the anti-Hitler coalition on May 8, 1995, yes or no?
- Are you for the reinstitution of Berlin as the German Capital, yes or no?

During the 19th century the individuals with the best characters, the college professors and their students in the fraternities, the poets and thinkers and the practitioners from the political and the economic sphere as well as the most capable minds of the liberal, the democratic and the labor movements stood together at the forefront in the struggle for the unity and liberty of Germany against the preponderance of Russian reaction, who had their dirty hands, their gold and their vile informers in all important German and European cabinets.

It was an irony of History that the closest friends of the Russians, the most reactionary Germans, those who wielded power in Prussia, would bleed to their death under the shots of the Democrats of Germany in the catacombs of Rastatt after the terminal fights of the revolution of 1848/'49 that was fought for unity and liberty, that these reactionary Germans became the executors of those patriots for freedom. The white revolutionary Bismarck forged the national unity of the Germans, whose national tradition began with the Holy Roman Empire of the German Nation and not, as the *ersatz*-Russian pen-wielders of the Socialst Unity Party S.E.D. today would have it – by the by, much in contradiction to their chief party ideologues, Marx and Engels – with the year 1870. History does *not* repeat itself in its concrete phenomenal forms, but it follows very well the inter-exchange of objective and subjective social laws! The factual coercion of the scientific-technological and the economic-financial development - used and accelerated by active and goal-oriented personalities, who willed and acted in a vigorous manner - paved the way, decades before Bismarck and the latter's forging of the imperial unity. A series of German universities, above all Goettingen - probably because there the influence of the English royal house and the English Political Economy were especially developed - gave orientation to the Prussian reformers around Stein and Hardenberg as to the wars of liberation with their perspectives on world and science. They and their followers were men who did not shrink back – in contrast to our pseudo-classic Marx – from the reactionary schools of the Halle or Berlin universities.

Among those scholars and practitioneers there was an excellent mind who managed to combine theory and practice in the interest of German unity and liberty like no other: Friedich List.

The vulgar economist Marx could never in the least equal this man who had the political and economic range of a true classic; for that very reason Marx vituperated and riled against the latter as much as he could.

I am turning to the Conference of University Deans of the Federal Republic of Germany [westdeutsche Rektorenkonferenz] with the plea and postulate to take the initiative to start at all German universities and colleges Friedrich-List Committees on a bipartisan and multi-partisan basis. Bring together the finest minds from those committees for a national convention that would found a central Friedrich-List Committee, to create a statute and program of this movement, which shall, proceeding from the educational institutions, integrate all cities, townships and communities, even down to the smallest village and hamlet and bring them to a genuine popular movement for peace, unity and liberty!

No party difference, no confessional or other difference may interfere, which would impede the reconciliation of the plebiscite. This popular movement shall not be a party and it shall disband as soon as its goal has been reached. This movement has to become, with mounting force, a concentration of all peaceful, ecological, social and national powers – nothing less is at stake than the physical rescue of land and life! Only the Peace Treaty and disarmament will release the ideative, financial and material means and possibilities that are necessary to avoid the ecological and demographic catastrophe which is lethally threatening Germany. There has to be an end in German politics of that leering toward sanction of the respective superpowers like a Doberman. First and foremost, the question of life and survival has to be asked!

For forty years we keep hearing from the superpowers on all sides: We want peace, peace, peace! The same slogans were repeated from both German governments. But what is the reality behind these slogans? Below this sloganeering for peace Germany, in

East and West, has been quietly put the atomic powderkeg of the world that can blow up any moment!

Is it not high time, instead of waiting for the general world regulator, to change the German conditions towards peace and security? Is it not high time to begin with the generally proclaimed disarmament in Germany in concrete terms?

The voice of the people – the voice of God: Let all young men and women who have reached majority, all older women and mothers, all older men and seniors, who still remember the last war, decide in a general plebiscite what should become of Germany! The victorious Allied Powers, all members of the United Nations, would deem the right of self-determination of a nation like Germany equal to the one of, for example, Papua, New Guinea?

I would like to appeal to the student associations of the Federal Republic of Germany: Powwow the issues in your councils, connect with other youth organizations and find a consensus! Become avant-guard fighters for you own peaceful future! Without peace you will have your life, as well as the lives of your children, behind you. Talk to the various Communist groups and to the *Free German Youth [F.D.J. – the Communist Youth organization]*. They will have to show their true colors, whether they would like to continue to engage in the peace cant to enforce Soviet, i.e., imperialist power politics, or whether they are concerned with German – and that means in this case – humanitarian values. Turncoat the *ersatz*-Russians ideologically, but be careful to distinguish between those loyal members that have been led astray and those Party functionaries paid by East Berlin!

For starters, as a discussion paper for the national Friedrich-List Convention I would like to submit the following thoughts:

The values from experience of History can be condensed. In this manner, temporal cycles can be accelarated and be made more economically effective. The development of the *Zollverein* [the Customs Federations of the small feudal German states in the 19th century] has worked well, even admidst belligerent conflicts. Why should a like enterprise not work today between the two larger German States, in spite of the ideological warfare that the Soviets still erroneously claim to be the prerequisite for coexistence? Ten years' time is not too little, fifty years were given to the Allied Powers to find a democratic and peaceful solution. It is inadmissible to put off the solution of the German Issue to the indefinite future, until the Atomic Big Bang, accidentally or deliberately induced!

The experiences of our 20th century Customs Association of the European Union bear many analogies with, but also a much larger experiential reservoir than the experiences of the 19th century German Customs Federation. Why should these experiences not be utilized for the temporal political union of Germany, the transitional state towards a unified statist whole, especially in the areas of economic and financial law? Creative performances of economists and legal experts will be much sought after, when the issue of an effective, qualitative innovative, economic legal framework arises, as the statist and cooperative sector brought in by the G.D.R. will have to be retained in a new pluralist economic constitution. The statist proportion of industry within the Western industrialized nations would be well comparable with the one of a newly-united Germany.

Why is not the unification of West Germany and East Germany a national shame and a peace-menacing fact, but, instead, the militaristically-maintained isolation of the German Democratic Republic or G.D.R. from the Federal Republic of Germany or F.R.G.?

Nobody knows how world history and German politics will continue to unfold: Will the S.U. or the U.S. achieve First Strike capacity in arms technology and will they make use of it? Will the U.S. achieve space superiority, or will the danger of a conventional war grow, which would be disastrous for Germany in equal measure? Would Russia, in the face of a complete military superiority of the West, possibly because of S.D.I./"Star Wars," return to its borders? Would there then be forces in Germany, who, as junior partners of the U.S., would demand and enforce the return of East Prussia, Silesia and the Sudeten territories? The Russians would be, in such a case, closer to their national shirt than to their Eastern European coat. Or in other words, would positive alternatives ensue from the negotiations in Geneva, Vienna and Helsinki, which would induce a turn towards disarmament and a furthering toward German unity?

Come what may, Germany has to prepare itself for the rejection of negative variants, i.e., any material for conflict needs to be reduced. For that reason, all neighboring states would have to receive a peaceful safeguarding of its borders. The *Ostvertraege* or Eastern Treaties oblige the Federal Republic. The *Ostvertraege* do not oblige a unified Germany, which will come one way or another. A border issue would stop being one, once it is regulated within the framework of a Peace Treaty. A Germany peacefully united by 1995 would guarantee all borders, would relinquish arms of aggression and would put revanchist demands and propaganda under the punishment of the Law. Neighbors should consider that such a solution would banish the peril of nationalist extremisms. On the other hand, a revengist government could very well rise in Germany. Nothing is impossible in matters of History: it is not possible to trample into the dirt the national honor of a people. A patriotic renewal, comparable to the one engendered by Reagan in the U.S., would be conceivable in Germany. What would be the consequences for East and West? We are always told that fire and water don't mix. But there is much water in the mix already. Do the Italian and the French Communists exist within a national community, have they not a state capitalist and a private capitalist sector within their economies?

Would it not be better if the German people decided themselves whether to live together under one political roof? Who actually has empowered a handful of anti-German Central Committee secretaries, to execute sycophantically the Russian policy of G.D.R. isolation? A half dozen figures, a committee that keeps perpetuating itself - an institution, indeed, which even Montesquieu deemed the most appropriate to perpetuate ad infinitum existing injustices – presumes to conduct the fate of the German nation upon Russian directives. The German people will never accept this!

What should the Peace Treaty stipulate? The outer boundaries in their present shape, the disengaging from both military blocs, the withdrawal of all occupational troops, the removal of all atomic, biological and chemical weaponry from German soil, the abolition of the German Army and its replacement by a people's militia or national guard, geared towards defensive measures and border control, but no limitation of future technologies of space travel and rocket science for peaceful purposes!

Furthermore: Abolition of all paramilitary forces, special forces, civil defense; guarantee of the inviolability of the German borders by the U.N. Security Council, lifting of the separating of Germany into the four zones and the Four Powers Administration for Berlin. The Peace Treaty would bring Germany safeguard from nuclear holocaust, which neither the S.U. nor the U.S. missiles would be able to prevent, on the contrary, they would both assure their respective use.

History has no example of weapons systems that continued to grow and grow, to be scrapped, in turn. The real-socialist order is no exception to this rule. See Ussuri, see Vietnam and China, see Cambodia, see Afghanistan. The maxim that Socialism and peace be identical is a propaganda lie, parroted by the German *ersatz*-Russians. Allegedly, Marxist-Leninists are for intellectual and not for belligerent dispute. If someone now actually does seek an intellection dispute, he is deported, detained, or murdered – all in the name of perpetual peace!

We strongly reject such anti-German propaganda, which could be found in the *Red Banner [the Communist Party Organ]*, as late as July 1932, and welcome, on the other hand that the *Young World*, the publication of the F.D.J., did republish the same in its Thaelmann Quotes Column in March of 1984. It brings out the fact that the C.P. Marxist Thaelmann helped the Nazi and anti-Marxist Hitler to come to power via anti-German Soviet propaganda and it highlights, who today does not represent German interests of survival, but Russian interests of world hegemony: "We do not know any other fatherland than Soviet Russia ...the defense of our Socialist fatherland, the Soviet Union ...

means the defense of the innermost life interests of the working class
..."

Enough of that, once and for all! Our homeland was, is and will be the land of our ancestors! Germany to the Germans, the Gulag Archipelago to the Russians and all *ersatz*-Russians! The Russians, Russian missiles and the half German *ersatz*-Russians be gone! Dear Soviets, we are giving you the Chekists back as a gift with all editors of the *Young World*, you may resettle them in Kazakhstan for fruitful labor services! Let them found a new republic there: Moscow be hailed! And we would like to do that by peaceful means: remove yourselves after the signing of the Peace Treaty!

The West German government and the pluralistic democracies of the West have to be won over for this solution. This means that the overeager Marxist-Leninist preachers of peace have to be exposed as enemies of the peace. Russians and *ersatz*-Russians alone will refuse to extinguish the remaining embers of World War II and they will refuse to honor their own treaties and promises.

The Peace Treaty would entail that the Soviet Russians would have to withdraw to their own national boundaries and that, precisely, they have been, as yet, unwilling to do for reasons of neocolonialist military hegemonial ambitions, because that would mean the end of the administrative exploitation of their satellite states. The Peace Treaty would entail that the Marxist-Leninist ideology would be reduced to zero in Germany and that, precisely, the *ersatz*-Russians are loathe to allow, as they would shrink to microscopic proportions in legal elections and one would have to look for them with a magnifying glass then to find traces of them at all.

The Peace Treaty would entail that peace in Europe would become a tangible quantity, as the Soviets' ideological and military aggression would be reduced significantly in geographical terms.

The Peace Treaty would entail that Western-style pluralistic, liberal democracies vanquished Eastern-style dictatorships and that would enable to begin with a life worth living for millions of Germans within East Germany.

The Peace Treaty would entail that the possibility of genuine coexistence between Eastern and Western Europe were to become a reality. In spite of all ideological adversity of the Soviet Russians – which has to be expressed clearly and unequivocally as long as Russia continues to hanker after the utopian, reactionary, Marxist-Communist template - Germany has to develop excellent economic, financial, cooperative relations, in other words, a real coexistence with the U.S.S.R.

The Russians have to understand that the Peace Treaty would be in their own interest, as well. They have to understand that Germany, in accordance with a millennial historical tradition, is a country of the West and intends to and will remain so, as well. Their Stalin was perfectly correct in his judgment: Soviet Communism fits Germany like a horse saddle would fit on the back of a cow!

The Russia have to understand that peace for themselves will become possible only once they relinquish the maniacal Marxian idea of world hegemony, which Hitler had, as well. They will have to give up any notion of war and civil war. They will have to relinquish the past practice of fanning conflicts militarily in other countries and try to eradicate socialist opposition within their own borders. They should confine themselves prudently to bring order into their chaotic economic and agricultural affairs and to democratize their societal relations; that will give them more than enough to do for the weal of their own peoples. Germany has as much right for self-determination as any other country on the planet.

The Peace Treaty will entail that Germany will become a country to establish equilibrium between East and West, with a free determination of all Germans for the interior constitution of their country. Which outward parameters would support such an equilibration? A positive solution and resolution of the negotiations in Geneva, Vienna and Helsinki could bring further disarmament and the securing of peace in Germany. What would happen, however, if everything continues along negative lines as it has done up to now? Then the following would have to be stated:

For forty years Moscow has been proclaiming: Peace, peace, peace. Result: A maniacal arms race, life, in general, skirting a nuclear catastrophe.

For forty years Moscow has been proclaiming: German unity. Result: Division in concrete, Berlin Wall, death strip along the border.

For forty years Moscow has been proclaiming: Every nation their own way toward socialism. Result: Near complete Russification.

Does all this not signify that it is high time to confront those people who are trying to blow the Russian bugle in an independent Germany? To confront those who let themselves be hoodwinked by Russia and talk about the "irredeemability" of the status quo and who, thus, strenghthen the potential of Russian ideological aggression and their military application? If irredeemability of the European status quo is to signify that the outside borders of Germany are to remain as is, then the answer is: Yes, very well, but the domestic conditions of Germany have to be changed completely by way of the peaceful means of international law: Self-determination via plebiscite for the future of the German nation!

What would happen if all present negotiations would come to nought? In this case, the German people will have to oblige their respective two governments to initiate decisive steps toward the following actions: The Allied powers should be obliged via plebiscite and through both governments to leave the country simultaneously. Would they in that case declare war on Germany?

Certain political preachers maintain the anchoring of the respective Germanies within the two large power blocs would be necessary to ascertain military balance. Germany, however, does not weigh in the nuclear dispute at all. Ten minutes after the initiation of nuclear war there will be no Germany and no Germans left. That is all that can be said about it. This is a conviction I have gained in many conversations with Russians, not only slightly - or fully - inebriated Russians, but very sober and clear-minded ones, with military men as well as civilians, namely, that the Russians would welcome this solution of the eradication of Germany if war has to be. That poses the question whether we would have the right of national self-defense or not?

What would be the consequences of the plebiscites for the Constitution? The conditions of the Peace Treaty would have to be anchored constitutionally, equally international obligations of the political or economic kind would have to be settled. Domestically, instead of the Communist dictatorship the principles of a free Constitution would have to apply.

What would be the consequences of the plebiscite for the transitional state? Free, unimpeded travel, unimpeded exchange of literature, newspapers, journals, abolition of the off-limit border zones, free choice of the location of study, vocational training and work, no inhibition with regard to marriage, abolition of all blackballing of professionals from certain careers in East and West [Berufsverbot], full amnesty for all political prisoners in East and West. Imperative is further the reinstitution of the German local culture of the federal states [Laender] as, say, the Federal states of Thuringia and Bavaria would be able to solve many things in a more timely fashion than the Federal governments of Bonn and Berlin. An example would be the canal built between the two townships Neustadt and Sonneberg of the two lands and which is now popularly called after its founder, the former Bavarian governor, Franz-Josef Strauss.

Further interim solutions would have to be instituted in the following areas: free trade and exchange of goods and services, convertibility of the mark in East and West, balancing of possible mutual deficits in the domestic German trade, reopening of all ways of traffic via land, water, rail, reopening of all local "accross-the-border" trade and traffic, abolition of all customs controls and duties, rights of all economic and municipal units of the G.D.R. to deal autonomously with companies, banks and communal units on the other side; formation of a German domestic investment bank, institution of counselling units for the sectors of the economy, currency, finance, industry, agriculture, craftsmanship, traffic, legal coordination, etc.

Which economic, social and ecological advantages would ensue for the working population in Germany after these regulations have been, by and by, put into practice?

The economy would be bilaterally liberated from its present disproportionality, unemployment could be abolished. The G.D.R. is laboring on the environmentally damaging mining and energy production of brown coal; the F.R.G. is suffocating from its own coal deposits; the G.D.R. needs construction craftsmen; the F.R.G. has those as an unemployment contingent. The G.D.R. needs coal, steel, energy, environmental protection, high technologies, infrastructure – a qualitative economic growth would be preprogrammed over decades if a unified economic policy were assured. The G.D.R. needs ships, as domestic production barely covers export demand, F.R.D. shipyards are closed simultaneously – why should Germany not have the right to utilize the potential of their country for the benefit of their workers, but also, to conserve their natural habitat? Are the damaged or dying East German forests less German forest than those of West Germany? How much longer can we be passive onlookers in face of the destruction of nature in Germany? Should we wait 'til damage going into many millions would go into many billions? Should we wait 'til today's national resorts have been so ecolocially devastated that they would turn into deserts? In the later case, of course, the Communist Party planning commission could start drilling for oil there and all unresolved issues of currency imbalance and economic disequilibrium would then be solved directly, if not miraculously!

Would a greater settlement of the sparsely-populated regions of Mecklenburg not disencumber the densely-populated urban areas? Why should there not be, in areas where the air is still unpolluted, electronic factories erected which would not further contribute to pollution? Could the hinterland of the Baltic shores not be developed as world-class weekend resorts for the urban populations farther South to be reached by rail? Why use congested routes or highways to further pollution? Could that not become the location of a new building and construction boom?

Proletarians of Germany, unite! Unite in the List Committees, unite in the East and West German labor unions! Then you would achieve not only peace, but also democratic conditions, rights and security in the political and societal areas, as well! Do away with the sycophantic mentality of the G.D.R. functionaries, cooperate with the West German union, D.G.B., on all levels, create ideative and real-political alternatives to the mania of total militarization of society from kindergarden to retirement homes!

In all of Germany there is enough work and there are enough apprentice positions available for all young people; no young person in Germany should be without an individual perspective for the future, if we are able to give Germany a national future! Together we can brave all problems!

It remains for Russia to decide whether they would not want to transfer such an experiment unto East and West in general: Should they not join the World Bank, should they not assume their rights and obligations within the International Monetary Fund and the G.A.T.T., should they not agree with the regional financial, ecological and economic cooperation between COMECON and the E.U., should they not utilize convertible currencies and partial economic regulation for the relaxing of their overly stiff, inflexible State Capitalism in guarding globally-coordinated and agreed-upon parameters – in short, should they not engage in peaceful economic and social competition, instead of ruining themselves through hyperarmament economically and socially! Gorbachev, the likeable sweeper with an iron broom, should verily not listen to me. That not withstanding, it might not hurt if he were to look again at Lenin's directive for Geneva and ask himself why Comrade Vladimir had wanted to invent the International Monetary Fund back at that time?

Would anyone in East and West, in North and South be disadvantaged, if the tensions and confrontations between the Marxist ideology and policy and democratic pluralism in general were to disappear and if in Germany the inhuman Iron Curtain were to be dismantled? Germany would then become too powerful economically, you say? All the better, all the more it would be able to contribute to the all-European process of unification to the E.U., to the COMECON and to the so-called "Third World" countries. The rivalry of the superpowers would then be deflected to the Pacific coast. To that extent, the line of confrontation between East Berlin and West Germany could also be relaxed, this to the advantage of the Germans, but also to the advantage of the superpowers. The greatest gain would obviously be the deflection of the peril of a nuclear war. Let there be a Peace Treaty with Germany – half a century of non-peace is more than enough! Halt the state of war by May 8, 1995!

It would be nice to see effective treaties, after all, and Talleyrand may be remembered. Diplomacy is akin to music: a motif that is not set to a score has no value. We have had enough yada - yada – yada, enough of those empty and mendacious phrases and slogans! Germany has waited and hoped enough. Should we be made fools of for all eternity?

Nobody is going to come to our rescue if we don't come to our rescue ourselves first: Help yourself and then God will help you also! Political illusions are uncalled for. Only a powerful endeavor of the overwhelming majority of the German people in East and West against, precisely, certain politicians of East and West will clear the way for the Peace Treaty.

German intelligentsia, our academics and scientists, engineers, lawyers, lawmakers, historians, educators and, above all, our writers, publishers and, last but not least, our journalists in all media shall assume the position of the vanguard.

Intellectual theorists are less encumbered than politicians. They can both say and do more. They should not only confront every citizen of the Federal Republic, but also every citizen of the Democratic Republic, with the issue of the plebiscite. They can contact the genuine peace movement through the Friedrich-List Committees, but also with the National Council and the party-directed peace council of the G.D.R.

In East Germany signatures have to be collected also to that end. Nobody may punish a German who demands the conclusion of a Peace Treaty and the withdrawal of foreign troops and the clearing of all atomic, biological and chemical weapons from German territory.

The East German Chairman of the State Council has declared himself that he is prepared to make the G.D.R. zone free and clear of such weapons. That would mean, further, that the Russians have become redundant and that they can leave! It is they, alone, who can produce, store and operate all this devilish machinery, the East German National People's Army [N.V.A.] cannot do this. And the Russians can leave only, once everything connected with their leave has been organized, and that can happen only - see the Four-Power Agreement of Berlin and the Military Missions - through a Peace Treaty.

Our government is wise. It articulates prudently. The fullest harmony between it and its adoring people would, nevertheless, be engendered without words. Where genuine policies of peace become state policies all friends of peace will be well sheltered.

We Germans have three possibilities to fail as a nation. But we have only one option to survive with human dignity: through peace to unity, through unity to liberty of Germany as a whole!

Endnotes:

[With the exception of notes 54, 67, 124, 144, 167 all other endnotes are those of the author. The other five endnotes have been added for the convenience of the American reader by the translator].

[1]. Compare *Karl Marx Biography*, Berlin, 1983, editor: Institute for Marxism-Leninism of the Central Committee of the Communist Party of the Soviet Union. For these and further tirades see p. 5 - 11

[2]. According to Marx ideology is a false reflection of reality, theory on the other hand is an adequate reproduction of it, therefore, it is science. But if one has to write non-sense then with method please: Today in the Socialist Unity Party of Germany theory and politics, agitation and propaganda, science, ideology and economics do not only blend, no, they form "an inseparable unity". One may only marvel why language has such diverging terms for such diverging areas, if everything ends up being the same Marxism-Leninism potpourri?

[3]. Perhaps the bio party hacks, whose high remunerations are not quite matched by their intellectual and educational level, may learn when exactly Herschel became the protestant Heinrich, from the *Jahrbuch des Koelnischen Geschichtsvereins*, 1932, or from the standard Marxist secondary literature

[4]. Cf. letter of H. Marx to K. Marx from November 18, 1835, copied in the mother's handwriting. This letter, as well as all following ones, are quoted from *Marx Engels Complete Works*, 1927, I, ½. There also the following lyrical effusions can be found which will not be noted separately each time.

[5]. op. cit., p. 182

[6]. Quoted from Auguste Cornu: *Karl Marx and Friedrich Engels – Life and Works,* East Berlin, 1954, Vol. I, p. 55

[7]. Quote from Karl Obermann: *Deutschland von 1815 – 1849, Beitraege zum Lehrbuch der Deutschen Geschichte,* East Berlin 1961, p. 24. F. List, *Das natuerliche System der Politischen Oekonomie - Oekonomische Studientexte*, East Berlin 1962, which is – next to Lavergne-Peguilhen and Schulz authors who we have to deal with later on – a treasure trove to refute the lie Marx had been the creator and originator of the

materialist conception of History. Obermann is citing Marx in connection with List, so one would have to assume Marx had assessed the situation in a much more informed and differentiated manner. Actually, exactly the contrary happens to be the case. Obermann does not cite Marx as List's contemporary, but the older Marx. Forgers, thus, have many creative techniques.

[8] . M.E.G.A., East Berlin, 1983, volume IV/6

[9] . Walter Ulbricht: *Die Bedeutung des Werkes "Capital" von Karl Marx fuer die Schaffung des entwickelten gesellschaftlichen Systems des Sozialismus in der DDR and der Kampf gegen das staatsmonopolistischeHerrschaftssystem in Westdeutschland,* East Berlin 1969, p. 11., i.e. "The significance of the work 'Capital' for the creation of a developed social system of Socialism in the G.D.R. and the struggle against the state-monopolistic hegemonial system in West Germany" Does that strike us not as a peace-loving title of a pamphlet? Would it not be revengism if the Chancellor of West Germany, in turn, would proclaim a struggle against the system of the G.D.R.? Long live the peaceful coexistence of all Germans!

[10] . Oddly enough those "socio-political crises in the development of socialist countries" recently are not hushed up anymore, possibly because they have become too many, cf.: J.A. Ambarzumow, *Lenin's Analysis of the Crisis of 1921,* in: *Sowjetwissenschaft, Gesellschaftswissenschaftliche Beitraege, Hefte 6/ 1984, p. 595*

[11] . Quoted from: *Karl Marx, Notstand, Staat and Presse.* Ed. Wilhelm Bracht, Trier 1968, p. 30. In the old *Marx Engels Complete Works* this quote from the *Rheinische Zeitung* from October 16, 1842: "The *Rheinische Zeitung* in which the Communist ideas *in their present form* ..."

[12] . Wilhelm Weitling, *Garantien der Harmonie and Freiheit*, Hamburg 1849, 3rd edition, p. XIII, quoted in the future as *Garantien*

[13] . ibid., p. XX

[14] . Quoted from: Lorenz von Stein, *Geschichte der sozialen Bewegung.* Second vol. *The Industrial Society – Socialism and Communism in France from 1830 – 1848.* Ed.: Dr. Gottfried Salomon, Munich, 1921, p. 471

[15] . Herder, *Collected Works,* Ed.: B. Suphan, vol. 32, Berlin 1899, p. 1

[16]. Marx/Engels Works [MEW], vol. 7, East Berlin 1964, p. 89. Blanqui's "Parisian dictatorship," the ruling of the capital over the country, has been implemented fully by Lenin, very much following Blanqui's original intentions, that this should be "a dictatorship of the avant-garde". Revealing as well as unintentionally embarrassing – cf, the analysis of the elections in which Blanqui mostly lost - is the study of Seidel-Hoeppner, *From Babeuf to Blanqui*, Reclam 1975

[17]. ibid., P. 568 - 570

[18]. *Die Neue Zeit*, vol. 2, 1895/96, p. 53. Cf. Furthermore L. v. Stein, vol. I *The Concept of Society and the Social History of the French Revolution up until the Year 1830*, Munich 1921, preface G. v. Salomon, p. XXXII f.

[19]. ibid., p. 19. Even the Russian censors would allow *Capital,* vol. I to be printed with the reasoning that it was a work incomprehensible except for a few intellectuals.

[20]. Karl Marx, *Historical Materialism – the Early Writings.* Ed. J. Landshut and J.P. Mayer, vol. I Leipzig 1932

[21]. ibid. P. 79

[22]. cf. e.g. B.H. Heitzer, W. Kuettler, *A Revolution of Historic Thinking – Marx, Engels, Lenin and Historical Science*, East Berlin 1983, the unreferenced quotes above are derived from this work

[23]. These works appeared in Stuttgart and Tuebingen. The study of Schulz comprises pages 20 – 98. Because of the mass of the material quoted I will confine myself to some general references. For the expert the text is of such importance that he has to take cognizance of it in full. To my knowledge Schulz is mentioned only in the volume edited and collected by Erwin Reiche: *This Book belongs to Freedom. German Documents from five centuries*. Kiepenheuer, Weimar. In the edition of 1950 the following can be found on p. 142: "Wilhelm Schulz – his life: never-ending police investigations, three years confinement and flight to Alsace, taking residence in Switzerland, a close friend of Georg Buechner, 1849 further flight and death in exile. Nine years after the *Hessische Landbote* the radical publication sympathizing with the French revolution published and written by Buechner, which bears a singular testimony towards human and civil rights Wilhelm Schulz wrote: *The Shame of German Justice*, 1843: "It may be remembered that Germany now more than appeased right now holds a larger number of

political prisoners and political exiles than France that has been so long been the stage of revolts and uprisings. One may also stop to think of the atrocities of the secret German inquisition in those interminable political interrogations – in that manner one will find sufficient material for a commentary of the popular German folk song: "What is the German's Fatherland?"

[24]. ibid., p. 31 - 32

[25]. ibid., p. 43 ff.

[26]. ibid., p. 85. After I had read that it became clear to me why in all books of the Humboldt University behind the writings of L-Peguilhen the laconic penciled note appeared: Lost in 1952. At this point the fuss had caught on to what explosive material was hidden here. It is also impossible to access other sources that I have quoted at the library of the university, that regards the literary estate of E. Gans as well as the works of L. v. Stein and other authors. The central library of the unions stamps the books of L. v. Stein the lend-out card with the following text: "Above work has only been lent for purposes of scientific research. I shall ensure with my signature to safe-guard it in such a way that abuse is not possible". This goes for other writings as well so those that would prove that even Engels only copied his own wisdoms, e.g. about the primeval societies. Cf. the copies of library lend-out cards in the appendix of the book. The German Democratic Republic follows here the Soviet Union as well. The Hamburg weekly *Die Zeit* has extensively documented how in the Soviet Union regularly after a change of power in the collective leadership all literature that does not fit the new course, is eliminated from the libraries. Soon we will have progressed to that same state of affairs everywhere not solely in the Humboldt library. As we can see the general progress cannot be stemmed. For further reading cf. *How Mehring Forges*, regarding: Salomon, ibid. endnote 17

[27]. ibid., p. 329 ff.

[28]. ibid., p. 350

[29]. ibid.

[30]. ibid., p. 29

[31]. ibid., p. 189

[32]. ibid., p. 232

[33]. ibid., p. 323

[34]. ibid., p. 43 ff.

[35]. ibid., p. Cf. F. Engels: *Letters about the Historical Materialism 1890-95,* East-Berlin, 1979, p. 55. To simplify things the text of Lavergne-Peguilhen has been completely omitted in the most recent edition, following the maxim, yes, there was something, but it was wrong. The G.D.R. Man is used to get only from the West what has been there.

[36]. ibid.

[37]. ibid.

[38]. ibid.

[39]. ibid.

[40]. in the Letter Edition of 1979 this turn of phrase is criticized self-critically by Engels as "too negligent" on page 61, Mehring should write that that "feudal societies engender a feudal world order" - that is to falsify even more against Lavergne-Peguilhen on a "world-historical" level so to speak.

[41]. ibid.

[42]. Gans, *Philosophical Writings,* ed. and introd. By H. Schroeder, East Berlin 1971, p. 221

[43]. ibid., p. 218, cf. also the introduction

[44]. ibid., Vol. I, p. 81, endnote 86

[45]. cf. *Hallische Jahrbuecher,* Leipzig, from no. 106 onward as of May 4, 1841. Koeppen only stresses the point without further elucidating it that the masses of the people should be honored. Gans receives high praise from him.

[46]. ibid.

[47]. ibid., p. 218

[48]. Cited from: *The Union of Communists – Documents and Materials.* East Berlin, 1970. Vol. I, p. 195, in the future quoted as *Documents*

[49]. ibid.

[50]. quoted from K. Chernenko, in: *Einheit [=Unity],* East Berlin, 2/1985 – To Fulfill the Requirements of Developed Socialism," p. 112

[51]. cf. Moses Hess: *Philosophic and Socialist Writings 1837 – 1850. A Selection.* Edited and introduced by Auguste Cornu and Wolfgang Moenke, East Berlin 1961 p. 346. Here are a few more verbatim quotes of Hess to show to what extent Marx plagiarized him down to the last turn of phrase, p. 336: "Human beings have … to sell themselves … to

live," p. 352: Modern industry has created the "unbridgeable gap between rich and poor, Capitalists and Proletarians," and it be evident that "this modern Monmouth industry paces towards its own destruction with giant steps," the "modern industry," p. 353: the "have this egotistical society come apart at the seams and then give them their surplus of productive forces as a Communist one," p. 358: "Pauperization is a consequence of private property and is developing simultaneously with it to an equal degree and measure."

[52]. Documents I, p. 654

[53]. cf. Documents I, esp. p. 470 – 488, 501 – 503, furthermore 214, 305, 309, 347, 362, 376, 386, 431, 451 – 457, 579, 589, 624. It is further instructive to read the *Prague Manifesto* of Thomas Muentzer, who by the way carried Thomas More's *Utopia* on him in Frankenhausen, Babeuf's *Manifesto of the Plebeians*, Cabet's *Communist Credo*, etc. This is just to underline how not only contents but forms get copied and plagiarized.

[54]. Till Eulenspiegel, popularized in word, print and music, most notably by the homonymous opera by Richard Strauss, was a kind of North German Robin-Hood figure and prankster said to have lived and played his practical jokes in the High Middle Ages on the high and mighty and overly well-to-do, although his 'ideology' would not have passed muster by the commissars and his unorthodoxy would have landed him clearly in the gulags in the Stalinist period, his sympathies and the thrust of jokes were clearly with the people and against the clergy and the landed nobles. Bakunin's remarks refer to the flakiness of Eulenspiegel's arguments that recruited victims through the taking literal of metaphorical meanings and the smokescreen-and-mirror quality of his speech; many a Bolshevik would have envied him for his gift of the gap.

[55]. Both names have been altered, for obvious reasons

[56]. Cf. *Neues Deutschland,* B issue from February 7th 1985, p. 4. Honecker declares upon the reception of the Karl-Marx-Order from the Ministry of State Security: "As we were fighting the brown-shirted hordes in the times of the Weimar Republic with the call 'Hail Moscow!'" This speech was published for the first time at the occasion of the first trial in the G.D.R. ever in which members of the Stasi were tried, and in which members of the Polish State Security were condemned to 25 years in

prison for murdering priests. By the by: Honecker has a rather disingenuous relationship to ideology: Officially the VII world convention of the Communist Youth had condemned this "Hail Moscow" as a strategically wrong orientation of the German Communist Party

[57] . N.D., Febr. 12, 1985, p. 1

[58] . ibid.

[59] . Cf. Marx-Engels, *Correspondence*, East Berlin 1949, vol. I, p. 120

[60] . Citation follows H.J. Steinberg: *How Marxist Really Was the Old Social Democracy?* In: *Die Neue Gesellschaft,* Bonn, 3/1983, p. 228. I would like to thank the Ministry of State Safety that it keeps these journals as well as those of the West German unions from me through regular confiscation. Otherwise there would have been the danger that I'd turn Social Democrat. To practice the due and necessary self-criticism I'm fully aware that it is only the highest councils of the Socialist Unity Party of Germany, East that can deal directly with the Social Democratic Party, West, and that it is dangerous to let the lower party rank and file of both Parties loose on each other willy-nilly. In case the old legal state should be reinstituted according to which in the occupied zones of Berlin all parties are again permitted and legal I would be grateful for the ever so solicitous Ministry of State Safety to be informed directly.

[61] . *Garantien*, p. V, VI

[62] . ibid., p. VI

[63] . ibid.

[64] . ibid., p. XXIV

[65] . J. Stalin, *Works*, East Berlin, 1954, vol. 12, p. 14/15 *About the right-wing deviation in the Communist Party of the Soviet Union.*

[66] . ibid., p. 17, 19, 21-24

[67] . "For the East German Zone, a Soviet Military Administration [S.M.A.] was formed on June 9, 1945, with [General] Zhukov at its head. Its chief concerns were to provide for the future security of the U.S.S.R. by setting up a pro-Soviet regime in Germany ... On April 22, 1946, after four months negotiation, the Communists and the Social Democrats of the Soviet zone were merged into a single Socialist Unity party of Germany [S.E.D.] ; Wilhelm Pieck and Otto Grotewohl were elected joint chairmen. This fusion was strongly condemned by the Social Democrats of West Germany, where the Allied authorities did not

234

recognize the S.E.D." quoted from Encyclopedia Britannica, 1970 edition. These political figureheads were as independent from Moscow as Captain Renaud, the Claude Rains character in *Casablanca*, was unaware that gambling was going on in *Rick's Café*.

[68] . F. Engels, *Letter from September 21, 1890, to Joseph Bloch*, quoted from: Engels, *Letters on the Historical Materialism*, East Berlin, 1979, p. 30

[69] . Ussuri is the river in Eastern Asia that is marking part of the border between Russia and China. It became a catchword that came to symbolize the Sino-Soviet border conflict between March and September 1969 in which both sides claimed victory

[70] . Rosa Luxemburg, *Collected Works*, East Berlin 1974, vol. 4, p. 359 ff.: *On the Russian Revolution*

[71] . ibid., p. 359

[72] . Herbert Wehner, *Change through Tribulations, Collected Writings and Speeches,* 1930 – 1967. Ed. by Count Finkenstein and G. Jahn, West Berlin 1968

[73] . For those who may have forgotten the extreme brutal features the system GULAG was endowed with from the beginning in the G.D.R., shall read in Wehner's book from p. 61 onward in his comments on Bautzen. Until the day of Wehner's speech in this prison alone "18,000 people were ruined and brought to death" under the most deplorable and human dignity defying circumstances all in the name of humanist Marxism

[74] . Authors' Collective: *German History*, East Berlin, 1983, vol. 3, p. 237

[75] . Completely without rhyme or reason are the economic postulates with regard to the middle class as well, one may compare only the project of the central or State bank: On the one hand, it was supposed to undermine the"rule of the big moneymen," on the other hand – and that verbatim in the same text - "the interests of the conservative bourgeoisie" was supposed to be "tied to the revolution". In this nonsensical style the whole document is drafted.

[76] . Authors' Collective: *German History*, East Berlin 1983, vol. 3, p. 439

[77] . Kant, *Collected Works,* vol. VIII, Berlin, Leipzig 1923, p. 23

[78] . *Documents II*, p. 160 - 162

[79] . cf. MEW, East Berlin 1964, vol. 7, p. 84, 33, 89

[80] . *Documents II*, p. 718 ff.

[81]. *Documents II, p. 11*

[82]. *Documents II, p.* 331 - 334

[83]. cf. *Author's Collective: German History.* East Berlin 1984, vol. 4, p. 258, 299, see the ideology and practice of Marx

[84]. Marx-Engels, *Collected Works in Six Volumes,* East Berlin 1970, vol. V, p. 279 in the future quoted as MEAW

[85]. ibid., p. 224

[86]. ibid., p. 221, vol. VI p. 235

[87]. Lorenz von Stein, edited with a preface by Dr. G. Salomon, Munich 1921:

Vol. I – The Concept of Society and of Social History of the French Revolution up to the Year 1830

Vol. II – Socialism and Communism in France between 1830 – 1848

Vol. III – The Empire, the Republic and the Sovereignty of the French Society since the February Revolution of 1848

[88]. Stein, *Vol. I, p. 2*

[89]. ibid., p. 3, 4, 7

[90]. ibid., p. 105, 106

[91]. ibid., p. 107, 108

[92]. ibid.

[93]. ibid., p. 130, 131

[94]. Stein, vol. II, p. 18, 19

[95]. ibid., p. 20

[96]. cf. ibid., p. 14, 21

[97]. ibid., p. 25

[98]. ibid., p. 27

[99]. ibid., p. 32

[100]. ibid., p. 75, 76

[101]. ibid., p. 85

[102]. ibid., p. 79, 86

[103]. ibid., p. 89

[104]. ibid., p. 98

[105]. *Documents,* II, p. 265

[106]. Quote following F. Mehring, *Of Historical Materialism,* East Berlin, 1950, p. 14 Marx to J. Weydemeyer

[107]. cf. K. Marx, *Das Capital,* vol. II, East Berlin 1951, p. 7, henceforth: *Capital*

236

[108]. ibid.

[109]. ibid., p. 8

[110]. Cited following Cornu: ibid. vol. I, p. 65

[111]. *Capital II*, p. 9

[112]. MEAW, VI, p. 202

[113]. cf. ibid. p. 8

Rosa Luxemburg has made excerpts of Rodbertus, as well, from which in the following relevant essentials are being quoted; cf. *Collected Works – Economic Writings*, East Berlin 1975, vol. 5 197 ff.: The working classes are "the creators of all societal wealth. *The workers* have been liberated naked or in rags, *with nothing but their labor power."* Labor power intensified "a hundred times by inventions" has exposed the workers "to the most dreadful outbursts of real misery.

Regarding the contradiction between productive forces and the conditions of production Rodbertus writes: "the creative force of the productive means will be increased, and their adjustment is its consequence. The state of society demands the raising of the material condition of the working classes to the same level of the political condition, and the economic state responds with their most abject abasement. - Society is in need of the unhampered increase of its wealth, and today's managers of production have to limit the same in order not to increase poverty. – Only one thing is harmonious! The reversed nature of these conditions corresponds to the reversed nature of the ruling part of society, to look for the root of the evil of that reversed nature where it does not lie at all. This egoism which all too often clads itself in the garb of morality, castigates as the origin and root of pauperism the unvirtuous nature of the workers. The alleged lack of economy and lack of sufficiency of the latter it burdens with what overwhelming facts commit in crimes against them, and even were it may not close its eyes of their complete innocence, it elevates the 'necessity of poverty' to become theory."

Rodbertus recognizes, as Rosa Luxemburg writes, "as early as 1850 that there is a periodicity of crises, and, furthermore, their recurrence in ever shorter intervals, but with ever increasing intensity." Furthermore, Luxemburg cites Rodbertus conception of how to avoid crises by way of a supreme macroeconomic planning commission, conceptions that were also presented in the "German workers' hall" of that same year in

Hanover. As a precondition Rodbertus mentioned the "complete reversal" of all proprietorial conditions. Rosa Luxemburg rejects Engels' criticism Rodbertus have plagiarized Sismondi in the crisis theory. Just to underline: Not only the theory of surplus value - but the thesis of increasing misery, and the issue of recurring crises, etc., were plagiarized by Marx.

[114]. *Capital II*, p. 13

[115]. ibid., p. 15

[116]. Quoted from F. Mehring: *Collected Works*, East Berlin 1960, vol. 3, p. 391

[117]. *Capital III*, p. 18

[118]. Ibid., p. 21

[119]. Ibid., p. 26

[120]. Ibid.

[121]. Ibid., p. 25

[122]. Ibid., p. 28

[123]. Ibid., p. 27

[124]. The contrast "Vulgar economists/not-quite-vulgar Marx" in the German original reads " den nicht gans-vulgaeren Marx". It should read "nicht ganz-vulgaer," but the author, here, plays with ganz = quite vs. Gans, the last name of Hegel's master student whose lectures Marx attended.

[125]. at the place indicated, p. 137

[126]. A. Smith, *An Inquiry into the Nature and Essence of Public Wealth*, Jena 1923, p. 10 [German translation: *Eine Untersuchung ueber die Natur und Wesen des Volkswohlstandes*]

[127]. MEAW, vol. VI, p. 202

[128]. A. W. Anikin, *Economists of Three Millennia*, East Berlin 1974, p. 375

[129]. Karl Marx, *Theories of Surplus Value*, in MEW, 26.3 East Berlin, p. 292, henceforth: *Theories*

[130]. *Theories*, p. 310

[131]. Ibid., p. 109

[132]. Ibid., p. 181

[133]. Ibid., p. 234

[134]. *Capital I*, p. 171, footnote 31

[135]. *Capital I*, p. 679, 680

[136]. Marx-Engels-Works, vol. 23, East Berlin, 1956 ff., p. 791, henceforth: MEW

[137]. MEW, vol. 16, p. 235

[138]. Walter Ulbricht, as quoted, p. 8, 9

[139]. MEAW IV, p. 503, footnote 166

[140]. cf. MEAW IV, p. 382-402

[141]. The West German government had the policy of often buying East German prisoners out, if they believed they were behind bars for political reasons

[142]. cf. MEAW IV, p. 207-210. Surprisingly Engels attacks Rodbertus here in his preface to the first edition of Marx's *Misery of Philosophy* as a "labor money" utopian. At this point two remarks are necessary, first: That is even the labor money utopia of Marx derives from Rodbertus and from the Communists prior to Marx, and second: How can it be that what is utopianism in the case of Rodbertus becomes science in the case of Marx? Cf. note 31 in part II. Engels is commenting on our real-existing Socialism, not on Rodbertus, when he writes: "Only by way of the devaluation or survaluation of the products the individual producers of commodities are being confronted with how much or how little of it society needs or doesn't need. However, just this sole regulator the utopia held as well by Rodbertus is trying to abolish. And if we ask which guarantee we have that of each product only the necessary quantity is produced and not more of it, so that we do not starve of grain and meat, but be glutted with sugar from turnips and drown in potato brandy, that we shall not have enough trousers to cover our bareness, while trouser buttons abound million times; so Rodbertus presents us triumphantly with his notorious calculation that for each superfluous pound of sugar, for each unsold barrel of brandy, for every useless trouser button the right certificate has been made out, a calculation that always "comes out exactly right," according to which all demands are rightfully satisfied and the liquidation has been brought about correctly. And for all those who remain incredulous they may turn to the governmental main treasury pension fund statistician X in Pomerania, who has been auditing the calculation and signed off on it as correct and who remains quite credible, as he has never been caught with a deficiency in the treasury."

Governmental main treasury pension fund statistician would make a nice title for Marx, but you may not send him to Pomerania, as Pomerania has been burned, brother Frederick.

[143] . Code NL 116/15. The user manual reads as follows: "The quoting of codes, stock marcations and page numbers is generally not permitted." – "The manuscript has to be shown for inspection." Even the oral communication of knowledge about the MS stock is *verboten*, that includes even a discussion with fellow scholars!

[144] . feud, feudum, also feodum, Latin, trust or fief, a right to lands and hereditaments (Webster').

[145] . Cf. Karl Liebknecht, *Thought and Deed. Writings, Speeches, Letters on the Theory and Practice of Politics.* Edited and introduced by Ossip K. Flechtheim, Frankfurt/Main, West Berlin, Vienna, 1976, p. 244, 245

[146] . Rosa Luxemburg, *Collected Works,* East Berlin 1974, vol. IV, p. 352

[147] . *Neues Deutschland*, November 9th, 1984, p. 4

[148] . R. Kossolapow, *Socialism and Contradictions*, In: *Soviet Science, Contributions to Social Science*, 6/1984, p. 593

[149] . K. Chernenko, *To Satisfy the Demands of Developed Socialism*, in *Unity*, II, 1985, p. 112

[150] . J.A. Abarzumow: *Lenin's Analysis of the Crisis of the Year 1921*, in: *Soviet Science*, ibid., p. 595

[151] . ibid., p. 597

[152] . ibid., p. 598

[153] . W. I. Lenin, *Works*, vol. I, East Berlin, 1955 ff., p. 246, henceforth: LW

[154] . ibid., p. 76

[155] . LW, vol. 24, p. 25, 337 f., 428, 518

[156] . LW, vol. 27, p. 285

[157] . ibid., p. 243

[158] . LW 26, p. 362

[159] . Cited from: *Soviet Science*, ibid., p. 607

[160] . LW 32, p. 218

[161] . C. Kritzmann, *The Historical Period of the Great Russian Revolution*, Vienna 1929

[162] . LW 27, p. 249

[163] . Cf, Friedrich List, *The Natural System of Political Economy*, Berlin, 1961, p. 240

[164] . LW 33, p. 44

[165] . List, *The Natural System ...,* p. 39, 40

[166] . ibid.

[167] . "ein Undink" in the German vernacular, the literate term would be "Unding," [derived from 'Ding' = thing, stuff] something manifestly impossible and hence highly undesirable.

[168] . LW 30, p. 515

[169] . LW 32, p. 222

[170] . MEAW, vol. I, p. 564

[171] . E. Apel, *Current Questions of Economic Research*, East Berlin, 1964, p. 17

[172] . ibid., p. 7

[173] . ibid., p. 13

[174] . ibid., p. 93, 94

[175] . LW 33, p. 69

[176] . ibid., p. 42

www.ingramcontent.com/pod-product-compliance
Lightning Source LLC
Chambersburg PA
CBHW022055210326
41519CB00054B/419